D0211101

Great Civilizations

ISBN 0-75258-224-0

This is a Parragon Publishing Book
This edition published in 2003

Parragon Publishing
Queen Street House
4 Queen Street
Bath BA1 1HE, UK

Copyright © 1999 Parragon

Printed in Indonesia

Cover design by Blackjacks

Great Civilizations

GENERAL EDITOR:
Brenda Ralph Lewis

Contents

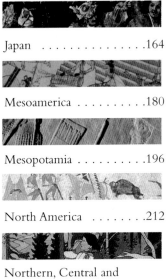

Introduction

'HISTORY,' IT HAS BEEN SAID, 'repeats itself'. This is not entirely true, for history never repeats itself in all its detail. If it did, there would be no change, no progress and no regress, either. It is very evident that the world today is fundamentally different in all sorts of ways – philosophically, spiritually, socially and technologically – from the ancient world, and the world of the second millennium has seen radical change even in so short a time, historically, as the years which have passed since the start of the twentieth century. However, in very broad terms, the ways history *does* repeat itself are also very clear. In both ancient and modern times, as this Micropedia shows, Empires have risen and declined. Wars have been fought for the sake of power, resources or vengeance. Religion has brought out the best in mankind – and the worst. What has been called 'Man's inhumanity to Man' has threaded its way through the centuries.

The Micropedia outlines the origins of the world's peoples, their politics and power struggles, wars, conquests and peacemaking, explorations and empires, trade and industry, science and technology, societies and cultures, religions, myths, art and creativity. None of this, however, deals with a dead past or with happenings and attitudes which have no relevance today. Today is the heir of the past and the past is full of lessons, some of which have been learned and some not. There are, though, substantial similarities between now and then.

For example, the need for religious faith, and the belief that some greater power than Man both controls and protects the world and its existence has been fundamental throughout history, regardless of the actual faith involved. In this sense, there is little basic difference between the pagan faiths of Ancient Egypt, Greece, Rome or Mesopotamia and the monotheistic religions of Judaism, Christianity or Islam. Monotheism, the concept of the single invisible God, may be the predominant type of belief today, but it has its roots in the pagan past when the overwhelming power now ascribed to one almighty deity was shared by several gods, each of which had his or her own area of operations.

The recourse to war, another unchanging element of life on Earth, which as yet shows no sign of lessening, sprang from similar motives – survival, gain, independence or the urge of one nation to impose its will or its ideology upon another – whether it was the Pelopponesian War (431–404 BC) in Ancient Greece, the Crusades to the Holy Land (1096–1303), the American Civil War

(1861–65) or the First (1914–18) and Second (1939–45) World Wars.

Revolts and revolutions, too, have had similar sources; as protests against injustice or the desire to topple ineffectual and neglectful governments, from the removal of the degenerate last king of early Rome (509 BC) to the French Revolution (1789) to the Communist victory in China in (1949).

On the other hand, one example of the great difference between the past and present lies in today's attitude towards violence in any of its forms – national, international, institutional or personal. Today, war and violence are seen as undesirable, even though both continue unabated. Yet before the First World War, when weapons made it possible to wreak widespread slaughter and destruction, war was regarded as natural, necessary and, for a long time, glorious. This is one reason why wars so regularly punctuate the history told in this Micropedia. Though war is now regarded as a failure of diplomacy, in the past, diplomacy was rarely considered and war was an almost routine recourse.

Social attitudes have also changed enormously over the centuries. For instance, in Biblical, Ancient Greek and Roman and also more recent times, slavery was seen as the natural fate of the defeated or the poor and weak. By contrast, it is now widely regarded as an appalling crime to be expunged wherever found.

Likewise, what is now called racism, the persecution of one race or one religion by another, is now generally regarded as an affront to humanity. This would have been inconceivable in past times when 'dislike of the unlike' – whites for blacks, Christians for Jews, Muslims for Christians, Muslims for Hindus, Catholics for Protestants – was thought to be a natural and justified response to the challenges posed by different cultures or beliefs and, what is more, that the response, however brutish it may appear today, was the correct one.

It is very tempting to believe that the modern world has at last 'got it right', that today's way is a permanent improvement on the cruel, mistaken and misguided beliefs of the past. History, however, teaches differently. Every age, including our own, has been marked by the surety that its own ways, beliefs and actions are the best. The Ancient Romans who conquered the greatest empire known up to their time believed themselves superior to those they vanquished, which gave them a right to rule over them. The absolute kings and emperors of the past were sincerely convinced that it was their destiny to rule over the 'lesser' beings who were their subjects. Every generation has grown old in the belief that the youth of their time is worthless, and when, in its turn, that youth matures, it has repeated the pattern. Paradoxically, every age has also bemoaned the 'glories' of the past in the light of the 'undesirable' present.

What this means is that history can be meaningful only if present day ideas are temporarily set aside, and the events and people of the past understood by their own lights. This Micropedia therefore makes no judgments in its efforts to span history with particular reference to human civilisations in their most formative centuries. Some of it will make uncomfortable reading, some of it will shock, but some of it will sound very familiar. All of it recounts the ongoing adventure of humanity through time, of which today's world is only the latest episode.

BRENDA RALPH LEWIS

Africa

Humans Evolve

ABOUT 20 MILLION YEARS AGO, somewhere in Africa, ape-like
creatures – whom anthropologists call Proconsul – came down out of
the trees and began to live on the ground, searching for their food on
the broad savannahs. In time, they adapted to this new life, began to walk
upright, fashioned tools, made fire and eventually, think and talk. Now
markedly different from their ape-like ancestors, they became Hominids,
the first creatures to be noticeably human-like.

Modern anthropology has confirmed their existence in Africa
through the discoveries of the Leakey family. In 1959, Professor Louis
Leakey (1903–72) discovered the skull of Australopithecus Robustus in
the Olduvai Gorge, Tanzania. Five years later, he uncovered more human
remains, those of Homo Habilis, and in 1976, his wife Mary Leakey

(1913–96) found fossil footprints which proved
that our ancestors walked upright 3.6 million
years ago. Although the Leakeys at first
encountered resistance to their idea that humans
originated in Africa, this contention is now
generally accepted.

Once humans began to evolve there, the
way was open for gradual development towards
organised bands of hunter-gatherers and cave-
dwelling families little different in basic essentials
from families today. However, as the species grew
in numbers, their increasing demand for food
meant that Africa could not contain them.

◀ *A scientific reconstruction of a prehistoric Neanderthal Man.*

Homo Neandertalensis

Humans Migrate

WITH THIS, THE EARLY HUMANS became nomads, wandering further and further away in the quest to find new and better opportunities. Eventually, these migrations took them to every part of the world that it was possible to reach by land and sea. In the course of this development, humans encountered different climates, conditions and environments. Gradually, as is the way of Nature, they began to adapt in order to survive. Those who remained in Africa, with its broiling climate and strong sunshine, developed black or brown skins and thick, wiry black hair for protection. Further north, where the sun was less strong, human skin became pale or pinky-white and hair was fair. In Central Asia humans encountered fierce cold and developed an extra fold of skin on the eyelid to shield their eyes. This fold gave them the typically slant-eyed Asian look of today's Japanese, Chinese or Koreans. Racial differences, the cause of so much later conflict and hatred were, therefore, no more than a matter of geography, environment, climate and time, created by the paramount driving force in all living creatures: the need to survive.

◄ *Civilisations developed hunting skills using man-made tools.*

Power, Politics and War in Africa

THE USE OF POWER, strength and aggression has always been a characteristic of human life, and one that was closely tied in to the urge for survival which all living creatures possess. The early wars, for example, often had as their basic purpose the preservation of water supplies, the one resource which was indispensable to life.

It was a short step from that to aggression as a power game designed to achieve supremacy, and Africa, with its proximity to southern Europe across the Mediterranean, was often the stage on which such contests were played out. North Africa, with open shores that were relatively easy for invaders to reach, was the target of frequent incursions. Phoenician traders, who founded the city of Carthage in Tunisia arrived late in the ninth century BC. Ancient Greek colonisers followed, and after them the Romans who crushed Carthage in 146 BC and extended their own power into the area. Later invaders included Vandals, Byzantines and the Muslims.

In the more impenetrable central and southern areas of Africa, continuous tribal wars became characteristic. With intervals of peace, or rather intervals when no actual fighting took place, raiding rival villages, stealing cattle or carrying off prisoners became virtually a way of life. It remained this way for many centuries.

◀ *Dramatic illustration of the fall of Carthage to the Arabs.*

Organised Warfare

TRIBAL CONFLICT WAS not a form of warfare which required military genius, but in South Africa, the Zulu chief Shaka (1787–1828) preferred a more organised concept. In 1818 – hundreds of years after the first battles took place on African soil – Shaka created a near-invincible army based on the 'Impi' of about 1,000 strictly disciplined, unmarried men. Among other strategies, Shaka trained the Impi to charge in a close-knit body which made hand-to-hand fighting more effective and shattered the enemy's formations. With these tactics, Shaka soon drove other tribes out of Natal and created a powerful, centralised Zulu kingdom. It did not, however, outlast its century.

After 1878, the 'Scramble for Africa' – in which Belgium, Britain, Germany, France, Italy and Spain carved up the continent to extend and enrich their own empires – created pressures which inevitably led to war. Shaka's kingdom was an apparent threat to adjoining British possessions in South Africa, and the danger it posed was proved in blood when the Impi slaughtered six companies of British soldiers at Isandalwhana in 1879. Subsequently, the Zulus were driven off at high cost by a small force at Rorke's Drift hospital station and were finally defeated by the British at Ulundi. This was the end of Shaka's kingdom, which was annexed to British-ruled Natal.

▲ *British defending Rorke's Drift against the Zulus in 1879.*

Europeans Fight Natives and Each Other

FOUR YEARS LATER IN 1883, in the western Sudan, the British were under attack by the forces of the Mahdi, a Muslim messiah who declared Jihad, or Holy War, against the Christian infidels. In the course of this war at Khartoum in 1885, General Charles George Gordon was slaughtered together with his entire garrison.

The two Boer Wars, fought in 1881 and 1899–1902, were conflicts of a different nature. Here, the Dutch Boer settlers in South Africa fought the British for independence from British rule. Though the Boers appeared to be simply civilian farmers, their use of the wickedly accurate Mauser 10-shot pistols made them formidable enemies. They were, however, principally guerilla fighters confronting a large, organised professional army and inevitably, in 1902, British might prevailed.

These struggles for power and possession had been made possible by explorers from other countries, who ventured into the tangled jungles and broiling deserts of the 'Dark Continent', so called because it was as yet unknown to Europeans. Exploration in Africa was, however, a tremendous challenge, considering its harsh terrain, punishing climate, the presence of hostile natives and the virulent fevers to which Europeans had no natural resistance. This was venturing into uncharted territory at its most dangerous.

▲ *Muhammad Ahmed, the Mahdi.*

Discovering Africa

MANY CENTURIES BEFORE EUROPEANS set out to penetrate the 'Dark Continent', its edges had been explored by Phoenician sailors on the orders of the Ancient Egyptian pharaoh Necho (610–594 BC.) They sailed along the east African coast and, on a later voyage, apparently took their ships through the Straits of Gibraltar and back into the Mediterranean. In 425 BC, a Carthaginian merchant named Hanno sailed through the Straits and on south down the coast of west Africa. It is possible that Hanno got as far as Senegal and maybe Gabon.

However, where Europeans were concerned, the shape and extent of Africa remained unknown until the pioneering voyages inspired after 1418 by Prince Henry the Navigator of Portugal (1394–1460) in the quest the discover a sea route to Asia. Over the next 80 years, successive voyages by Portuguese navigators pushed further and further down the west African coast – a terrifying region which sailors believed led to the end of the world – until in 1488, Bartholomew Diaz (c. 1450–1500) rounded the Cape of Good Hope and so opened the way for Vasco da Gama (1469–1524) to complete the sea route to Asia by crossing the Indian Ocean and landing on the Indian coast in 1498.

◀ *Portuguese explorer, Henry the Navigator.*

Exploring Africa

THE INTERIOR OF AFRICA WAS, of course, much more perilous, but this did nothing to deter exploration. The Scots doctor Mungo Park (1771–1806) searched for the source of the River Niger. In 1824, another British explorer, Alexander Laing (1793–1826) became the first known European to cross the Sahara Desert north to south. Richard Burton (1821–90) and John Speke (1827–64) discovered the lakes Tanganyika (1857) and Victoria (1858). The Scots medical missionary David Livingstone (1813–73) helped map much of southern and central Africa.

Several motives lay behind these explorations. There was scientific and geographical interest in uncovering Africa's many unknowns. For missionaries, Africa offered the chance of thousands of potential converts to Christianity. For abolitionists, penetrating Africa enabled humanitarian missions to find where slavery persisted and to rescue Africans from slavers and the slave trade.

By the nineteenth century, intrepid explorers had some protection from the worst effects and dangers of African exploration. Medical advances helped Europeans triumph over some formerly fatal diseases. Quinine, developed in 1827 by the French, preserved them against malaria and dramatically reduced the once-heavy death-rates. Small steamships provided the means to navigate inland waterways, and enabled explorers to open up great rivers such as the Niger, Zambezi, Nile and Congo.

▼ *Rivers such as the Nile provided a means of penetrating the African interior.*

Explorers exploited animals such the elephant for skins and ivory.▶

Riches in Africa

AT A TIME WHEN EUROPE was suffering the depredations of the so-called Dark Age that followed the collapse of the Roman Empire, parts of Africa were enjoying a golden age of prosperity through trade. On the east coast, for example, the city of Axum, the ancient capital of Ethiopia, whose churches made the traveller Cosmas marvel at their splendour in AD 525, conducted a rich trade in ivory.

On the west coast, the Kingdom of Ghana, founded some time before ad 750, traded in the alluvial gold from its rivers which was sent along trans-Saharan routes in exchange for salt, textiles, weaponry, copper goods and horses. Known as the Land of Gold, the scope of Ghana's trade also included feathers, leather, kola, ivory and solid gold weapons. Later, between 1400 and 1700, the Kingdom of Benin traded in kola nuts, palm oil (for soap) together with ivory and pepper.

To the south-east, in Zimbabwe, extensive mining operations were carried out between AD 700 and 1400 and the rock-built city of Great Zimbabwe, constructed in the mid-fourteenth century, was the centre of a powerful and wealthy empire, trading as far afield as China. Cotton cloth was produced here, and gold, iron and copper were manufactured.

Trading in Slaves

SLAVES, HOWEVER, PROVIDED one of the richest and most universal trading commodities in Africa. Slaves were among the exports of both the Kingdoms of Ghana and of Benin, where they were also used as sacrifices at the festival of Agwe, the feast of new yams at harvest time in November. The neighbouring Kingdom of Dahomey, which is now part of the modern Republic of Benin, grew extremely rich by selling slaves to Europeans in exchange for weapons. Dahomey had plentiful recourse to slaves, since it was a military state organised for war, and prisoners taken in the course of hostilities were either sold into servitude or were kept to work on plantations which supplied food for the royal court and the army.

There was also a long-standing trade in slaves elsewhere in Africa, mostly conducted by Arabs who were taking slaves across the Sahara Desert and into east Africa in medieval times and for several centuries afterwards. In this context, however, the activity which most readily springs to mind was the selling of African slaves to Europeans, for transport across the Atlantic to America. This was the trade, both abominable and cruel, which was later termed 'the greatest crime in the world'.

▼ *An Arab trader leads slaves across the African desert.*

The Slaves in America

AFTER THE SPANIARDS conquered their empire in America in the sixteenth century, and the Portuguese claimed Brazil, they discovered that too many natives died when put to hard physical work. Africans, by contrast, were physically strong, accustomed to working long hours in intense heat and were therefore ideal for labour on farms and estates and down the mines. With that, slave ships began to appear off the west African coasts where African chiefs were willing to sell captured enemies and even members of their own tribes to the slave traders, who soon included the British and the French.

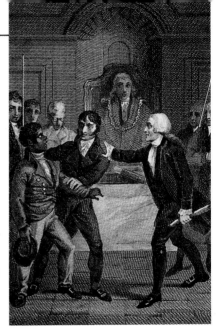

Over the next four centuries, millions of African slaves were exported to the plantations in America. Countless slaves died in transit or were thrown overboard during the appalling 'Middle Passage' across the Atlantic. Countless more perished from the ferocious punishments, such as being thrown into vats of boiling sugar, which were imposed on them by their masters. Those who tried to escape had their toes chopped off as a deterrent against future attempts.

By the time the British abolished the slave trade in 1807 and slavery itself in 1833, it is estimated that some 15 million Africans had been sacrificed to a practice that brought huge prosperity to its perpetrators.

British abolitionists, such as Granville Sharp, fought to end the African slave trade. ▲

Black and White in Africa

THE SLAVE TRADERS WHO BROUGHT such misery to so many Africans between the sixteenth and nineteenth centuries were not necessarily evil or cynical men. They felt no need to justify the fact that they were selling other human beings because they did not regard Africans as properly human at all. In their eyes, Africans were uncivilised heathens, and this belief may lie behind the fact that the British laid down no rules about the humane treatment of slaves. The French and the Spaniards did, and the Spaniards also forbade the breaking up of families. The British, however, had no such qualms, and terrible scenes of grief and violence took place at slave markets when husbands, wives and children were sold to different owners, never to see each other again.

The Boers, the white South Africans of Dutch descent, had a similar attitude. They believed blacks to be inferior, at first because they were not Christians, and later because they were so markedly different in appearance from Europeans. The Boers had, in fact, found justification for this idea in the Bible. These beliefs were solidly in place long before they manifested themselves in the apartheid laws introduced in South Africa in 1948.

The Boers believed they found justification for the slave trade in the Bible. ▶

African Myth and Magic

MANY EUROPEANS IN AFRICA – and that included the missionaries who sought to convert the natives to Christianity – found it hard to comprehend the nature of African faith and belief. Africans were certainly pagans, in that before they became Christian, they were not monotheists in the Jewish, Christian or Muslim sense.

The vastness of Africa ensured that there were many native religions, just as there were many different peoples and social and political systems. What most Africans have in common, however, is a veneration for a single, supreme, creator god. Parallel to this is belief in ancestors and nature gods whose task it is to intercede with the deity on behalf of humans. This intercession is not seen as all-pervading, however. In most of Africa south of the Sahara, there is a belief that the one god intended human beings to live for ever, but by an unlucky chance death intervened and has made human life finite ever since.

African faiths do not, however, rely solely on the one god or the intercessors. There was a strong belief in the powers of certain human beings – kings, rainmakers and witch doctors – to effect benefits through rituals, or by their personal power.

Wooden African double figure, a tribute to the ancestors. ▶

Witch Doctors, Rainmakers and Other Beliefs

AMONG SEVERAL AFRICAN PEOPLES, witch-doctors or shamans play an important part through their ritualistic power to exorcise malevolent spirits, thought to be responsible for illness or bad luck. The shaman acts as an intermediary between the human and the supernatural worlds and is believed to possess special powers to fend off misfortune, and to control good and evil spirits. Several cultures in Asia and native America share similar beliefs in seers, sorcerers or medicine men.

African rainmakers also work on the basis of personal power, and through the use of ritual and dance to conjure up the rain which is so vital to the continuance of life on the continent. The ability to make rain was deemed to be of such importance that in many African tribes, only the king was endowed with the requisite powers. This, in its turn, bolstered the royal position, an important factor in a continent where rule by one 'strong man' was a long-standing tradition.

Sacrifices, too, have their place in African religious beliefs and among the Nuer, a pastoral people of the Sudan, offering up an ox to their god Kwoth, is a central part of their faith.

Myths and Mythmakers of Africa

IN THE STORIES WHICH MAKE UP the African myth traditions, there are beginnings – the origin of the universe – and there are endings – the onset of death. Between the two is the struggle to re-achieve the first and to avoid the second. If initial connections between heaven and earth are severed, separation between God and man is the result. To recover those connections, a conflict erupts on earth between contending forces. Sometimes, they are given form in mythical heroes, at other times they feature the ritual struggle of ordinary human beings.

The African mythmaker has a repertory of stories built around an initial sense of oneness that has been lost. African myth systems contain

A statue of Nimba, the Baga's goddess of fertility. ▶

numerous different stories, but a number of common threads are present in most of them. Myth can be found at the heart of all stories, including tales and epics. Sometimes stories begin as tales, but since mythical elements are always involved, these frequently end as myths. Myth plays an important part in human belief, since it becomes a constant metaphor for what humans can become, moving from the chaos of their everyday life on earth towards a kind of eternal order.

The Divine Trickster

IN AFRICAN RELIGIONS, the one creator god takes various forms. The 'divine trickster' is a symbol of the period of transformation characterising the age of creation. As he moves from the perfect or 'golden' age to the present era, the trickster embodies certain changes. The move is from the perfection of God, that is, the creative side of the divine trickster, to the flawed human being, who represents the destructive side of the divine trickster.

There is, however, another facet to the trickster. In the present era, his divine part has gone. What is left is the profane trickster who is an unpredictable character. His residual creativeness is seen in the illusions which he establishes, but there is an amorality here evidenced by his outrageous and often anti-social behaviour. This dualistic god typifies ordinary men and women, each of them caught in a perennial struggle with the two sides of their nature.

They hope to overcome chaos and to order the world, but the divine and the profane trickster are always there to obscure order with chaos, and so complicate the task. Some of the African myths are actually tales on a huge cosmological scale, with gods taking the roles of human beings.

▲ *This pair of masks may have been used to illustrate the dualistic nature of the African gods.*

The Battle for Oneness and Independence

IN AFRICAN BELIEF, the linkage to the gods is typified by a ritualising of everyday life. However, while humans may long for that much-desired sense of order, there are dangers in yearning for a oneness with God. That would bring a 'golden age' but would also mean loss of free will.

African myths often begin with a domestic scene as the setting for action with which audiences can easily relate. It might be some outrageous human activity or the search for a bride or groom, or it could depict someone who is under attack. However, new life can emerge from these often anti-social happenings. Outrage has a purpose because it represents chaos. The contrasting creation which emerges represents order.

Yet, the battle rages on within them, the struggle for oneness on the one hand and independence on the other. This is a parallel between the human situation and the relationship between the trickster and the hero of

the story. Between them, the struggle wages between free-willed humanity and God-related unity. However, that unity is lost as they move closer to their world, and the profane trickster becomes the spectre of what humans could become if they move away from God.

Statues of male and female ancestors. ▲

Asia

The First Asians

THE ORIGINS OF SOME OF the many and varied peoples of Asia are intimately tied into myth, and a great deal still remains to be discovered about their ancient past. However, civilisation came very early to Asia, first on the Indus River, in north-eastern India, where it was probably established around 2500 BC. With its cities of Mohenjo-Daro and Harappa, the Indus Valley civilisation lasted for nearly 1,000 years before disappearing suddenly in around 1700 BC. The reason for its destruction is not precisely known, although over-use of natural resources, especially the surrounding forests, and an overwhelming attack by enemies have been named as possibilities.

Around the Pacific Ocean, where Southeast Asia today consists of mainland Mayanmar (Burma), Thailand, Cambodia, Laos, Vietnam and Malaysia, the great arc of the Indonesian archipelago and the Philippine and other islands, the great majority of the population are descended from the Mongol pastoral nomads of Central Asia. This is the result of the continuous drift of people into Southeast Asia from the north and possibly from southern China between 500 and 1000 BC. The settlers practised shifting agriculture in remote upland regions, while others settled in river valleys and along the coastal strips.

▲ *Cloth worn in Indonesian ritual ceremonies; the two figures are symbols of male achievement.*

Myths and Nomads

IN ABOUT 1000 BC, Bronze Age warriors of the Tungusic racial group invaded Manchuria and the Korean peninsula and mixed with the existing inhabitants. In appearance and culture, their Korean descendants are distinctively Chinese, and their language includes a substantial amount of Chinese vocabulary. Yet Korean myths reflect a non-Chinese culture, apparently deriving from a much earlier period.

The people of Tibet, another region influenced – and ruled – by China have gone further into myth to explain their origins. Before the dawn of history, Tibet was held together by a succession of immortal rulers. Eventually, the first human ruler 'descended from the sky' onto a mountain in Kong-po and was proclaimed king by an enthusiastic people.

The origins of the Persian peoples appear much more clear-cut. Originally horse- and cattle-nomads on the steppes of Central Asia, they came to the Iranian plateau in around 1000 BC. Other Iranian tribes – Medes, Parthians, Scythians – were migrating at the same time. Some Persian tribes took up a settled existence, and eventually adopted many customs of the older urban cultures of West Asia. Others remained nomads, but later became rulers of a multi-ethnic empire stretching from the Mediterranean to the Oxus and Indus rivers.

▲ *The Tibetan mystic and poet Milarepa, founder of the Kagyu order.*

The Hittite Empire

FROM EARLIEST TIMES, parts of Asia became known for their ambitious and warlike inhabitants. For instance the Hittites, an ancient people of Asia Minor, invaded what is now Anatolia in Turkey in around 1900 BC and imposed their language and culture on the natives. Their

powerful, well-equipped armies maintained the Hittite empire at a size rivalling that of Egypt, Babylonia or Assyria, until it fell in about 1200 BC. While it lasted, however, the Hittite charioteers, who were masters at deployment of this powerful weapon, were the military scourge of both Egypt and Mesopotamia. Their weapons were made of iron, of which the Hittites enjoyed a long monopoly in Asia. Hattusa, capital of the Hittite Empire was, predictably, a citadel within a massively fortified city. Its Lion Gate, featuring huge monoliths, was designed to impress as well as to provide powerful defence.

The neighbouring Phoenicians, whose empire thrived from about 2000 BC until Alexander the Great (356–323 BC) sacked its capital of Tyre in 332 BC, were people of a quite different calibre. They were great seafaring traders, establishing trade links through Asia and into Africa, where they founded Carthage in Tunisia, and on as far as Spain and, it is believed, to the south-west coast of Britain.

▲ *View over the great city of Carthage.*

Empires in India

INDIA, TOO, WAS THE SCENE of conquest and the setting up of powerful empires. In the Punjab of north-west India, the Mauryan Empire (321–185 BC) founded by Chandragupta Maurya, eventually covered most of the north and south-central regions of the subcontinent and had a population of some 30 million. Asoka (273–228 BC), the third and greatest of the Mauryan kings and a devout Buddhist, turned his empire into a Buddhist state.

Much later, the Muslim Mogul Empire (1526–1858) was established in northern India and became known for its magnificent buildings, its wealth and the sumptuous luxury in which its emperors lived.

When, as all empires do, this one began to decline, the militaristic Hindu Mahrattas, set themselves up as rivals to the Moguls and inflicted a heavy defeat upon them in 1761. By then, however, another empire had intruded into India and like its predecessors, gained its power by military conquest. The British, who had originally come to India as traders, destroyed Mahratta power between 1779 and 1871 and annexed their territory to the British 'Raj'. By that time, the Mogul Empire, too, had succumbed to the British, who ruled India as the 'Jewel in the Crown' of their empire until independence in 1947.

Indian painting of Buddha. ▶

The Mongols

UNTIL THE END OF THE twelfth century, the Mongols of Central Asia were warring nomads, their clans forever rivalling and intriguing against each other. This changed after 1206 when Temujin (1167–1227), who later took the name Genghis Khan, unified the clans and turned them into the Horde, an almost unstoppable military force. In 1221, the Horde broke through the mighty defences of the Great Wall of China. Subsequently, the Mongol conquest of China brought Genghis's grandson Kublai Khan (1216–94) to the throne as the first emperor of the Yuan dynasty (1279–1368).

The Mongols did not stop at China. They turned west and conquered lands all the way to Russia and Persia. They were so greatly feared that when news of Mongol presence on the Russian steppes reached Britain, there was widespread panic. The Mongols did not penetrate far into Europe, though. They reached Poland, Hungary and Croatia in 1240, but came to a halt when their great military leader, Ogodai, died in 1242. Subsequently, in 1260, the Muslim armies prevented the Mongols from conquering the Middle East. The Mongols were so impressed by their Muslim enemies that they adopted their Islamic faith, which they regarded as the 'religion of the strong'.

The Mongol conqueror, Genghis Khan. ▶

Japan

JAPAN, RULED AFTER THE TENTH century by the samurai warrior caste, was an isolated island country of many curious contrasts – militaristic yet artistic, strictly disciplined yet prone to ferocious in-fighting, curious about the outside world, yet suspicious of it. When Europeans first made contact with Japan in 1543, the Japanese had been embroiled in civil war for two centuries. European weapons enabled Nobunga to become Shogun (military ruler) of Japan in 1573. He established a firearms industry and built European-style ships.

Later, after many years of renewed civil war, Ieyeasu (1542–1616) one of Nobunga's generals, established the Tokugawa dynasty (1603–1868). In 1636, however, an Isolation Decree was issued principally as a protection against the activities of Christian missionaries, and so cut Japan off from the outside world. As a result, Japan remained in medieval stasis until, in 1853, the United States demanded that its ports be opened to foreign trade and that treaties be made with foreign powers. Japan complied, but after 1868, when the enlightened Emperor Meiji (1862–1912) came to the throne, the Japanese went even further and began to modernise at such a phenomenal rate that they absorbed modern institutions and technology within only about 40 years.

▲ *Warlords had been exercising strict control over Japan since the first shogun Yorimito.*

Farming and Cultivation in Asia

SOME OF THE WORLD'S GREATEST INNOVATIONS originated in Asia. Among them was farming, the seminal development which allowed humans to leave behind their previous nomadic life of hunting and gathering, and settle down in cities. Farming originated in Asia between 10000 BC and 7000 BC and by 4000 BC it had spread to Europe.

Subsequently, food-gathering was refined to improve yield and lighten the physical work involved. Wild cereals were being harvested with flint sickles in Palestine in 8000 BC. By 7000 BC, farmers living in settled villages in eastern Anatolia had domesticated some cattle and sheep, and wheat, barley and pulses were being grown in Jericho. Anatolia was the scene of metalworking in 6750 BC, and pigs had been domesticated in Iran by 6000 BC.

As early as 3000 BC, the growing of rice, the staple diet in Asia, developed out of the conditions caused by the heavy monsoon rains of south and Southeast Asia. Rice paddies were developed, in which the maturing plants were kept under a shallow sheet of water for several weeks on end. Rice growing proved very labour intensive, but animal labour was not required, and the yield from the paddy fields could be very high. This had obvious benefits for feeding dense peasant populations.

▲ *Terraced rice paddies in the Indonesian mountains.*

Inventions and Innovations

CIVILISATION, WHICH MEANS 'LIVING IN CITIES', enabled people to specialise in certain tasks and these included several important inventions. In the Indus Valley of north-eastern India, for instance, artisans produced distinctive black and red pottery, metal ornaments and tools, and ceramic toys. Writing on seals was used possibly to mark goods for export, and the Indus also produced a standardised system of weights and measures.

Much later, after 100 BC, the horse, with its obvious uses for transport – a purpose which lasted until the advent of the motor car – acquired a new importance. This arose after the Parthians of west Asia noticed that horses fed on specially grown alfalfa grew larger and stronger. This introduced the horse to warfare, especially cavalry warfare, since the animal could now carry a much heavier load of armour. Civilian life, too, gained from the improved horse, as an aid to farm communities in defending themselves from raiders, and as protection for the caravans which ran along trading routes.

The Asian trade routes needed heavy policing, since the goods carried over great distances could be hugely valuable and were greatly desired in Europe. They included silks, gold, jewels and the spices which were necessary for preserving meat.

▲ *The impression made by a seal that may have been used to mark goods destined for export.*

Religion in Asia

ASIAN RELIGIONS SUCH AS THE Hindu, Buddhist, Sikh and Jain faiths, are intensely spiritual and, in the case of Hinduism, of extremely ancient origin. India in particular is a land of many faiths, some of them mutually inimical, as the long, often violent, rivalry between Hindus and Muslims has shown. Buddhism, a supremely pacific faith, was introduced into the Maurya Empire of India by its third king, Asoka (273–228 BC) as a shock reaction to the slaughter involved in expanding his empire shortly after he succeeded to the throne. The religion was taken into Tibet in about AD 8 by an Indian monk, Padmasambhaval, and also became the religion of Thailand (Siam).

Although Hinduism is seen principally as an Indian faith, it spread to Sri Lanka and further afield to Cambodia or Bali in predominantly Muslim Indonesia. Islam made great inroads into Asia, dominating Malaysia and accounting for eight per cent of the population in Sri Lanka, where the majority faith is Buddhism.

India is also host to Zoroastrianism, a faith of Persian origin, and to Christianity and, though to a far lesser extent, to Judaism. The Portuguese who first came to western India after the pioneering voyage by Vasco da Gama in 1497–98, converted many Indians to Christianity, and small communities of Jews, now much reduced by emigration, were established in Bombay and Cochin.

Different schools of Buddhism have appeared throughout Asia since the sixth century. ▶

Hindus, Sikhs and Jains

HINDUISM, ONE OF THE WORLD'S oldest religions, teaches that samsara, the cycle of reincarnation, can be eluded by acquiring spiritual knowledge through meditation or by performing good works. The religion is enshrined in the Baghavad Gita, the 'Song of the Lord' and in the four Vedas, of which the Rig Veda is the most sacred. Hindus have a great pantheon of hundreds of gods and goddesses, which include the beneficent Krishna, but also the terrifying skull-garlanded goddess Kali.

Often regarded as a development from Hinduism, Jainism, founded by Mahavira (599–527 BC) preaches total non-violence and maintains that once the soul is liberated from karma, the sum of previous existence, it is able to reach the perfect bliss of nirvana. Jains, like Hindus, are vegetarians and like them recognise a pantheon of gods, although Jains worship none of them as a saviour.

Sikhs, whose religion was founded much more recently, in 1469, believe by contrast in a single incarnate god, the immortal creator of the universe. Sikhs wear five symbols to denote their faith – uncut hair, a comb, a steel wristband, a miniature sword and shorts – and all Sikh men share a common surname, Singh, meaning 'lion'.

▲ *One of the key Hindu gods, the beneficent Krishna (left).*

Buddhism

SIDDHARTA GAUTAMA BUDDHA, born a prince in Nepal in about 586 BC, abandoned all his wealth and privileges at the age of 29 in order to live a humble life, searching for solutions to the problems and sufferings of existence. Buddha, which means 'enlightened one', devoted his life to study and austerity and during meditation under the sacred bo tree, was finally liberated from fear and suffering.

Within two centuries, Buddhism spread throughout India and later into the Far East, to become the first world religion disseminated beyond its original society. The central concept of Buddhism is enlightenment. Understanding of the nature and causes of suffering can bring suffering to an end with that, perfect consciousness. The Five Precepts and Four Noble Truths of Buddhism, together with the Noble Eightfold Path as the way to enlightenment, define the ethical conduct Buddhists must observe, and though they believe in free will, they also consider that actions have consequences which can be expunged only if desires and suffering are allowed to lapse.

Though Buddha himself did not deny the existence of gods, Buddhism is a religion without a deity, and one which regards physical phenomena as impermanent, unsatisfactory and lacking in soul or other vital essence.

▲ *Bust of the 'enlightened one', Buddha.*

Zoroastrianism

AT THE AGE OF 30, ZOROASTER (638–553 BC), also known as Zarathustra, the Persian prophet and religious teacher, believed that Ahura Mazda, or Ormuzd, the Good God, had come to him in a vision. Later, he formulated the apocalyptic faith named after him, teaching that there was an eternal struggle between Ahura Mazda, representing the forces of light and the forces of darkness of Mangra Mainyu, the Evil God. This belief is at the core of Zoroastrianism, which was the state religion of the Persian empire from 600 BC to AD 650, and was brought to north-west India by Persian immigrants in the tenth century. The struggle, Zoroastrians believe, centres on sacrifice and fire – fire being considered sacred and the repository of Ahura Mazda – and that the Good God will always prevail in the end.

Zoroastrians, also known as Parsees, maintain eternal fires in both their temples and their homes. They keep the sayings of Zoroaster in the holy book, the Avesta, in a series of hymns known as Gathas, together with other sacred texts. They traditionally dispose of their dead by chopping up corpses in special buildings known as Towers of Silence and leaving the remains to be disposed of by birds and animals.

▲ *Zoroaster, the Persian prophet and religious teacher.*

Christianity in Asia

AFTER THE ROMANS DESTROYED THE Jewish Temple in Jerusalem in AD 70, many followers of Christianity, sect of Judaism, fled to neighbouring Syria. Centuries later, Nestorius (AD 381–451) created the Syriac or Nestorian church, which taught that Jesus was not himself God, but was a human made divine by God. After reaching Chaldea in Mesopotamia, Nestorian Christianity spread rapidly to Central Asia, China and India. By the third century, the Christian sect based on the teachings of St Thomas became active in southern India.

The arrival of European traders from the end of the fifteenth century led to further input of Christianity into Asia. The Portuguese established themselves in enclaves such as Goa on the western coast of India. Together

with the Spaniards, who later colonised the Philippines, their missionaries converted many natives to Catholicism. The British in India, Malaysia and elsewhere brought the Protestant Church of England to Asia and other missionaries brought Christianity to Japan and China. where their work at first met savage resistance. In 1521, in fact, Ferdinand Magellan (1480–1521), the Portuguese navigator, then engaged in the first round-the-world voyage, was killed in the Philippines while attempting to convert the islanders to the Catholic faith.

◀ *Early illustrative map of the city of Jerusalem.*

Myths and Mystics

AS ELSEWHERE IN THE WORLD, Asia has myths depicting human descent from a semi-divine common ancestor or, among Muslims, legends of semi-historical kings and warriors. Tibetan Buddhist myths tell of the religious texts and images which fell from the sky onto the roof of the palace of Lhatho tho-ri, their first human king. In the creation myths of Central Asia, the world was made and sustained by huge numbers of gods and demons, residing unseen in countless locations of power. There are also myths concerning shamans who can travel the three realms of land, sea and sky, and understand the intricate workings of the Universe.

Mystics have long played an important part in Asian religion. For instance, Ramanuja taught that humans come from God and can return to God. Lord Chaitanya, born in Bengal in 1485, following the Ramanuja tradition, advocated passionate devotion, or bhakti, towards the god Krishna. Another Hindu mystic from Bengal, Sri Ramakrishna (1836–86), also taught bhakti, but with Kali as the centre of devotional prayer. Kabir of Benares, the teacher of Guru Nanak (1469–1539) the founder of Sikhism, sought to reconcile mystical Hinduism with the Sufi Islam through worship of Rama-Allah as the one supreme god.

Red Yama, the Tibetan Lord of Death is shown here turning the Wheel of Life. ▶

Australasia

The First Inhabitants

THE FIRST HUMANS, OR ABORIGINES, settled in Australia during the time when the island continent was linked by land to what is now Indonesia and Papua New Guinea. Their earliest traces, found by archeologists in the Upper Swan river region of western Australia date to about 38,000 BC.

The origins of the Australian Aborigines lie in southern Asia and, within some 2,000 years, they had spread over the entire continent, living a hunter–gatherer life which persisted until Europeans arrived after 1788. Their nomadic lifestyle served not only for the purposes of gathering food, but also to establish and maintain political, marital and ceremonial alliances between the various scattered groups. Their intricate kinship organisation consisted of divisions into categories called sections and subsections, based on the intersecting of male and female descent principles. The sections and subsections were also vital for fulfilling important ceremonial functions, such as initiation and the passing on of secret religious knowledge.

Compared to the Australian Aborigines, the Maoris of New Zealand were comparative newcomers, first arriving in about AD 850 but, like the Aborigines, establishing themselves throughout the area. Maori ancestry, however, was Polynesian and their arrival in New Zealand reflected the considerable Polynesian navigation and seafaring skills.

▲ *The Calendar Stone.*

The Coming of the Europeans

ONCE EUROPEAN NAVIGATORS BEGAN TO open up the world between the fifteenth and eighteenth centuries, the search was on for Terra Australis Incognita, the great southern continent which geographers believed 'balanced' the great land masses in the northern hemisphere. Dutch and British navigators landed on its coasts and explored in the general area after 1605, but it was not until 1788 that the first European settlers began to arrive, in the form of convicts transported to Australia from Britain. They arrived at Botany Bay on the east coast and settled around Sydney Cove in the territory that became known as New South Wales.

New Zealand, in its turn, was colonised from Australia and in 1815, the first Christian missionaries arrived. Among the first immigrants were escaped convicts and traders who sold guns to the Maoris. Despite the depredations of the European diseases the newcomers brought with them, the Maoris presented a formidable challenge to the establishment of permanent settlements and the British were at first reluctant to undertake the wars that might result. Only fears of French claims to the area prompted the British to declare formal sovereignty over New Zealand, and a treaty was signed with Maori chiefs at Waitangi in 1840.

◀ *Captain Cook arriving in Botany Bay, Australia, in 1788.*

Developing Australasia

THE TERMS OF WAITANGI WERE, HOWEVER, constantly breached and fierce disputes over the possession of land arose between the Maoris and the colonists, including full-scale Maori rebellions in 1845–47 and 1860–72.

Colonisation nevertheless went forward, with the development of the large-scale sheep farming which became the principle source of income by 1875. By then, there were 10 million sheep on the South Island of New Zealand alone and shortly afterwards, the Maoris on North Island were forcibly suppressed. With that, North Island began to develop a trade in dairy produce and in frozen lamb, using the refrigeration ships introduced in 1882.

Sheep-farming, based on the merino, was also established in Australia, where settlements like Perth (1829) and Melbourne (1835), and exploration into the interior began with the first crossing of the continent in 1860–61. The conclusion reached after further ventures was that the punishing heat and harsh terrain of the 'outback' made it unsuitable for settlement. It was, however, the 'outback' which provided riches after 1851, when gold was discovered in the state of Victoria. As a consequence, the population of nearby Melbourne trebled within three years.

◀ *The sheep population in Australasia soon began to rival that of the indigenous kangaroo.*

The Natives Disinherited

AS WHITE AUSTRALASIA GREW RICH and thrived, the native Aborigines and Maoris were largely disinherited of the land which they had occupied for so many centuries. The Maoris fared rather better, obtaining representation in the New Zealand parliament in concessions made to them after their second rebellion ended in 1882. The loss of their tribal lands still rankled, however, and today, the Maoris are demanding a review of the Treaty of Waitangi, and have laid claim to some 70 per cent of New Zealand.

The Aborigines suffered a great deal more. They were not only dispossessed, but hunted, misused and sometimes murdered. The death rate was so high that by the 1870s, there were no Aborigines left on the island of Tasmania. Today, Aborigines represent only 1.5 per cent of Australia's population and suffer discrimination in employment, where their unemployment rate is three times the national average. In 1995, the death rate among male and female Aborigines in the more remote regions of northern Australia was reckoned to be three and four times

the average for men and women respectively. The average Aboriginal life span is, in fact, some 20 years less than it is for the white population.

Such statistics have fuelled Aboriginal demands for human rights, and for the restoration of their ancestral lands.

▲ *Today the prospects are still bleak for aboriginal children due to discrimination against them.*

Creator Beings

THROUGHOUT AUSTRALIA, most myths deal with the journeys and actions of ancestral creator beings. They created the waterholes, mountain, rock formations and also brought living creatures into being. The creators also named the places they visited and the species they placed there to inhabit them.

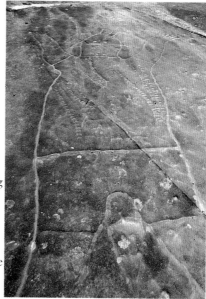

The tracks they made during their travels went across and through the lands of different groups of people. Therefore, no local group, clan or language group owns or knows a complete myth, but only a segment of it. This is why Aborigines come together periodically in order that the ritual recreation of the entire myth can be accomplished.

The time when the ancestral creator beings made the world is known as the Creation Time, more commonly called the 'Dreamtime' or 'the Dreaming' in Australia. The Aborigines believe that the act of creation still continues to this day and still exerts power over human beings. Access to the significance of ancestral creation is often gained through the power of dreams, which is why the term 'Dreamtime' is used to describe it. Ayres Rock, a 335–metre (1,100-ft) high mass of pink rock in northern Australia, is one of many sacred sites for the Aborigines who look back to the Dreamtime.

▲ *Figure believed to have been created by clan ancestral beings who formed the landscape during the Dreamtime.*

The Beliefs of the Maoris

THE POPULAR RELIGION OF the Maoris, which bears close resemblance to that of Polynesia, recognises many gods of Nature, such as Tane-mahuta, deity of trees, birds and forests, or Tangaroa who, like Neptune, guards the sea and its fish. Maori chiefs and priests, however, have an extra dimension to their faith. They also venerate Io as a supreme god and one whose powers are conjured up during ceremonies of birth, baptism or marriage among the Maori aristocracy. Ordinary people were for many years excluded from knowledge of Io. However, both high and low in Maori society believed in malign beings called *atua* who made omens, motivated black magic and punished those who broke *tapu*, the overriding law of proper behaviour, which incorporates strong overtones of prohibition.

Like the Australian Aborigines, dreams play an important part in Maori faith. Maoris believe that humans have been endowed with the *wairua*, a spirit which wanders in dreams, as well as the *mauri* and the *hau* which represent the principles of life. The *mauri* and *hau* disappear at death, but the *wairua*, or soul, travels to Te Reinga, also called Te Po, the Underworld beneath the sea where life continues in a peaceful environment.

Carving of the Fisherman's God, from the Cook Islands. ▲

Britain

A Frequently Invaded Island

THE PEOPLE OF BRITAIN do not have a single origin, but many, because the island country was the most frequently invaded territory of ancient and early medieval times.

The first Britons wandered, probably in small groups, over the land bridge which, until about 5000 BC joined Britain to Europe. The first newcomers with a name were the Celts, who came from southern Europe and arrived in several waves after about 1900 BC. They were followed by the Romans, who invaded Britain in AD 43. As Britannia, the country became the northernmost province of the vast Roman Empire for the next four centuries.

In the third century, while the Romans still held Britannia, new invaders, the Angles, Jutes and Saxons (or Anglo-Saxons), mainly from northern Germany came raiding and terrorising the population. Later, though, the Anglo-Saxons returned as settlers, driving the established British population westwards towards Wales.

History appeared to repeat itself after AD 793, when the fearsome Vikings from Scandinavia staged their first major raid across the North Sea. However, like the Anglo-Saxons before them, they eventually settled in Britain and at one stage, in the ninth and early tenth centuries, their 'Danelaw', where Vikings law and customs prevailed, covered about one half of Britain.

▲ *The wealth of Celtic artefacts, such as this bronze statue, give an insight into this ancient civilisation.*

Becoming One People

IN TIME, AND IN turn, the invaders mixed with the established population until they lost their original identities and became simply Britons. In 1066, it was as Britons that they faced the last successful invaders, the Normans from northern France, who were themselves descendants of the Vikings. Although the

▲ *The expulsion of the Huguenots from France: one example of the conflict between Catholics and Protestants that occurred throughout Europe.*

Normans subsequently took over the country as their own, they too blended in with the existing population in the course of time.

With the Normans, the age of invasions was over and the multi-origin peoples of Britain settled down to become a single, but very variegated, nation. The next people to arrive as immigrants came under different conditions. They joined an established culture and brought to it their own particular traditions. The first to establish themselves firmly were the Protestant Huguenots from France who first arrived in 1572, and afterwards in 1685 as refugees from religious discrimination. The Jews, on the other hand, had a chequered history in Britain. They were invited to settle in 1070, expelled in 1290 and invited in again, this time to stay, in 1655. More recent immigration, by Indians, Pakistanis, Caribbean peoples and others, have helped turn Britain into the multi-cultural, multi-racial society it is today.

The Sovereigns' Powers

EVER SINCE THE REIGN of Alfred the Great, the first ruler who could properly be called Sovereign of all England, the monarch has been the lynchpin of British political life. His or her powers have varied over time. However, they were never absolute but were always subject to the input of a body of advisers, such as the Anglo-Saxon Witangemot, the Norman and later nobles who believed they had a natural right to advise the monarch, later forming an increasingly influential, and ultimately paramount, Parliament. Relations, good or bad, often centred around the ability of monarchs to commend themselves to their nobility. Until the sixteenth century, for instance, a king achieved popularity by success in war. Those who failed in this important regard, such as King John (1199–1216), or Edward II (1307–27) paid the penalty of deep hostility from their nobles. Alternatively, strong, forceful monarchs retained loyalty far more easily. William I (1027–87) for instance, held his barons in thrall by exacting homage from them in return for grants of feudal lands. Queen Elizabeth I (1558–1603) was held in high regard by her subjects for her total devotion to her realm and her own personal courage.

▲ *King Alfred the Great divides up Britain into smaller kingdoms.*

Parliament Supreme

THE POSITION OF PARLIAMENT as the focus of political power had a long, painful gestation. The most frequent cause of its disputes with the monarch was the taste of certain kings for personal power. King John's efforts in this direction were answered when he was forced to sign the Magna Carta (1216), which limited royal powers and protected the barons' rights. John's son, Henry III (1216–72) sidestepped his nobles and resorted to 'favourites' and was punished for it when Simon de Montfort (1208–65), Earl of Leicester, imprisoned him and forced him to call the first recognisable Parliament in 1265.

Subsequently, although with setbacks, an increasingly powerful Parliament persistently frustrated over-ambitious monarchs. Its resolve to prevail was brutally demonstrated to the Stuart king Charles I (1625–49) who believed kings had a Divine Right to rule. Charles was rudely

disabused in the Civil War with Parliament, which ended in his execution. After 11 years of republican rule, the monarchy returned, but Parliament's troubles with the Stuarts and their Divine Right were not yet over. After James II (1685–88) defied Parliament and attempted to restore Roman Catholicism to England, a constitutional monarchy was introduced, putting the monarch under parliamentary control. Britain has been a constitutional monarchy ever since.

◀ *King John is forced to sign the Magna Carta.*

Fighting Britain

IN A MUCH-INVADED COUNTRY like Britain, war was inevitably a frequent resort, and from the Celts to the Normans, newcomers were obliged to fight to stake their claim in bloody and destructive battles. Even after that, Britain has been obliged to take up arms over rivalries with foreign powers escalating all the way to the First (1914–18) and Second (1939–45) World Wars and beyond that to the Falklands War with Argentina in 1982.

Britain's greatest wars have included three civil conflicts. There were two before the Civil War between Charles I and Parliament (1642–49) and both of those, in 1139–54 and 1455–85 were contests for possession of the crown. Overseas, there were seven centuries of bitter rivalry with France which ended only as recently as 1904, when the rising power of Imperial Germany began to threaten western Europe. The rivalry, while it lasted, included the Hundred Years' War (1337–1453), in which the

French sought to reclaim British-ruled territories in France. Later, the Seven Years' War (1756–63) saw Britain and France fight for colonial supremacy in India and Canada. Subsequently, Britain fought to help suppress the ambitions of Napoleon Bonaparte (1769–1821), who had risen to power after the French Revolution (1789).

▲ *Manuscript illustration of the Hundred Years' War between the French and the English.*

Weapons of War

THE WARFARE OF THE EARLY BRITONS largely consisted of charging an enemy in a disorganised mass, brandishing swords and battleaxes and uttering fearful war cries. Roman discipline and tactics proved the futility of such methods, and so did the Normans when they brought mounted cavalry and massed archers into battle at Hastings in 1066.

Subsequently, British fighting methods became much more organised and, in the eleventh to fourteenth centuries, the strictly trained, armoured knight on horseback, carrying lance and long cavalry sword, became the beau ideal of British fighting men. Also admired for their skill were the longbowmen, first introduced into warfare in 1277. The longbow enabled a trained archer to fire four times for every single shot from a crossbow, and the resulting shower of arrows could decimate an enemy advance, as was proved when the English confronted the French at the Battle of Agincourt (1415).

However, the invention of gunpowder, reputedly the work of an English monk, Roger Bacon (1214–94), in 1260 signalled the end of this type of warfare and over the next seven centuries, the power of guns grew mightily until the two World Wars showed how they could obliterate an entire landscape within their line of fire.

▲ *The Norman invasion of England from the Bayeaux Tapestry.*

Reaching Overseas

THE TRANSATLANTIC VOYAGES OF Christopher Columbus (1451–1506) in 1492–1504, and the subsequent creation of a great Spanish Empire in Central and South America, whetted the appetite of other European powers for overseas riches and the power that came with foreign possessions.

England appeared to be a poor relation in these stakes, recently emerged from the enervating Wars of the Roses (1455–85) and later riven by religious disputes between Protestants and Catholics. English status, however, had no effect on English ambitions. English traders very much wanted to participate in valuable commerce with the Spanish American colonies, even though the Spaniards sought at maintain a monopoly and banned foreign intruders from their possessions.

However, impudent English sea captains like Francis Drake (1540–96), regarded by Spaniards as a pirate, resolved to force their way in. During an expedition which ultimately proved the first circum-navigation of the globe by an Englishman (1577–80), Drake sailed round South America, pillaging Spanish ports along the coast. This, together with the subsequent capture of Spanish treasure ships, eventually brought Britain its greatest threat of invasion since 1066, when the mighty Spanish Armada arrived in the English Channel in 1588. The Armada was vanquished, but the rivalry with Spain remained.

▲ *Christopher Columbus arriving on the shores of Watling Island.*

Planting Britain Overseas

BEFORE LONG, THE ENGLISH WERE setting up their own colonies in the New World of America. Though attempts by Sir Walter Raleigh (1552–1618) to found settlements at Roanoke and elsewhere in North America ended in failure, a colony was successfully founded in Virginia in 1607 and received slaves brought from Sierra Leone 12 years later. More American possessions followed, with the acquisition of formerly Spanish Barbados in the Caribbean in 1625 and Jamaica in 1655. English planters settled there to grow sugar and meet a constantly increasing demand from Europe. The profitability involved was immense.

Meanwhile, across the world, the Honourable East India Company had been established in 1600, with a monopoly of British trade with the Far East awarded it by Queen Elizabeth I. Here, however, they clashed with the Dutch and the Portuguese, both of whom resented English intrusion into their profitable trade in spices.

The East India Company set up several trading bases in India, notably at Surat in 1612 after English traders made contact with the powerful Mogul Empire. Japan, too, attracted the English, Portuguese and Dutch, but the Japanese feared foreign influences and in 1640 ejected all intruders, except a small colony of Dutch traders.

Many British explorers set off on voyages of discovery during the reign of Queen Elizabeth I. ▶

The Empire on Which the Sun Never Set

FROM THESE RELATIVELY MODEST BEGINNINGS, the British later acquired the greatest empire the world had ever known. It was said that the sun never set on it because it always shone somewhere in the territories of the British Empire which, at its greatest extent in the nineteenth century, ruled one quarter of the earth's surface and one quarter of its population.

After the Seven Years' War with France, the British acquired the prized French colony of New France in Canada and also came to dominate India – which later became the 'Jewel in the Crown' of the Empire. The American colonies, which became the United States, were lost after the War of Independence (1775–83), but the list of British possessions continued to grow, eventually encompassing fresh territories in Southeast Asia, the Caribbean, Africa, Central and South America and the Indian, Pacific and Atlantic Oceans. British African possessions also included Sierra Leone, where a colony had been established in 1808 from a settlement for freed slaves set up in 1787–92 by British abolitionists.

Australia and New Zealand became British colonies – and later self-governing Dominions – after the first ships carrying transported convicts arrived to set up a penal colony there in 1788.

▼ *Things were not always calm within the Empire: in 1773 Bostonians disguised as Indians threw tea into Boston Harbour in protest over Britain's trade restrictions.*

Trading Britain

TRADE BETWEEN BRITAIN AND EUROPE had been taking place since very early times and as early as 1150 BC, goods such as axes, spearheads, daggers and chisels were being brought across from France. Much later, and before the Roman conquest, Britons were trading across the Channel with the Roman Empire, and were acquiring gold coinage and beautiful pottery from Europe. Early

British merchants grew rich on trade such as this and in time, the merchant class grew to be a powerful influence. When the feudal system the Normans had brought to Britain after 1066 collapsed in the mid-fourteenth century, the cause was not only the decimation of the feudal work force during the Plague (1349–51), but the growing independence and wealth of the merchant class in the towns.

By the sixteenth century, foreign trade in wool and cloth was a particularly lucrative area. In the eastern Mediterranean, cloth was exchanged for luxuries such as sweet wines, olives and currants which could be sold in Britain at high prices.

Later, the British Empire made the country a mighty force in world trade, although unfortunately, the riches that made ports like Bristol or Liverpool into great entrepots came from the trade in slaves.

▲ *A London merchant at his books.*

Industrial Britain

INDUSTRIAL INNOVATION IN BRITAIN began well before the Industrial Revolution of 1733–1840. In the sixteenth century, paper and gunpowder mills, sugar refineries, cannon foundries and salt-evaporating enterprises were mechanising goods and materials, and inventions such as drainage engines and ventilation shafts made it possible for mines to be sunk to greater depths than before. This was especially important at a time when supplies of timber, which had provided wood for fires, were running short and greater emphasis was placed on coal.

The first factory, in fact the first factory in the world, also predated the Revolution when it was built in 1702 near Derby, to make silk. A special machine was employed to unreel the material from cocoons.

The change-over to coal brought distinct benefits, since coal yielded more energy per unit than any other known fuel. This meant that factories

could expand and so increase their output. The output from blast furnaces grew as well, after Abraham Darby (c. 1678–1717) showed the way by developing coke from coal. In 1709, Darby made marketable iron in a coke-fired furnace, and soon demonstrated the superior cheapness and efficiency of this fuel by building much larger furnaces than had ever been possible with charcoal.

▲ *The interior of a weaving factory. New skills in manufacturing were introduced by the different groups of immigrants that arrived in Britain.*

The Industrial Revolution

IN BRITAIN, THE MID-EIGHTEENTH CENTURY saw the start of a series of inventions which revolutionised both trade and industry. It began in 1733, when a weaver named Jon Kay invented the flying shuttle. This device could throw a weaving shuttle from side to side in a loom more quickly than weavers could do it by hand. This in turn led to more inventions, as other people strove to make the thread supplying the shuttle keep up with the increased activity. Thirty years later, the first machine to meet this challenge was created – James Hargreaves's Spinning Jenny (1764–67).

Driven at first by water-power, the new machines revolutionised production in the textile mills. Later, with the introduction of James Watt's improved steam engine (1775), production rates increased even further and the use of steam spread from textiles to the iron and pottery industries and corn grinding. This had a 'domino' effect on mining, which grew rapidly as the factories' demands for coal increased.

With more goods flowing from more factories, transport to the markets had to be improved. The roads were unfit for the task. Canals were therefore built, the first of them the famous Bridgewater Canal (1762–72) which ran from Worsley to Manchester.

▼ *Canals were built to transport raw materials and goods to and from factories.*
Tow paths enabled horses to pull the barges.

Railways

PROBABLY THE MOST SPECTACULAR innovation of the time was the development of railways, an entirely new form of transport that challenged the centuries-old monopoly of the horse. It was George Stephenson (1781–1848) who built the world's first successful railway. While working as an engine-wright at a colliery in northern England, Stephenson had begun to think about ways of moving large amounts of coal more efficiently than by horse-drawn wagon. The result was the steam-powered locomotive which could pull trains capable of carrying coal in large quantities.

Trains to carry passengers came as a natural development, and the world's first railway line, the Stockton-Darlington Railway was built in northern England. It opened for traffic when Stephenson's engine 'Locomotion' pulled 34 passenger vehicles along a 16-km (10-mile) track on 27 September 1825. This was soon followed by the Liverpool-Manchester railway line, built by Stephenson and his son Robert (1803–59).

These successes set off an era of 'railway mania' both in Britain and the United States. Between 1844 and 1846 alone, Parliament gave permission for the construction of more than 400 new railways, and among other engineers who followed the Stephensons' lead was the brilliant Isambard Kingdom Brunel (1806–59), who built the Great Western Railway after 1833.

▲ *Examples of freight and passenger trains used on the original Liverpool–Manchester railway.*

A New Technological Age

BEFORE LONG, RAPID COMMUNICATIONS became vital to the new industrialised world. The electric telegraph, a British invention introduced in 1837, spread speedily throughout the western world, its adoption facilitated by the relative economy of installing the necessary wires. The early telegraphs were mainly owned by Britain, and before 1900 submarine cables, including the first transatlantic cable laid in 1866, were also British-owned. Together with other, foreign, inventions such as the telephone and radio, worldwide contact on a scale never known before became possible by the end of the nineteenth century.

Sea transport had also been revolutionised by the introduction of steam-powered boats, of which the first reliable example was the tug Charlotte Dundas which operated on a Scots canal in 1802. Later, after 1838, Brunel's great steamships *Great Eastern* (1838), *Great Britain* (1843) and *Great Western* (1858) became the first great liners to use steam engines all the way across the Atlantic.

Parallel advances had meanwhile been made in agriculture, with the introduction of devices such as the seed drill (1701) and the threshing machine (1802). Calculating machines were conceived, among them the 'Analytical Engine' planned by the English mathematician Charles Babbage (1792–1871), and Michael Faraday (1791–1867) invented the dynamo.

▲ *HMS* Agamemnon *laying the Atlantic cable.*
This illustration shows a whale crossing the line.

Enter the Feudal System

AT LEAST FROM THE TIME OF THE CELTS, after around 1900 BC, society in Britain was strictly hierarchical and, within families, patriarchal. At the apex of this social pyramid stood the king. Then came the aristocracy and after them the mass of common people who were mainly farmers. Among the Celts, of course, the Druid priesthood was ranked second only to the king, a status which did not continue in quite the same way once Britain was converted to Christianity. It was no accident, though, that this was the sort of arrangement common in armed forces, with commander, officers and ordinary soldiers. War, contests for possession, rivalries for power and sheer lawlessness had to be taken for granted as a feature of everyday life in early Britain as elsewhere, and society organised itself accordingly.

This state of affairs was formalised in the feudal system which came to Britain with the Norman invasion of 1066. Feudalism, a mutual self-defence arrangement, was basically a response to the disorder that blighted Europe after the fall of the Roman Empire in about AD 476. It also proved to be a way of bolstering the class structure and underwriting royal and aristocratic power.

▲ *Druid priests and priestesses were revered members of Celtic society.*

How Feudalism Worked

THE FEUDAL SYSTEM WAS A PYRAMID. At the top was the king, whose vassals, the nobility, owed him fealty and the duty of providing forces for his wars. Soldiers were recruited from among the mass of ordinary peasants who, in their turn, were a noble's vassals.

Oaths of fealty were solemn, binding contracts, sworn before God. To break them was therefore blasphemy, an awesome crime in an age of superstition. However, in return for fealty and the labour of their peasant vassals, or villeins, the nobles were duty bound to protect them in times of danger, if necessary within their castle walls.

The position of a feudal lord was extremely powerful. A demanding lord could treat his villeins like slaves, and runaways were common. In the feudal courts, a lord's word was law and anyone who contravened it risked severe punishments.

The villeins, for their part, spent two days a week labouring on their lord's *demesne*, or feudal estate, and also did 'boon' work in late summer, at harvest-time. However, villeins, too, were landowners in a small way. Better-off villeins might have up to 30 strips of land, poorer ones only three or four.

▲ *Bodiam Castle, a traditional Norman castle with solid fortifications and a moat to render it nearly impenetrable to the enemy.*

Exit Feudalism, Enter Humanism

AFTER THE PLAGUE (1349–50), the feudal system could no longer be maintained. Former villeins who survived were liberated by this disaster, since they could now demand higher wages for their work. There was also a new mood abroad in society, typified by independent merchants who grew rich from trade and, subsequently, new ideas of human importance emanating from the Renaissance, the revival of classical learning that began around 1450. Previously, humans had been viewed as passive creatures, locked into pre-set social systems and subject to the will of God. The Renaissance promoted humanism, a new view of people as the masters and potential improvers of their fate.

Instead of simply accepting the trials of life, ways were now sought to lighten the burden. In Britain in 1601, the state signalled for the first time its duty to take care of vagrants, beggars and other unfortunates when a Poor Law was created to raise funds for poor relief. In 1712, Thomas Newcomen (1663–1729) invented an 'atmospheric engine' which, among other functions, protected miners underground by reducing the danger of flooding. Medical advances were made which improved treatments and reduced suffering and mortality rates.

▼ *In 1601 the Poor Law was introduced in England,*
to try to alleviate the suffering of the destitute.

Philanthropic Britain

HUMANISM DID NOT CREATE UTOPIA; many cruelties persisted. Philanthropists were, however, ready to meet this challenge. Their first great campaign was the abolition of the slave trade to British possessions in 1807, and afterwards the end of slavery itself in 1833. They also tackled the appalling conditions in factories, where workers slaved for 14 hours a day amid unfenced, and therefore dangerous, machinery, and in the mines where small children and pregnant women spent hours labouring underground. After 1819, legislation was passed by Parliament to limit hours of work and protect factory workers from machines as well as to forbid the employment of women and young children. Trade Unions were legalised in Britain in 1825, enabling them to press for better wages and conditions.

These measures, which for the first time promoted the interests of ordinary people on a country-wide scale, did not come about easily. Every single one was hard-fought as employers and others with vested interests in maintaining the status quo obstructed the philanthropists in every way they could devise. Nevertheless, philanthropy prevailed, and the reforms later led to old age pensions (1908), the enfranchisement of formerly voteless men (1918) and of women (1918/1928).

▲ *Children were valuable workers in mines: they were paid little but forced to work as long and hard as the adults.*

Religion in Britain

IN EARLY BRITAIN, AS EACH NEW INVADER settled the land, each brought with them their own pagan faith. Christianity came to Britain in the third century, while the Romans still ruled, though before the

Roman Empire itself adopted the religion after AD 313. At that time, it was a clandestine faith, forbidden by the Roman conquerors, and it had its martyrs as early as AD 259.

Later, from the mid-fifth century, after the departure of the Romans, the Celtic Church became established – mainly in Wales and western England, Scotland and Ireland. Its missionaries were energetic zealots, especially those from Ireland, and they were tireless in spreading Christianity around Britain and in Europe. After about AD 450, however, the pagan Anglo-Saxon invaders set about destroying Celtic Christianity from most of England and ultimately marginalised the Church in the south-west, Wales, northern England and Ireland.

The Anglo-Saxons, however, themselves became Christian after the mission headed by St. Augustine (d. AD 605) arrived from Rome and began its campaign of conversion in Kent. Subsequently, papal Christianity became dominant in Britain and received a boost with the arrival of the Normans in 1066 who had their own especially vigorous form of the faith. Or so it appeared at first.

▲ *Celtic crosses can still be found in church yards all over England and Ireland.*

Excluding the Pope

FROM THE ROYAL POINT OF VIEW, the one unacceptable feature of the 'Roman' Christian Church in England was the foreign, papal influence it involved. King William I and his Archbishop of Canterbury, Lanfranc (1010–89) made it quite clear that their jurisdiction over the English Church took priority over commands from Rome. This set a pattern. The struggle between Henry II (1133–89) and his friend, former chancellor and later Archbishop of Canterbury Thomas Becket (1118–70), who upheld papal rights in England, ended with Becket's murder in Canterbury Cathedral in 1170.

King John, in his turn, attempted to block the Pope's right to interfere in episcopal elections. Consequently, John was excommunicated and his realm was laid under interdict (1208–13).

Papal power in England finally met its match with the rise of the Protestant Church after 1517. Emulating several European rulers, though for his own purposes, Henry VIII (1491–1547) took the English Church out of papal jurisdiction after the Pope had refused to grant him a divorce from his first wife, Catherine of Aragon. Henry then pronounced himself its head in the Pope's place and annulled his own marriage. The Church of England has been Protestant ever since.

▲ *The murder of Thomas Becket in Canterbury Cathedral.*

The Celts

Origins

THE IMAGINATIVE, technologically brilliant, but reputedly disorganised Celts were one of the great founding peoples of Europe. However, their lack of written records has meant that their prevailing image comes from Ancient Greek or Roman observers who were not kindly inclined towards them.

The Celts' ancestors were already living in southern Europe in the early Iron Age. Excavations of the late Hallstatt culture have revealed major Celtic occupation from around 1100 BC in what is now northern Austria. By the late Iron Age and Bronze Age, the Celts were already well established at a time roughly contemporary with the traditional beginning of Rome in the eighth century BC.

Subsequently, the Celts spread over a large area, from the Balkans and across southern Europe to France and the Iberian peninsula and later, under pressure from Roman conquest, to the edges of the then-known world, to Brittany in north-west France, Ireland, Scotland, Cornwall and other parts of Britain.

The one-sided picture of the barbaric, uncivilised and compulsively warlike Celts left by the Ancient Greeks and Romans failed to note what archeology later discovered: artifacts which showed that the Celts were intelligent, complex and wealthy people, whose art and technical skills were unsurpassed in prehistoric Europe.

A bronze shield with glass inlay, probably dating back to the Roman occupation of England. ▲

The Celts at War

THE ANCIENT GREEKS AND ROMANS, for all their obvious dislike of the Celts, were not entirely inaccurate in their observations. They were right, for example, in the idea that the Celts were warlike. The Celts, in fact, were physically built for it. The Romans found they were generally tall and muscular – the build of warriors.

The spread of the Celts across Europe was probably achieved through a series of aggressions, as exampled by their presence in Italy before around 400 BC and certainly afterwards, when a great migration of Celtic tribes took place. Rome was attacked by Celtic Gauls in 390 BC and afterwards, bands of Celtic raiders roamed over the peninsula and reached Sicily.

Thanks to the account left by Julius Caesar (100–44 BC) after confronting the Celtic Britons in 55 BC and 54 BC, Celtic warfare became virtually synonymous with fighting from chariots. The Celts were certainly nimble charioteers, but their fighting style was likely to have been more of the violent-charge and hand-to-hand variety. There is some evidence that the Celts fought naked and also that they beheaded their enemies. No wonder that even the Roman army, the best of its time, feared them.

Bronze Celtic figure of a man. ▶

The Celts as Traders

THE CELTS WERE ENERGETIC TRADERS, bartering salt, furs and gold for wine, oil, mirrors and luxury pottery with the Mediterranean peoples of southern Europe. They were establishing contact with the Greek colonies of the western Mediterranean as early as 600 BC and their customers soon found that Celtic goods were worth acquiring. The Celts were skilled metalworkers in gold and bronze, fashioning exquisite torques and bracelets, hammered, embossed or set with the symbols of princely power, coral and amber. They also produced heavy, solid gold and bronze necklaces and decorated their wares with stylised animals. Celtic pottery, with its decorative lozenges, circles and chevrons was equally desirable.

Trade made the Celts rich. In about 520 BC, Celtic chieftains were being buried with a wealth of gold and bronze objects. Imports found in

Celtic graves included bronze cauldrons from Greece, Etruscan bronze vases from Italy and Athenian clay cups. The Celtic princes lived well, too. Their Greek and Etruscan imports included many luxury items, such as works of art and fine wines. Cultural influences also marked Celtic trading practice. Their long, double-edged iron swords were decorated in Etruscan style or were taken from their links with southern Russia.

▲ *Detail from the Gundestrup Cauldron, showing a magnificent bearded deity.*

Celtic Society

CELTIC SOCIETY WAS BASED ON CLANS and blood ties, with powerful princes and prosperous, outward-looking settlements which were frequently established on well-defended hilltops, where strong forts were constructed. The aristocracy was a warrior aristocracy; Celtic leaders were principally war leaders and the general structure of Celtic life was based on a patriarchy in which households consisted of a man, his wives and their children and grandchildren.

Basically, the Celts were a farming society so that ownership of land, vested in their kin, was important to them. Mixed farming was the foundation of their economy, though whether they cultivated cereals or kept cattle, or both, depended on their location in the wide and varied swathe of Europe which they occupied.

As might be expected of a fighting, farming society, horses acquired great importance in Celtic life. They were first introduced into Celtic Gaul (France) during the Bronze Age and Julius Caesar later wrote of the great passion the Celts felt towards them.

The Druids priests, who performed religious and magic duties in Celtic society and exercised enormous influence, were a class apart. Their importance was such that, although they were drawn from the warrior aristocracy, they actually ranked above them.

▲ *Roman soldiers massacre the Druids at Anglesey.*

The Celtic Druids

ACCORDING TO JULIUS CAESAR, Druidism was established in southern and central Gaul as the religion of the Celts from around 100 BC. The Romans looked very much askance at the Druids because of their superstitious influence and reputed human sacrifices, and they and their rites were banned by the Roman Emperor Tiberius (42 BC–AD 37) and Claudius (10 BC–AD 54).

However, Druidical beliefs were in some ways not all that different from those of other, less criticised, faiths. The oak, or *drus* in Greek, which gave the Druids their name was a sacred tree, and, in one of the most sacred of their rites, a golden sickle was used to cut mistletoe from it. The Druids taught that the human soul was immortal and subject to reincarnation. However, their reputation for offering human sacrifices may be speculative.

The Druids were not only spiritual leaders, but were expert in mathematics and astronomy, both of which had their place in the observance of religious rites.

It was through these rites that the Druids controlled access to the world of spirits. This was not, however, a monotheistic religion, for the Celts had many gods which, like those of the Greeks and Romans, were associated with important aspects of life.

▲ *Roman Emperor, Julius Caesar.*

Gods and Myths

WARFARE, HUNTING, HEALING AND good harvests had their particular gods and the Celts associated some of them with particular places such as sacred groves, remote mountains and lakes. In Britain, the goddess Sulis gave her name to the healing springs at Aquae Sulis, present-day Bath. In Celtic Gaul, the gods Borvo and Grannos were associated with wells.

Celtic gods and goddesses naturally feature in myths, and one of the most powerful tells of the invasion of Ireland by Tuatha Dà Dannann, the People of the Goddess Danu, who formed a divine race. Giants also occur in Celtic myth, as do giantesses, such as Bebinn who plays a part in the Fenian Cycle which tells of the poet-seer-warrior Finn mac Cool whose band of Irish warriors, the Fianna, are pledged to defend kings. Giants also feature in Sacred Head myths in which they and their enemies are beheaded or serve to challenge heroes in decapitation contests.

There is, too, the mystical Otherworld, usually sited on an archipelago of wondrous islands in the western or Atlantic ocean. In one myth, the land of Women in the Otherworld is sought as a place where there is no grieving, no winter and no want.

▲ *The boar is the most widely depicted animal in Celtic art; these figures were probably votive offerings.*

China

Origins

THE CIVILISATION OF CHINA, one of the earliest to be established, arose in the Hwang-Ho or Yellow River area of north-east China in about 1650 BC, but human settlement, of course, existed long before that. Homo Erectus, the first true human, who originated in east Africa, began arriving in China, at Shaanxi, in about 900,000 BC. By about 450,000 BC, they had made their homes in and around the Zhoukoudian caves at Dragon Bone Hill, north of the Yellow River. These humans were hunters, living in small groups of up to 40 in number, and were short, stocky and well-built.

Traces of the more advanced Homo Sapiens, immediate ancestor of humans today, have also been found in China not long afterwards. Rice cultivation came to China in about 5000 BC, during the Neolithic or New Stone Age, when several ethnic communities were in existence. By about 4000 BC, the Yangshao culture, with its distinctive geometrically-patterned pottery, was established in the north, in Henan. By 3500 BC, the Longshan people of the east and north-east had set up the first towns in China. and were producing equally distinctive black ceramics. In these areas, millet was grown, and dogs, pigs, sheep and oxen raised.

▲ *Rice is the staple diet throughout Asia. In mountainous regions terraced paddies use gravity to ensure the irrigation of all the fields.*

The First Chinese Civilisation Emerges

IN TIME, ONE OF THE MANY PEOPLES living in China became more advanced than the rest and grew to be the dominant power in the Yellow River region after about 1650 BC. From this, there arose the first Chinese state, ruled by the Shang dynasty. The Shang capital and the nucleus of its power was an Anyang, in the modern Henan province.

The Shang owed their success to their efficient military organisation, urban settlement, institutions of kinship and priesthood, methods of transport and communications and their high standard of art – all of which were superior to those of the surrounding peoples. The Shang were also more technologically advanced, with considerable expertise in metallurgy. This, of course, was a vital adjunct to military superiority and greater advance in material culture.

By 1200 BC, they had invented a writing system consisting of graphs or characters. This in its turn enabled the formation of a bureaucracy and an administration capable of controlling state affairs. Consequently, the Shang developed an improved social organisation and created healthy commerce, the regulation of agriculture by means of a lunar calendar with a cycle of 60 years which was devised in the Shang period and a sophisticated approach to foreign affairs and religious observance.

◀ *Chinese plate decorated with a green and red dragon motif. Dragons are often central to Chinese mythology.*

A Warlike Civilisation

FROM THE FIRST, THE overriding characteristic of Chinese civilisation was its warlike nature. As dynasty followed dynasty, right up to the last of them, the Qing (1644–1911) and on to the Kuomintang Republic (1912–49) and the present-day People's Republic, the pattern of succession was all too often one of power seized by aggression. The Shang, for instance, were overthrown by the Zhou from western China in 1027 BC. In 403 BC, the Zhou Empire broke up into small kingdoms which were at war until the Kingdom of Qin vanquished all rivals and set up their own empire in China in 221 BC. The Qin, in their turn, succumbed to the Han (202 BC–AD 20) and the Han fell to widespread, long-lasting rebellion before they were replaced by the Sui in AD 581. This was a history of constant upheaval, punctuated by periodic disintegration and reunification of empires and regular rebellions and invasions. The overall scenario was one of endemic disorder and the impermanence of power.

Remarkable advances were nevertheless made despite all this political mayhem. For example, the world's first system of printing was developed while the T'ang empire (AD 628–907) broke up into the period of 'Five Dynasties and Ten Kingdoms', and China went into economic decline.

▲ *Chinese wooden drinking vessel on a carved tripod stand.*

Organising an Empire

THE VASTNESS OF CHINA created its own problems of administration, and these were solved most successfully when there was a strong, centralised government.

The centralisation principle became fact very early on in Chinese history. The first Qin emperor, Shih Lung Ti, effected some surprisingly modern reforms, aided by the authoritarian status that Chinese emperors enjoyed. He set up 36 regions, or *chun*, each with civil, military and governing civil servants. Laws and weights and measures were standardised, and so were the characters of the written Chinese script. The reforms included some fine detail. For instance, axle lengths on carts were strictly controlled in order to make commerce easier.

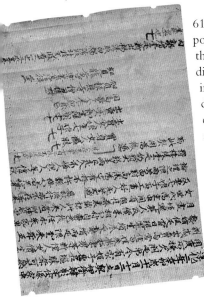

A thousand years later, after AD 618, when the T'ang came to power, China was reorganised again, this time into 10 – later 15 – districts which were sub-divided into prefectures. Each prefect was directly responsible to the imperial court for the administration of his area. The Grand Council met with the emperor on a daily basis and there were six ministries and 10 other offices. One was a flood prevention bureau, another a national college for the training of officials. Two state universities trained civil servants who had to sit written examinations to gain promotion.

▲ *A page of a sutra, discourse of a Buddha.*

The Great Wall of China

CHINA WAS SUBJECT TO INVASIONS, mainly by Mongol and Turkish nomads who ranged free across the vast Gobi desert. This led to the building in the north of a great defensive wall, the Great Wall of China, which was so extensive that today, it is the only artificial construct on earth which can be seen from outer space. The Qin, who built the Wall in the reign of their emperor Shi Huangdi, were ideally suited such a massive enterprise. They knew how to erect strong fortifications and were also great exponents of siege warfare. The Qin developed catapults, scaling ladders and other equipment of a kind that was widely copied and was in use many centuries later, both in Ancient Roman times and in medieval Europe.

Built after 214 BC, the Great Wall extended 2,600 km (1,615 miles).

along the monad frontier south of the Gobi desert, and was a standard 7.6 m (24.9 ft) at the base and 5 m (16 ft) wide at the top. The Wall, an average 7.6 to 9 m (24.9 to 29.5 ft) in height, had crenellated parapets 1.5 m (5 ft) above the walkways with defensive watch towers at regular intervals. Afterwards extended by the Han dynasty, the wall was made of earth and stone faced with brick.

◀ *One of the most amazing feats achieved by mankind was the construction of the Great Wall of China.*

The Mongols

THE GREAT WALL served its purpose for over 1,000 years, a tribute to the soundness of both its concept and its structure. It kept the Mongol raiders out of China for all that time, but could not do so forever. The early Mongols who struck at the Chinese empire were nomads wandering the grassy plains of Mongolia with their sheep, camels, goats and cattle. The later Mongols, who finally succeeded in breaking through the Wall in 1211, were far more formidable. They were mighty warriors with unparalleled skills in fighting on horseback and a strong military structure converted from warring clans into a near-unstoppable force by their great general Temujin (1167–1227), who later took the much-feared name of Genghis Khan.

Genghis organised his army into multiples of 10, with the *touman* of 10,000 men as the largest tactical unit. After unifying the Mongol tribes under his leadership by 1206, Genghis led the Horde, as his army was called, through the Great Wall and into the Chinese countryside which they devastated at will, creating universal panic. Afterwards, Genghis added China to his empire, which ultimately stretched from eastern Europe to the Pacific Ocean and was the greatest land empire ever known.

The mighty warlord, Genghis Khan. ▶

The Mongol Emperors of China

THE CONQUERING INSTINCT evidently ran in Genghis Khan's family. Genghis' great-grandson, Babar (1483–1530), conquered the Mogul Empire in India in 1526 and Genghis's grandson, Kublai Khan (1216–94), became Emperor of China in 1259. Genghis had left the subjugation of northern China unfinished, but Kublai completed it after 1240 and 19 years later established the Yuan dynasty which was to last more than 100 years, until that great enemy of so many Chinese emperors, rebellion, drove the Yuan from the throne.

While it lasted, however, the Yuan reached great heights of wealth and splendour. Europeans learned of it after the Venetian travellers Marco Polo (1254–1324) and his uncles crossed the Gobi Desert to reach the court of Kublai Khan in 1271. Polo's later account of the stunning riches in gold, jewels, fine cloth and spices later whetted the appetites of European merchants for trade links with China.

As emperor, Kublai Khan established his capital at Cambaluc (modern Beijing) and made Buddhism the state religion in China. His empire stretched to the River Danube in the west, and he later extended his rule into Indochina, though what the Japanese called *kamikaze*, a 'divine wind', prevented his fleet from invading Japan in 1281.

▲ *Marco Polo wearing the traditional costume of the Tartars.*

Voyages of Discovery

ALTHOUGH THE RULE OF THE YUAN emperors was comparatively shortlived in China, Mongol incursions created a dislike of foreigners and foreign influence. This chauvanism, however, did not prevent overseas explorations, and in around 1400, Chu Ti (1360–1424), third emperor of the Ming dynasty which supplanted the Yuan, appointed a court eunuch, Zheng He, as commander-in-chief of missions to the western oceans. In 1405, Zheng embarked on the first of seven voyages which ultimately took him to Malacca in present-day Malaysia, Ceylon (Sri Lanka), Calicut in India, Sumatra in Indonesia, Hormuz in the Persian Gulf and along the east coast of Africa. The fleets Zheng commanded

were considerable. On his first voyage, he sailed with 62 ships manned by 27,800 sailors.

However, in 1424, a new Ming emperor, Chu Kao-chih (1378–1425) forbade the building of seagoing vessels and suspended expeditions abroad in the belief that imperial resources should not be squandered on distant enterprises, but mustered in defence against the nomads. Chu Kao-chih died the following year, though, and Zheng's voyages appear to have resumed, lasting until 1433.

The effect of Zheng's endeavours was to encourage the Chinese to emigrate abroad, notably to Southeast Asia, where Chinese presence has remained ever since.

Chinese exploration, especially of overseas regions, began tentatively in the early fifteenth century. ▲

Europeans Reach China

THE DEATH OF THE INTREPID Zheng He in 1434 ended the brief period of Chinese maritime exploration. However, exploration in the form of European ships, came to them and the intrusion was not entirely beneficial.

Portuguese explorers reached Macao on the south China coast in 1516, established a trading post in 1537 and 20 years later obtained a lease from China which was to persist for nearly five centuries, until 1999.

Despite their urge for isolation, the Chinese had traded with Europeans before, but not in this intrusive manner. The discovery in 1498 of the sea route to Asia as a substitute for the land route blocked by the Ottoman Turks after 1453, brought explorers and would-be empire-builders into the Chinese orbit rather than the more co-operative merchants who had come before. The pressure soon told.

The Chinese tried to confine foreign trade to a few ports and deliberately heaped humiliations on the few Europeans who reached inland. They were required to stamp on the Cross or crawl on hands and knees in front of officials. After 1793, however, the British in particular grew impatient and decided to take stronger measures to open up more trade. The weapon they chose was opium.

▲ *The English sell goods to the Chinese at designated trading posts along the coast, despite the efforts of the Chinese to stop foreign trade.*

The Humiliation of China

OPIUM WAS COPIOUSLY CULTIVATED in Bengal by the British East India Company. This supplied European traders who introduced the drug into China, where the number of addicts soon mounted alarmingly. When, in a series of attempts to put a stop to it, the Chinese destroyed an entire cargo, the so-called Opium War (1839–42) between Britain and China broke out.

Faced with modern military technology, the Chinese were helpless before the onslaught. In the treaty of Nanking (1842), they were forced to open up five 'treaty' ports for foreign trade and lease Hong Kong to Britain. After their defeat in a second Opium War (1856–60) in which

Beijing was seized by an Anglo-French force, the Chinese were forced to agree to a foreign enclave on their territory where merchants acquired extraordinary privileges, including exemption from Chinese law.

Despite the ferocious Boxer Rebellion of 1900, which attempted to expel the foreigners, this profound humiliation of the Chinese emperor and empire lasted until well into the twentieth century and later served as a spur to Mao Zedong (1893–1976), the Marxist Communist leader who resolved, while still a young man, to make China once more respectable and respected in the world.

◀ *The British and the Chinese meet face to face in Nanking during the Opium War.*

The Silk Road

DESPITE CHINESE DISLIKE OF FOREIGNERS, Emperor Han Wu-ti (141–87 BC) opened what later came to be called the Silk Road for trade between Europe and China in about 100 BC. This 6,000-km (3,728-mile) highway, connecting the Mediterranean to Asia, was a series of routes, one of which ran from the Chinese capital of Chang'an (now Xi'an in the Shaanxi province) across northern China to the Middle Eastern ports of Antioch and Alexandria. Some of the most luxurious

trade in the world travelled along the Silk Road, including Chinese silk, clocks, gunpowder and spices, gold, jewellery, metals, glass and coins.

Under the T'ang dynasty (AD 618–907) Arabian, Persian, Korean and Japanese merchants also brought spices to China and these soon found their way into Chinese food, while the Chinese menu was augmented by Persian cakes and sweetmeats.

Outside events, however, had their effect when the Road fell into disuse with the rise of the militarised and belligerent Muslim states which grew up during the rapid spread of Islam. The Mongols revived the route in the thirteenth century, but after 1453 it was closed for good, when European traders were prevented from using it by the Muslim Ottomans in Turkey, who were sworn enemies of the Christian faith.

▲ *The opening of the Silk Road led to the introduction of many new materials, objects, foods and spices to Europe.*

The Inventive Chinese

THE CHINESE WERE EXTREMELY INVENTIVE people, displaying an originality that owed nothing to outside influences, and inventing sophisticated devices and methods long before they came into use elsewhere. They learned early on how to irrigate the soil and make silk; they developed smelting and metalworking industries. Paper was another Chinese invention, and its production involved the world's first mechanised industry. This was an essential for a highly literate and bureaucratic society that left minutely detailed records. The Chinese also devised a system of weights and measures, established a calendar and invented a 'weathercock' which was an early warning system for the detection of subterranean seismic disturbances.

A further invention from China, before 450 BC, was the crossbow – a deadly weapon, and one that later helped transform the firepower of European armies. The crossbow was dangerously accurate and of especial use in sieges where long-range fire from a steady 'platform' was vital in repelling the enemy.

Firearms, including cannon, were known in Europe by 1327, when a primitive cannon-like device appeared in an English manuscript kept in the library of Christ Church, Oxford. This development, too, had filtered across from China and with it, the Chinese discovery of gunpowder.

Chinese Buddhist saint from the Qing dynasty. ▲

Gunpowder

ALTHOUGH THE EVIDENCE is considered inconclusive in some quarters, it is believed that the Chinese knew about gunpowder, or 'black' powder, for at least two centuries before Europe became aware of it. There are, in fact, several other claimants, including Roger Bacon (1214–94), an English monk who is credited with inventing gunpowder in 1260.

It appears, though, that the Chinese chanced on the formula for making it some 200 years earlier, during the early eleventh century, after experiments with various ingredients such as oil, pitch and sulphur. The first Chinese recipe, recorded in 1044 by Ching Tsao Yao, outlined the making of saltpetre. The Muslims may have learned the formula from the Chinese, or possibly invented gunpowder independently. The formula appeared in about 1200 in the writings of an Arabian, Abd Allah, and the Arabs produced the first known operational gun in 1304.

The potential of gunpowder as a propellant was realised only when Europeans used it in their own wars, in the form of an upturned 'bells' called 'vasi', from which large stones could be fired. This gave a new slant to catapults and other siege engines which had performed the same task mechanically, by means of torsion.

Using Chinese Inventions

THE ARABS, WHO WERE KEEN TRADERS and travellers, frequently acted as 'agents' to bring Chinese inventions to Europe. In AD 751, for instance, the Chinese set up a factory for making paper in Samarkand, east of the Caspian Sea in present-day Uzbekistan. From there, the Arabs took it to Muslim-ruled Spain. The invention spread and by the thirteenth century, water-powered paper mills were in operation in Italy. Another example was the water-powered clock with mechanical escapement and gear mechanism, invented in China by 1088. By the late thirteenth century, full mechanical clocks with weighted drives and verge and foliot escapement were being constructed in Europe.

Technological progress in Europe was also fuelled from China by developments in printing, the introduction of the horizontal loom, the spinning wheel, the lateen sail, the sternpost rudder and cast iron. All served to maintain the momentum of European technology, where their potential appeared to be better realised than in China itself. This was hardly surprising since the cultural ethos of China was relaxed and collectively orientated, and invention for its own intellectual sake had a value. Europe, by contrast, was a place of thrusting ambitions where practical need was more energetic.

From the very early, simple punts such as this, the Chinese went on to invent the lateen sail and the sternpost rudder. ▼

The Son of Heaven

THE POSITION OF THE CHINESE EMPEROR could not have been more exalted. He was regarded as the 'Son of Heaven', a divine being who mediated between the earthly world and the spiritual world, and was customarily described in glowing and reverential terms. This was so despite the fact that the 157 emperors and reigning empresses of China were all too human, with vices and eccentricities as well as virtues. On occasion, they could be weak and ineffectual rulers, willing to delegate control of their vast empire to dowager empresses, eunuchs and even concubines. Others were seriously corrupt. For example, the Han

emperor Chengdi (r. 33–37 BC) was fond of visiting cock-fights in disguise and got rid of his wife, the empress Xu, for the sake of a low-born concubine, Zhao Feiyan, with whom he fell in love. Later, to preserve Zhao's position, Chengdi had his two sons murdered.

Even so, some emperors, such as Kublai Khan, were brilliant military commanders, and others, such as the T'ang emperor Taizong (r. AD 626–649), were fine scholars and capable administrators. Taizong, in fact, was one of the great Chinese emperors, a hard worker who lived frugally and cared for the welfare of his subjects.

The Chinese Peasants

ALTHOUGH THEY EXISTED AT THE OTHER end of the scale, and were a vast distance away from their emperors, Chinese peasants were regarded as one of the indispensable pillars of Chinese society. This was only logical when peasant labour on the farms fed the empire. The peasant farmers received state aid, including technical aid, for food production, yet paradoxically, they were also exploited and mercilessly overworked by their feudal overlords.

Peasant life was hard and could be gruelling. Poverty, despite state help, was common, and it was said that a Chinese peasant could work all year round and still not earn enough to feed himself and his family. Many fell so far into debt that loans from money-lenders became an inheritance that was passed from one generation to the next. Farming was not all the peasants were required to do. They were also duty bound to work on public building projects such as irrigation and drainage systems, reservoirs and other water-control works, and they had to perform military service, too.

This situation helped account for the many peasant rebellions that punctuated Chinese history, many of them set off by bureaucratic procrastination in mounting relief measures in times of disaster.

◀ *Marco Polo and his brothers present the Pope's letter to Kublai Khan, the emperor of China.*

Confucius

IF THE PEASANTRY WAS ONE indispensable pillar of Chinese society, the philosophy of K'ung Fu Tzu (551–479 BC), the 'Master' better known as Confucius, was the other. Confucius was regarded as a superior being and after Confucianism became the official ideology of China in the second century BC, under the Han dynasty, sacrifices were made to him as well as to the heavenly bodies, the imperial ancestors and several nature gods. From the seventh century AD, public observance of Confucianism became obligatory.

Confucian philosophy emphasised ethical conduct and moral example, and its teachings were essentially conservative. Great emphasis was placed on moral order, the established patriarchal family structure and on the importance of authority, obedience and mutual respect. In Confucianism, the Superior Man was the ideal and filial piety was the greatest virtue.

Confucius was born in Lu, in the present-day province of Shangdong, and after a poverty-stricken youth, became a minor official and then a teacher. Confucius was greatly concerned by the suffering of the poor, but he was 67 years old before his philosophies became widely known. When he died five years later, he was buried with great ceremony and his grave became, as it remains, a place of pilgrimage.

◀ *The teachings and beliefs of the scholar and philosopher Confucius, are the basis of the school of thought, Confucianism.*

Taoism

TAOISM, IN SOME WAYS A PARALLEL philosophy to Confucianism, in others a rival to it, was expounded in the sixth century BC by Lao Zi. Somewhat older than Confucius, Lao Zi was termed the 'Old Master' according to Taoist tradition. He served the Zhou king, K'ung Tzu, but was so disgusted with the problems existing in China that he left the country. Lao is supposed to have reached India where, Taoists claim, he became known as the Buddha. The Taoist scriptures, Tao Te Ching, have been ascribed to Lao Zi, but were apparently put together three centuries after his lifetime. The tao, or 'way,' denotes the hidden principles of the universe.

Taoism shares with Confucianism a belief in 'ying and yang' – bright and dark – which keep the universe in balance. Taoism, however, challenges the Confucian principles that order and harmony can be imposed, and teaches instead that they can be achieved only if they are allowed to happen naturally. To Taoists, disorder comes about through human attempts to interfere with Nature, while correct behaviour and well-being come through living spontaneously. Taoist awareness works in harmony with the circumstances of life, and the highest virtues are humility and lack of self-consciousness.

▲ *Yin and Yang are opposing forces which must interact and contain an element of the other to produce harmony.*

The Origin of the Chinese World

CHINA HAS A RICH TRADITION of cosmic myths. There is the world picture of the primeval earth covered by a sky cupola fastened together by cords, mountains and pillars. Another myth tells how the universe was created from vapour. A third myth relates how the world was created from matter which resembled a chicken's egg and separated into the sky and the earth. A further Chinese creation myth tells how the goddess Woman Gua created all things by undergoing 70 transformations.

A minority ethnic group in south-west China relates how the world and humans were formed from the ding body of the first-born semi-divine being, the giant Pan Gu. His breath became wind and clouds, his voice became thunder, his eyes the Sun and Moon and his limbs, the mountains. Pan Gu's bodily fluids turned into rain and rivers, and his flesh became the soil. The hair on his head became stars, and his body hair, the vegetation. Teeth, bones and marrow became minerals. The bacteria in his body turned into humans. This myth, recorded in the third century AD, and probably originating from Central Asia, is a series of metamorphoses and is called the myth of the cosmological human body.

▲ *Spectacular statue of the sky god.*

Mythical Themes in Art

MYTHS AND MYTHICAL FIGURES have provided the inspiration for art in many cultures. In China, the earliest artistic expression of myth occurs on funereal stone carvings and murals. Favourite themes are the acts of the gods, flood and fire myths, the tree of life, the paradise of the Queen Mother of the West and the trials endured by heroes, such as the filial Shun.

The most popular poetic theme features the two tragic stellar lovers. The military heroes of antiquity and intelligent animals, such as the Monkey, are recurring figures in novels. Temple architecture colourfully represents deified figures like that of Confucius and the life-giving symbol of the dragon appears on textiles and ceramics. A famous picture, 'Nine Dragons' by Ch'en Jung, painted in ink and muted colour on paper in 1244, shows the mythical beasts of China emerging and disappearing among mountain crags, mists and water.

Chinese sculpture, too, borrowed from myth. A third to fourth century AD culpture in stone, for example, shows a chimera, a fabulous beast formed from parts of various animals, while a stone relief from Sian in Shensi province, dating from the seventh or early eighth century depicts the 11-headed female Bodhisattva Kuanyin.

▲ *As in other regions of the world, the occurrence of a catastrophic flood is central to Chinese mythology.*

Egypt

Origins

IN PALEOLITHIC OR OLD STONE AGE times (3,500,000–8500 BC), the earliest stage of human technology, humans were living in the valley of the River Nile and in the desert bordering the Nile swamps. The swamps gradually dried up over a period of about 4,000 years and new immigrants came in from Africa and possibly from Mesopotamia. Inter-marrying and mingling over the centuries produced the Egyptians whose later civilisation was one of the earliest glories of the ancient world.

The earliest Egyptians lived in simple village communities, gradually developing the techniques of agriculture, weaving, animal domestication and the manufacture of stone and pottery vessels. The settlements grew in time and their inhabitants became more adept, building houses with sun-dried bricks, irrigating their land, fashioning glass and working with copper.

By around 10,000 BC, the Halfan folk of Egypt were harvesting the wild cereal grasses which began to grow in abundance as the Ice Age came to an end and the climate became more moist. At the same time, the population grew. The Halfan used grinding stones to reduce the crops to powder while in Nubia, on the upper Nile, limestone was used to make the stones, and reaping was done with flint-bladed knives.

◀ *Modern Egyptian Papyrus showing nobles hunting in the rushes along the banks of the Nile.*

Civilisation Takes Shape

BY 5000 BC, THE VILLAGE COMMUNITIES in Egypt were cultivating
wheat and barley, and boats carrying short-masted square sails began to
appear on the Nile. For some time, primitive reed boats had sufficed for
travelling along the river, but now, in about 4500 BC, much larger boats,
equipped with oars and featuring hulls streamlined for speed were
replacing them.

By 4000 BC, two
distinct groups had
settled along the Nile
Valley. One was
concentrated in the
Nile Delta with cultural
links to Mesopotamia,
the other further south
and basically African in
character. This
arrangement
characterised the
division of Upper and
Lower Egypt that was to be fundamental to later Ancient Egyptian
history. Copper, bronze and iron were being imported, probably from
Mesopotamia, but although metallurgy was established, the Egyptians
continued to use finely polished stone or flint for farming tools.

Writing, too, had arrived in Egypt in the form of hieroglyphs.
Archeologists have discovered tombs at Karnak, on the east bank of the
Nile, where walls were covered with hieroglyphic inscriptions, carved in
stone. These inscriptions were arranged in vertical or horizontal lines.
Paper for making records was made from reeds, notably papyrus reeds
which were soaked, pressed and then dried in the sun.

▲ *Model of the boat that would have transported Tutankhamen along the Nile.*

The First Pharaoh

MEMPHIS, WHICH STOOD AT THE TOP of the Nile Delta, provided the first of a long line of pharaohs in Horus Narmer – or Menes in Greek – the king of Upper Egypt, who united his realm with Lower Egypt in about 2950 BC. This first Egyptian royal dynasty was named Thinite, a name possibly taken from This el Birba in Upper Egypt, where Horus Narmer was born. The two halves of Horus's kingdom were symbolised by his two crowns, one white and one red, and he appears wearing them on a Hierankonpolis slate palette.

During the reigns of subsequent 1st Dynasty kings, high officials and possibly the monarchs themselves were buried in mastabas constructed of brick with panelled façades. The Ancient Egyptian practice of burying important people with a mass of possessions was already apparent at this

early stage, for the *mastabas* contained storerooms full of furniture, tools, hunting weapons, equipment and food and drink, which the deceased could use in the next world. Jars made of ivory or ebony were also buried with their owner and these carried labels outlining the principal events of the year, most of them religious, in pictograms and hieroglyphs.

◀ *Horus, the hawk-headed sky god.*

Old and Middle Kingdoms

THE THREE 'KINGDOMS' OF ANCIENT EGYPT – Old, Middle and New – began when the 3rd Dynasty King Zoser founded the first in about 2615 BC. The Old Kingdom was a strongly regulated and organised realm, divided into 42 districts, or nomes, each ruled by the king's representative.

Kingship in Egypt was a very personal thing, and the monarchs ruled as if the country was their own personal property. However, they had to establish their authority by the force of their own personality and this weighted success in favour of strong kings.

The weakness of a system that depended on a king's character became all too apparent in about 2175 BC, when royal authority in the Old Kingdom collapsed and their representatives in the *nomes* acquired independence. This, inevitably, led to civil wars and unrest as rival families contested for power.

This troubled period ended with the succession of King Ammenemes (r. 1991–1962 BC) who smashed the power of the nobles, secured Egypt's borders and founded the Middle Kingdom. This was followed by a time of welcome prosperity, and both artistic and literary development. History, however, repeated itself about 1785 BC, when the monarchy once again lost power and so lay open to invasion from the north.

Egyptian art depicting the Fields of Iahru, or the Afterworld. ▲

The Armies of Ancient Egypt

THE DISCOVERY OF COPPER in about 5000 BC – and the subsequent development of bronze, its alloy with tin – combined with Egyptian metalworking skills to create new and more effective weaponry for the army. In around 2500 BC, copper was being used in Egypt to provide better cutting edges on weapons, such as the axe. The axe displaced the former primary weapons of the Egyptians, which became ineffective after soldiers were issued with metal helmets and caps studded with metal discs.

Bronze replaced copper and, after about 2000 BC, the sturdier blades that could now be produced meant that the Egyptians were armed with effective swords, some of them sickle-shaped.

Although swords replaced spears and javelins as primary weapons, they were not redundant. The armies created by the pharaoh Ahmose I, who established the New Kingdom (1570–1100 BC), were equipped with spears and battleaxes. Ahmose also instituted volley fire by bowmen, and created new divisions of chariots and infantry that worked in mutual close support. This was the first time sophisticated strategy and tactics had become an established element in warfare.

The New Kingdom also saw the use of speedy light chariots, that had highly trained crews armed with bows and javelins for long- and close-range attacks.

◀ *Statue of one of Tutankhamen's guards, found in the pharaoh's tomb.*

Trouble Abroad and at Home

AGGRESSIVE INCURSIONS into Egypt became a fact of life, as ambitious outsiders sought to secure for themselves footholds in this supremely fertile area.

The Semitic Hyksos people, whose name meant, ominously, 'rulers of foreign lands', were among the first of these intruders. They established their own dynasty in the Nile Delta in about 1750 BC, bringing to Egypt their skills in bronze metallurgy and their war chariots. Nevertheless, they were unwelcome, and in about 1570 BC, they were successfully evicted by the 18th Dynasty pharaoh Ahmose I.

Two, however, could play the invasion game. Egypt was reorganised as a military state and the monarchs of the New Kingdom embarked on series of conquests in Syria, Palestine and Nubia. Eventually, the empire of Egypt extended as far as the River Euphrates. Due to its lack of natural borders, though, these far-flung territories were themselves open to invasion, and for a very long time, regular campaigns had to be undertaken to keep out intruders and preserve the empire intact.

There was also trouble at home, where, in the fourteenth century BC, Akhenaten, a pharoah of the 18th Dynasty trod dangerous ground when he altered a fundamental tradition of his realm.

▲ *The Egyptian god Thot with Seti, in the tomb of Seti I, dating from the 19th Dynasty.*

Akhenaten

AKHENATEN (r. 1353–1335 BC) came to the throne as Amenhotep IV, a name meaning 'Amen is Satisfied'. However, he changed his name to Akhenaten, which meant 'He who is acceptable to Aten', when he altered the deity worshipped in Egypt from Amen to the new sun god, Aten. The priests of Amen were enraged, especially when Akhenaten had Amen's name erased from all monuments.

The pacifist pharaoh became entirely absorbed in his new religion, and took no action when his realm was threatened by the Hittites from Anatolia and northern Syria. The Hittites created an empire of their own in Egypt, and all the Asian provinces conquered by previous pharaohs were lost. In addition, political chaos loomed as Akhenaten isolated himself in his desert capital, Akhetaton, draining the taxes and tributes that had enriched the former capital, Thebes, and supported the Amen priesthood.

Akhenaten was such anathema to the priests, that he was severely punished after his death in 1335 BC. His name was removed from the list of Egyptian pharaohs, the seals on his tomb were defaced and he became known as 'that criminal of Akhetaton'. His faith did not survive him. Egypt returned to worship of Amen, and the capital to Thebes.

Egypt in Decline

ALTHOUGH EGYPT DID NOT GO into an immediate decline after the damage inflicted by Akhenaten, the empire was greatly weakened. The price later paid was an inability to resist the onslaughts of new, ambitious foreign invaders such as the Greeks, who massacred an entire Egyptian army in 570 BC. Next came the Persians who conquered Egypt in 526 BC. Afterwards, there were intervals of independence, one of them attained with Greek help, but the Persians returned to rule in 454 BC and 342 BC.

Rome battled and eventually succeeded in conquering the mighty Egypt. ▶

After them, Egypt was conquered yet again by the Macedonian king of Greece, Alexander the Great (356–323 BC), who carved up the empire between his generals. Ptolemy, who received Egypt in this share-out founded his own dynasty of pharaohs in 305 BC.

The rulers who succeeded Ptolemy did little or nothing to halt Egypt's decline; the country was rent by internal fighting, military crises and a tottering economy. Finally, this once-great civilisation came into the orbit of Rome, the mightiest power in the vicinity and, in 30 BC, was made a province of the Roman Empire. It remained so for over four centuries, until the fall of Rome after about AD 476, to be conquered once again, in AD 641, by the armies of Islam.

Exploring for Trade

ONCE EARLY URBAN CIVILISATIONS like Egypt learned of the existence of other lands in which valuable products were produced, the next logical move was to explore the possibilities for trade. The Egyptians began to enquire into these opportunities in around 2600 BC, when a fleet of some 40 ships was sent north along the Mediterranean coast to the ancient seaport of Byblos, in modern Lebanon.

The people of Byblos proved willing to trade and the fleet brought back shiploads of timber, which was an especially valuable commodity in the Nile valley, surrounded as it was by parched desert. The arrangement was, of course, mutually beneficial. Byblos, already a flourishing city from about 5000 BC, later became a centre for the export of cedar and other valuable woods to Egypt.

Encouraged by this initial success, the Egyptians set about exploring southwards, along the River Nile and the Red Sea. They were seeking a land called Punt, where a supply of incense was available. Incense, too, was a commodity of great interest in Egypt, where it had uses in religious practice and in the home.

Two major expeditions south are known to have taken place before 1000 BC, one of them led by an Egyptian navigator named Hennu.

◄ *Excavations, such as this one of Egyptian boat remains, have revealed much about ancient seafaring techniques.*

Egyptian Voyages to India

THE PTOLEMY PHARAOHS OF EGYPT, the last independent dynasty to reign there between 305 BC and 30 BC, became interested in the opportunities offered by India and mounted at least two expeditions to reach this far-off destination. The navigator Eudoxus of Cyzicus made two voyages into the Indian ocean, one at a date sometime between 146 BC and 116 BC, and another after 116 BC. This, of course, was a different and much more challenging enterprise than the coastal voyages to and from Lebanon.

Euxodius appears to have accomplished his goal, but on the return voyage of his second expedition, his ship was blown off course. Euxodius arrived off the coast of East Africa – then termed Ethiopia – and here, he discovered the figurehead of a vessel which he identified as one originating from Gades (modern Cadiz) in southern Spain. This, by inference, indicated voyages of exploration which were even more adventurous than his own. It also suggested that it was possible to sail from Gades and round the long coast of the African continent. Later, Euxodius sailed to Gades across the Mediterranean and made three voyages trying to discover the route that led round Africa to India.

▼ *The Nile provided the main route into and out of Egypt as navigation improved and exploration began in earnest.*

Pharaohs and Pyramids

IN 2620 BC, THE ARCHITECT IMHOTEP built a great stepped pyramid at Saqqara, the burial ground of Memphis, for the 3rd Dynasty pharoah Zoser. The mummification of dead pharaohs, a method of ensuring that the monarch would reach life after death safely and accompany the sun god during daytime, was already being practised in 2580 BC. Two centuries later, the Egyptians were protecting their dead pharaohs by means of special inscriptions on the walls of their tombs; in around 2250 BC, when the Old Kingdom was at the height of its power, the largest and most magnificent of the ancient Egyptian pyramids at Giza were constructed.

The Great Pyramid of Cheops – or Khufu – at Giza was built from two million limestone blocks, covering an area of more than 5 hectares and rising, originally, to a height of over 150 m (492 ft). The huge blocks of stone were measured with amazing accuracy, using the simplest of tools – levers, pulleys, rollers and human muscle. The whole effort was gargantuan, for pyramid-building could occupy some 20 years and involve the labour of 84,000 workers. Consequently, a pharaoh's pyramid tomb was started when he succeeded the throne, and continued throughout his reign.

◄ *The embalmed mummies of the dead pharaohs of Egypt were placed into ornate golden coffins for their journey to the Afterlife.*

Mummifying a Pharaoh

THE EGYPTIANS BELIEVED THAT LIFE was a preparation for death. Consequently, they took enormous trouble to embalm, or mummify, the bodies of their pharaohs and so preserve them intact for their future in the next world.

The Egyptian method, which took 70 days, began by removing the brain, then the viscera. The body cavity was washed out, the corpse was folded to its smallest extent, then, except for the head, it was placed in a large jar filled with a solution of salt or natron which, over the next weeks, dissolved the fatty tissue and peeled away the skin.

After removal from the jar, the body was washed and dried. Finally, the body cavity and skull were packed with preservatives and the body plastered with paste made of resin and fat. It was then wrapped in bandages. The internal organs were preserved separately and placed in four vases known as canopic jars.

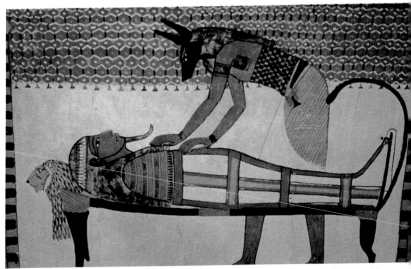

▲ *Egyptian illustration showing the jackal-headed god, Anubis preparing a body for the Underworld.*

Hydraulic Farming

THE ROMAN HISTORIAN HERODOTUS (484–424 BC) called Egypt the 'gift of the Nile', but without a certain amount of ingenuity, the 'gift' could not have been effectively used. To get the most from their crops, they used a system of hydraulic farming based around the rise and fall of the Nile waters.

First of all, seed was planted just before the rains began so that the crops had a good start and a good chance of being plentifully supplied with water. Next, the river would rise following the rains, and irrigation channels were used to supply the crops with river water over the vital growing period. A device called a *shaduf* was used to counter the progressive lowering of the Nile over the next few months by raising as much water as possible into the irrigation channels. The *shaduf*, which is still being used today, is a long pivoted pole with a bucket at one end and a counterweight the other. The water was lifted up a series of stepped tanks until it was elevated high enough to reach the irrigation system. This method was all the more important because rainfall in the eastern Mediterranean was both infrequent and seasonal.

Archeology in Ancient Egypt

THE WORK OF ARCHEOLOGISTS has accounted for most of the vast store of modern knowledge about the life, customs, appearance, diet, furnishings, art and religious practices of Ancient Egypt. However, the extent of this knowledge would have been far less but for the discovery in 1799 of the Rosetta Stone, a slab of basalt dating from 197 BC and inscribed with the same text in three languages – Greek, demotic (a colloquial form of Greek) and hieroglyphs. This enabled archeologists to decipher the many hieroglyphic inscriptions they discovered while excavating the tombs of the Egyptian pharaohs. The great age of Egyptian archeology came somewhat later, around the end of the

Tutankhamen's boat, one of the many treasures that were discovered in his tomb. ▶

nineteenth century, and the finds that were made proved stunning. None was more so, however, than the tomb of the young 18th Dynasty pharaoh Tutankhamen (r. 1333–1323 BC), which was excavated after 1922 by the British archeologist Howard Carter (1874–1939). Tutankhamen's tomb was untouched by robbers and the astounding display it contained of gold, jewels, art objects and other treasures caught the imagination of the world. The magnificent golden mask that covered the face of Tutankhamen has become a symbol of the splendour and magnificence of Ancient Egypt.

Religion in Ancient Egypt

THE ANCIENT EGYPTIANS NEVER FORGOT that their prosperity, in fact their entire life, depended on the River Nile. When its waters were low, it brought famine when high, disaster. These contrasts were conceived as the moods of beneficent or angry gods. Even so, the general regularity of the Nile, and the rising of its waters each year to deposit fertile mud on the land, gave a stability to Ancient Egyptian ideas about life and death. The concept of Ma'at, the goddess who embodied stability and law, therefore governed all aspects of Egyptian life and religion.

In the huge pantheon of 2,000 Egyptian deities, Amun-re was the chief of the gods, but others frequently took animal forms. Herodotus wrote that in Egypt the animals 'are without exception held to be sacred'.

Surprisingly enough, unlike those of India or the Mediterranean, Ancient Egyptian mythology did not contain a great number of stories. Essentially, Egyptian myths were concerned with the Creation, the Destruction of Mankind, the story of Isis and Osiris and the journey of Re, the sun god, across the sky by day, after which he spent 12 terrible hours in darkness before being safely reborn in the east next morning.

Horus, god of the Underworld, was frequently depicted in the form of a hawk. ▶

The Creation Myths of Egypt

EGYPT HAD FOUR CREATION MYTHS, each of them connected with a major city: Heliopolis, the 'City of the Sun'; Memphis; Hermopolis; and Esna. Each concerned a major god, Atum, who was later assimilated into Re, Ptah, Thoth and Khnum respectively.

In the Heliopolis myth, Atum was alone on a muddy bank which had emerged from the primeval Waters of Nun, that covered the world. Creation, he realised needed the assistance of other gods. Atum therefore produced them from his own semen. They were Shu, god of the sky and his sister Tefnut, goddess of moisture. Their children were Geb, god of the earth and Nut goddess of the sky.

◄ *Turquoise decoration in the form of a winged Isis, dating from c. 1000 BC.*

In the ancient papyri Nut appears arched over Geb while Shu separates them to their two spheres. Geb and Nut had five children – Osiris, Isis, Horus the Elder, Seth and Nephthys. They were born on five consecutive days that were not part of the calendar. This was due to a prophecy that Nut's children would surpass the power of Atum. Being born on epagnol or non-calendar days overcame the problem of the curse which foretold that Nut could not give birth on any day of the year.

Osiris and Isis

THE MYTH WITH WHICH ANCIENT EGYPTIANS identified most told the story of Osiris and his wife and sister Isis. Osiris was a good king, but he had a jealous brother, Seth, who contrived to have him killed and his body floated out to sea, where it ended up on the shore close to the city of Byblos. The grieving Isis searched long and hard for her husband's body. She eventually located it and brought it back to Egypt. Hidden in the marshes, Isis hovered over the body in the form of a hawk, and became pregnant with their son, Horus.

Seth, however, discovered the body in the marshes and tore it into 14 pieces, which were scattered far and wide across Egypt. Once again, Isis set off to retrieve Osiris's now fragmented corpse. One version of the myth tells how she buried each fragment where she found it and built a temple on the spot. Another recounts how she brought all the pieces together except for his phallus which had been lost when the oxyrhyncus fish swallowed it. Osiris was buried at Abydos, which became the most sacred site of Ancient Egypt and where the most beautifully decorated temples was erected.

▲ *A bronze statue of the oxyrhyncus fish.*

The Creator God Ptah

AT MEMPHIS, WHICH HORUS NAMER of the 1st Dynasty of Ancient Egypt established as his capital, the major deity was the creator god Ptah. According to the legend, Ptah took precedence over Atum because he had created Atum's heart and tongue. Ptah was particularly revered as the god of craftsmen and workers, and among his many titles, he was called 'the father and the mother of all gods'.

Another legend was identified at Hermopolis, the much-revered cult centre of the god Thoth. Thoth was frequently represented with the head of an ibis bird, and the baboon was also a sacred animal associated with him. Thoth was the god of wisdom and learning, for he had invented hieroglyphs which meant literally 'sacred writings'. Thoth was also the patron god of scribes and was associated with the Moon.

In the creation myth which featured Thoth, the primeval mound emerged from the Water of Nun at Hermopolis, not Heliopolis, as in the myth of Atum. The sun-god emerged from an egg lying on the mound or, in an alternative version, a lotus flower grew from it, and its leaves opened to reveal the young god of creation, Nefertum.

The creator god, Ptah. ▶

Esna

THE RAM-HEADED KHNUM was the god of the Esna creation myth, and here, a temple was dedicated to him. Khnum created man on his potter's wheel, and did so in duplicate, since everyone had a *ka* or double. The *ka* was the spirit which remained close to a dead man's tomb, while his *ba*, his soul, flew away at death to the next world as a human-headed bird. The fullest version of Khnum's creation can be found carved on the walls of the temple at Esna. This tells of a goddess called Neith, who was associated with the city of Sais in the Nile Delta. She came into being even before the primeval mound, emerging from the Waters of Nun to create the world.

◄ Obelisk portraying the god, Thoth.

In Ancient Egypt, there was no problem with having several basic versions of a particular creation story. Each legend took precedence at its appropriate place – Atum at Memphis, Thoth at Hermopolis, Khnum at Esna. Generally speaking, however, the version centred at Heliopolis held prime position because of its association with the sun and the chief of the gods, Re. Re was later assimilated with Amun of Thebes and became the great god Amun-Ra.

Journey Through the Underworld

WHEN THE SUN SET – OR DIED – in the west each evening, it was imperative that it should be reborn at the next dawn. To ensure this, the god Re had to travel underground through the dark hours of the night. Each hour had a doorway guarded by a terrifying demon. Re, however, succeeded in getting past them safely. Three major compositions acted as safeguards to make Re's journey possible: the book of Am-Duat, also known as the book of That Which is in the Underworld; the Book of Gates and the Book of Caverns.

Another well-known Egyptian composition was the Book of the Dead which consisted of some 200 chapters, designed to help dead people on their journey from this life to the next. The most important were Chapter 125 relating to the weighing of the heart in the Hall of Judgment, Chapter 30, in which the heart would not speak evil against the dead person and Chapter 6, also found as a text on the *ushabti* figure provided at a burial. The *ushabti* answered the summons, and stood in place of the deceased if he was called upon to carry out any tasks in the afterlife.

▼ *Chapter 134 of* The Book of the Dead, *plea for entry into the boat of Re.*

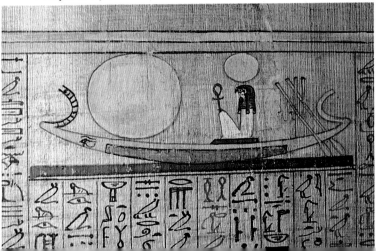

Greece

Before the First Civilisation

HOMO SAPIENS, OR INTELLIGENT MAN, the immediate ancestor of humans today, was living in various parts of Europe, including Petralona in Greece, in around 450,000 BC. The named forebears of the Greeks, however, arrived a great deal later in about 2000 BC when Hellenic tribes wandered in from central Europe.

The Hellenes, who gave their name to the country, settled in the mountains and valleys to live by farming and goat and cattle herding. It was a tough life. The terrain was arduous, and farmers had a hard time wresting a living from the unyielding earth.

Soon after the Hellenes arrived the Ionians from beyond the Black Sea in southern Russia invaded Asia Minor. The Hittites, however, drove them back and subsequently the Ionians settled all over Greece, the greatest number of them in the region of Greece named after them – Ionia on the west coast of Asia Minor, which bordered the powerful Hittite Empire.

Their importance, however, was reduced when the Achaeans, the first Greeks in the Aegean, migrated into Greece some time before 1200 BC. In time, they dominated both the mainland and the western isles, and with it, the Mycenaean civilisation.

◄ *Early man, having learnt to hunt animals and gather fruits, gradually progressed to a more settled way of farming with livestock.*

The Mycenaean Civilisation

THE MYCENAEAN CIVILISATION, which centred around the Achaean kingdom of Mycenae, had originated in around 2000 BC. Its greatest days came later, after about 1580 BC, and modern archeology has uncovered the superb artistic and architectural skills which marked this civilisation. Among the evidence were vases decorated with delicately executed figures, daggers from the sixteenth century BC with blades inlaid in gold and silver, the fourteenth century BC Lion Gate guarded by two lions which led into the citadel at Mycenae, the Treasury of Atreus, a beehive tomb dating from about 1350 BC and richly-appointed royal palaces. Royal life – and death – in Mycenae was opulent in the extreme. Both men and women were buried with gold and silver bases, crowns and tiaras and gold rings and necklaces.

By around 1300 BC, Mycenae was the greatest fortress in all Greece, dominating the fertile Plain of Argos with its rich cornfields and horse ranches. Yet within a century, the Mycenaean civilisation had collapsed due to invasions by the Dorians, who entered Greece from the north and not only destroyed Mycenae but seized most of the Peloponnese from the Achaens. The disaster had a sombre effect on the city of Mycenae: after about 1120 BC, it was largely uninhabited.

Highly decorative Greek amphora showing Herakles capturing Cerberus. ▶

The Minoan Civilisation

THE WONDERS OF MYCENAE owed a great deal to the Minoan civilisation, established at Knossos on the island of Crete in around 3000 BC. Named after its king, Minos, this civilisation was unknown before 1895, when the British archeologist Arthur John Evans (1851–1941) began 40 years of excavation and discovery. King Minos had been considered a mythical figure and the son of the Greek god Zeus. Evans, however, revealed that Minos had in fact existed and the extent of the magnificence in which he lived became evident after Evans uncovered the Palace at Knossos, where there were buildings up to five storeys high, an elaborate throne room, beautiful friezes, gilded stone roofs, stone conduits and clay water pipes for drainage, staircases constructed on wooden columns and light wells designed to illuminate the palace interior. In addition to Knossos, great palaces were discovered at Phaistos and Mallia. The Minoans used copper and bronze weapons and their pottery was intricately decorated.

The end of the Minoan civilisation was, however, sudden and violent. In about 1400 BC, it seems to have been largely destroyed, either because of an earthquake, or perhaps through invasion and war. Its remnants persisted until about 1100 BC, but its great days were well and truly over.

◀ *The mighty Zeus, king of the gods.*

The City-States

THE SETTLEMENTS FOUNDED BY the Hellenes grew, after about 850 BC, into city-states, a natural development when the mountain terrain of Greece isolated communities in their valleys. Just as naturally, the city-states became tight-knit, individualistic societies that were markedly different from one other. For example, Athens, with its vibrant intellectual and political life, was a complete contrast to militaristic Sparta. Ultimately, there were about 30 city-states, including Thebes, Corinth, Thessaly and Argos. Athens, the main city of Attica in eastern Greece, and Sparta, also called Laconia, which lay in the southern Pelopponese in the south, were the main city-states, and also the main rivals among them.

Rivalry, fostered by their differences and isolationism, was an inevitable development, and often a ferocious one. The city-states fought each other for territory for some two centuries, and formed themselves into leagues to try to gain the advantage over their opponents. By the mid-fifth century BC, two main leagues had emerged – the Athenian and the Peloponnesian.

The city-states nevertheless possessed a sense of their 'nationality' as Greeks, forgot their mutual enmity and banded together when the country was attacked from outside.

The magnificent remains of the Acropolis, Athens.▼

The Persian Civilisations

THE PERSIANS, THEN A MIGHTY military power, invaded Greece in 492 BC. They conquered the north before they were obliged to return home after their fleet was destroyed in a storm. They were soon back, however, and invaded again in 490 BC. Led by Darus I, the Persians landed at Marathon, some 32 km (20 miles) north-west of Athens. This, however, was a feint intended to lure the Athenians and their Plataean allies from Thebes towards the landing site, while a second Persian amphibious force stood by to land at Phalerum and seize Athens.

The Athenians were hopelessly outnumbered, with a force of only about 11,000 men. Realising the risk of being outflanked and overwhelmed by the Persians, they extended their lines across the whole of the Marathon valley. When the fighting started, disaster seemed to loom for the Athenians when their centre collapsed, but the wings stood firm and drove the Persians back in confusion. They took to their ships and escaped, having lost 6,400 soldiers.

The Athenians turned back and fought off the second invasion force, with the loss of only 192 men. The threat from Persia was not over, however. In 486 BC, they invaded Greece again.

Intricately decorated pillar relief from the Palace of Darius. ▶

The First Sea Battle

KING XERXES (519–465 BC), who succeeded Darius the Great in 486 BC, determined to succeed where his predecessor had failed. Harpalus, a Greek engineer working for the Persians, bridged the Hellespont – the strait now known as the Dardanelles connecting the Sea of Marmara and the Aegean Sea – and in the spring of 480 BC, with support from 1,200 ships, a massive Persian force of 160,000 troops crossed over and advanced into northern Greece.

The Athenians, Spartans and other Greeks who had combined forces to counter this dangerous invasion, met the Persians at the narrow pass of Thermopolyae, 129 km (80 miles) north of Athens, with only 1,700 of their crack troops, the Hoplites. The Greeks staked everything on the chance that the Persians would send their fleet southwards to outflank Thermopolyae. They won their wager. The Persians landed near Athens and the Greeks sprung the trap.

After a long, hard battle, they scattered the Persians. In the sea battle at Salamis, the outnumbered Greeks trapped the enemy fleet in a narrow strait and destroyed half the Persian ships. This crushing defeat was later classed as the first real sea battle. In 479 BC, the Greeks defeated the Persians again at Plataea, finally freeing their country from the Persian menace.

▲ *The great Persian battles were frequently won or lost at sea.*

Glittering Athens and Sombre Sparta

IN ATHENS, INTELLECTUAL accomplishments went hand in hand with the good life. Athenians were equally fond of comfort and good food as they were of art, music, poetry, theatre, philosophy, mathematics and astronomy.

Athenian craftsmen and artists created beautiful vases, statues and jewellery. Athenian architects designed elegant buildings with fine pillars and decorated walls and roofs, in styles which have survived the centuries, and can still be seen in many modern cities today. Democracy, too, emanated from Athens when its ruler Solon (638–559 BC) decreed in 594 BC that through an assembly where citizens were entitled to speak, they could reject or approve legalisation. Solon also laid down a code of laws that applied to rich and poor alike.

In complete contrast, Sparta was a severely disciplined authoritarian military state, where the people were either *perioeci* – tributaries without political rights – or helots or serfs. From childhood, both sexes were trained in special schools to toughen them and make them strong in both body and mind. Weaklings had no place in Sparta, and infants who were handicapped or not perfectly healthy were left on a mountainside to die.

▼ *The hedonistic lifestyle revolving around food, music art and pleasure is clearly portrayed in this picture entitled* The Banquet of the Gods.

The Pelopponesian War

ATHENS BECAME THE GREATEST power in Greece during the rule of Pericles (495–429 BC), whose ambitions were both suspected and feared in Sparta. Pericles came to power in 443 BC and transformed the Delian League, originally formed in 478–447 BC to avenge the losses Greece had suffered in the Persian wars, into a vast Athenian empire. The Spartans reacted violently, and in 431 BC, the Pelopponesian war broke out. This extremely destructive conflict lasted for 27 years and all Greece suffered.

The Athenians adopted a defensive strategy, allowing the superior Spartan army to range over the countryside while Athens itself remained inviolate behind strong defensive walls. This tactic, however, proved self-defeating when, in 429 BC, plague ran riot through Athens, which was overcrowded due to the influx of people from the countryside who had sheltered there.

The Athenians, though, took the initiative at sea, where their fleet ravaged the Spartan coastline. Disaster, however, occurred in 404 BC when the Spartans, led by Lysander (d. 395 BC) thrashed their navy in the land and sea battle of Aegospotami in the Hellespont. Subsequently, Lysander's forces starved the Athenians into surrender. Athens survived, partly through the respect it had earned as the fount of Greek civilisation, but its political power was severely compromised.

The battle was finally lost by the Athenians as the superior strength of the Spartan navy forced them to surrender. ▶

Alexander the Great

ALEXANDER THE GREAT (356–323 BC), still accounted one of the greatest of all military leaders, was the son of Philip II of Macedonia (382–336 BC), who took advantage of the perennial warfare between the city-states of overrun Greece. Philip had ambitions to invade Asia, but this was prevented by his murder in 336 BC, and it fell to Alexander to accomplish this feat.

First, however, he had to deal with the Persians, whom he finally thrashed in 331 BC. The Persian king, Darius III (d. 330 BC) fled eastwards. Alexander pursued him, but their rivalry ended when the Persian king was assassinated.

The way was now open for Alexander's great conquests. He founded colonies in Afghanistan, then turned south into India, where he conquered most of the Punjab after 327 BC. However, his ambition to push on to the River Ganges was thwarted when his soldiers, exhausted and too far from home, mutinied. Reluctantly, Alexander returned to Babylon on the River Euphrates. He was preparing for the invasion of Arabia when he contracted malarial fever from which he died in 323 BC. His vast empire had relied almost entirely on his dominant personality and presence, and with his premature death, it was divided up among his generals.

▲ *Floor mosaic showing Alexander the Great in battle against the Persians under the leadership of Darius.*

The End of Greek Glory

THE DIVISIONS THAT OCCURRED after the death of Alexander the Great caused considerable political instability in Greece. The city-states attempted to regain independence from the Macedonian monarchy by rebellion and war, but the monarchy clung on and later dragged the states into the in-fighting between the Diadochi, the successors of Alexander, who fought each other for power.

A century after Alexander's death, the Macedonians were still struggling to regain their hold on Greece, just as the city-states still struggled to shake off their yoke. In 205 BC, the city-states made the grave mistake of asking the Romans for aid. This, as it turned out, was an invitation to conquest. The Romans annihilated the Macedonian army in 168 BC, and afterwards dealt brutally with those who had supported the monarchy. Some 70 towns were destroyed and 150,000 men taken away as slaves. Even the Achaean League of cities in the Pelopponese, which had backed Rome, lost 1,000 of its leading citizens, when they were deported to Italy. From there, it was a short step for the Romans to add Greece to their empire, and it remained a Roman province for over 600 years, until the Roman Empire itself fell after AD 476.

▼ *Dramatic battle scene, with the triumphant Alexander the Great.*

The Greeks as Traders

PLANTING COLONIES OVERSEAS was an early recourse among the Greek city-states. Even before 500 BC, the population had increased to the point where emigrants left to found colonies in southern Italy, Sicily, southern France and Spain. Collectively, these were known as Magna Graecia, 'Great Greece', and here the Greeks served as middlemen in the trade between the 'barbarians' of outlying ares and the old cities of the mainland.

Trade received a boost when some Greek cities began specialising in producing wine and olive oil, which could be exchanged for grain, timber and other raw materials, as well as luxuries such as alabaster from Egypt. Through this rich commerce, large cities were able to grow in the olive- and wine-growing coastal areas. Greece and Crete also exported pottery and metalwork, and exchanged spices, gold, grain, silk and wool with the Romans.

The exchanges, however, were not purely material. The existence of the Greek colonies, together with the conquests of Alexander the Great, spread Greek ideas and influence to a wide area outside Greece. In Egypt, where a Macedonian dynasty of pharaohs ruled, a distinct 'Hellenistic' culture grew up, typified by the city of Alexandria, that Alexander had founded in 331 BC and named after himself.

▲ *Gold coins, such as this bearing the portrait of Julius Caesar, facilitated trade between the colonies.*

Voyages Overseas

EVEN BEFORE THE OVERSEAS EXPLOITS of Alexander, the Greeks were not content to confine themselves to the Mediterranean. Several long voyages of exploration took place as Greeks ventured into the Black Sea, across Asia to India and south into Africa. One of the most important Greek cities, and a regular sailing point in this exploratory movement, was Phocaea on the coast of Asia Minor. One Phocaean may have sailed through the Straits of Gibraltar, once known as the Pillars of Hercules, to reach as far as Britain, in about 600 BC. Others went west to found colonies, and the most important of these in Greek explorations was at Marseilles, on the south coast of France.

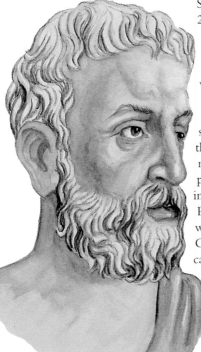

Some time between 320 and 240 BC, a Greek navigator called Pytheas sailed from Marsailles and headed north. Pytheas reached the south-western coast of England, something which had been done before by Phoenician seamen, but he did not stop there; he went further northwards and made landfall, probably in the Faeroe Islands in the north Atlantic Ocean. Pytheas's account of his voyage was later used by Eratosthenes of Cyrene (276–194 BC) to help calculate latitude and longitude and create the first scientific map in European history.

◀ *Eratosthenes, one of the earliest geographers.*

123

Maps and Ocean Voyages

ERATOSTHENES HAD A powerful influence on the science of navigation – an influence that persisted long after his death. He was the first cartographer to make charts that were practicable for use at sea. In his maps, lines of longitude and latitude created a grid, which meant that different locations were referenced in relation to one another. These were invaluable tools for understanding the overall layout of the then-known world, and made vital equipment for venturers such as the Greek merchant Hippalus, who sailed to India in the first century AD.

Hippalus had discovered a secret that Arab traders with India had jealously guarded for centuries – that the monsoon winds of the Indian Ocean reverse themselves. This allowed him to sail directly across the Indian Ocean, the first European to do so. It proved a much faster and more convenient method of getting there than the tortuous process of hugging the coastline.

However, what lay beyond India was no mystery to Mediterranean merchants and geographers. They knew of lands far to the east, and a geographer writing in the second century ad described several places in Southeast Asia, including Malaysia and possibly even Hanoi in Vietnam.

Despite the advances made by Eratosthenes, it was not until the sixteenth century that Gerardus Mercator realised a cylindrical projection was needed to show the world map. ▲

Logic and Science

THE GREEKS WERE THE FIRST EUROPEANS to develop a cursive script, a vital adjunct to logical analysis and philosophical thought. Subsequently, it became possible to formulate the principles of astronomy, mathematics and other sciences. Aristotle (384–322 BC), a strict, even obsessive, logician, propounded theories on the motion of heavenly bodies, which he conceived as being contained in crystalline spheres. Aristotle was remarkably versatile, encompassing not only astronomy but physics, meteorology, biology, psychology, ethics, politics and literature.

Euclid (330–260 BC), a mathematician and geometer, wrote influential books on plane and solid geometry and number theory, which became the basis for mathematical thought and expression for 2,000 years.

Hippocrates (460–377 BC), whose oath is still sworn by doctors, and Galen (AD 129–200), who formulated the theory of the three 'humours', which explained physical and mental characteristics, were both honoured for centuries as 'fathers' of medicine. Many of Hippocrates' ideas had a distinctly modern ring – cleanliness, moderate eating and drinking, and the benefits of good air.

Galen especially, retained a position as the prime authority on medical matters for almost 1,500 years and though some of his ideas have since become outdated, the debt that modern medicine owes him has never been questioned.

▲ *Bust of the Greek physician, Hippocrates.*

Socrates and Plato

THE ATHENIAN PHILOSOPHER SOCRATES (469–399 BC) became a martyr to his own logic for putting forward the view that dialogue and systematic questioning paved the way to true knowledge. Socrates believed that nothing could be immortalised and that uncritical claims to knowledge should be discarded.

Unfortunately, Socrates's philosophy challenged the ideas of the sophists, who used fallacious arguments as the basis for discussion. Condemned for subverting the youth of Athens, he was ordered to kill himself by drinking the poison hemlock.

Socrates's philosophy lived on, however, in the teachings of his pupil Plato (427–327 BC), whose dialogues formed a memorial to him and contained many discussions ascribed to him. Plato argued that knowledge can exist only if there are eternal things to which knowledge can refer. Plato believed in Forms such as Good, True and Beautiful, which all things expressed to a greater or lesser degree.

Plato's most famous work, the *Republic*, depicted a state based on his ideals and ruled by philosophers. This type of philosophy later became known as Utopian, the title of a book written in 1516 by Sir Thomas More (1478–1535), which was inspired by Plato's work. Like Socrates, Thomas More, ironically, was executed for his principles in 1535.

◄ *The Greek philosopher Plato, one of the earliest exponents of political ideas.*

Aristotle and Other Philosophers

ARISTOTLE, A PHILOSOPHER AS WELL AS A SCIENTIST and astronomer, was one of Plato's pupils and, in his turn, became tutor to Alexander the Great. Aristotle, however, rejected Plato's theory of Forms, and argued that the prime reality lay in material things, and that their properties, such as colour or taste, were simply aspects of them.

In addition to the giants of philosophy Socrates, Plato and Aristotle, several rival schools of thought existed in Ancient Greece. Two opposing theories were those of Epicurus (341–270 BC) and Zeno (334–262 BC), who founded the Stoic school. Both believed that neither the world nor the fate of human beings were controlled by the gods.

Where they differed was in the way they believed humans should conduct themselves during their mortal span on earth. Epicurus favoured a good life of reasonable pleasure and freedom from responsibility and physical pain. Zeno, by contrast, taught that the world was controlled by the mind and that life had no purpose other than to exercise reason in order to live rationally. He advocated that the trials of life should be confronted with dignity and emotional self-control. Zeno's 'school' acquired the name Stoic from the *stoa*, or porch, in which he taught.

▲ *Bust of the philosopher and scientist, Aristotle.*

Myths in Ancient Greece

IN ATHENS, MYTHS WERE IMPORTANT to philosophy and science, and were often portrayed in art, from images on vases and jewellery to the sculptures and statues in Greek temples. The myths usually involved extraordinary circumstances in which human beings flouted established norms, as, for example, Oedipus did when he killed his father and married his mother.

Myths also involved superhuman feats, performed by superheroes. Theseus, for instance, killed the Minotaur, a man-bull hybrid who lived in a labyrinth and terrorised Athenian youth. Herakles, one of the earliest mythological figures featured in Greek art, exemplified a problem presented by heroes, that he was not a perfect being.

Herakles's most famous exploits were his Twelve Labours, a punishment imposed by King Eurystheus for killing his family in a fit of madness brought on by the goddess Hera, who was jealous of the affection between Zeus, Herakles's father, and his mother Alkmene. Herakles accomplished the Twelve Labours – all extraordinary feats of stamina and strength – but was still afflicted with lust, drunkenness and gluttony. Herakles died, however, after his wife Deianeira, distressed at Herakles's fondness for Iole, tried to win him back with a love potion. It turned out to be poison.

Greek amphora showing Herakles capturing Cerberus, one of the Twelve Labours set for him by King Eurystheus. ▶

The Gods of Greece

THE GREEKS PICTURED THEIR GODS as a family, with loves, hates, rivalries and loyalties. Father was Zeus, whose dominion was the sky. Mother was Hera, Zeus's wife and sister, and goddess of women and marriage. Their brother Poseidon ruled the sea, and another, Hades, was sovereign of the Underworld. A sister, Hestia, was goddess of hearth and home. Of the children of Zeus and Hera, Ares was god of war, Hephaestus god of fire and metalworking, Hebe was goddess of youth and Eileithyia the goddess of childbirth.

Zeus, however, was not a faithful husband. Athene, the patron goddess of Athens, was the issue of his liaison with Metis; and Persephone, goddess of the Underworld, was his daughter by Demeter, goddess of agriculture. Hermes, messenger of the gods, Dionysus, god of wine and religious ecstasy, Artemis the huntress and her brother Apollo, god of music and poetry, were the children of Zeus's other liaisons.

One Greek creation myth tells how Zeus threatened to send a flood to destroy mankind. This prompted the Titan, or giant, Prometheus to warn Deucalion and Deucalion's wife Phyrra to build an ark. After the waters subsided the couple walked along throwing stones over their shoulders. Deucalion's became men and Phyrra's, women.

◄ *The father of all the Greek gods, the mighty Zeus.*

Homer and the Trojan Wars

THE EPIC POEM *THE ILIAD*, attributed to the blind poet Homer
(eighth century BC), tells of the war with Troy, once considered mythical.
It was not until the German archeologist Heinrich Schliemann
(1822–90) excavated a site at Hissarlik in Turkey in the nineteenth
century that the existence of Troy and the Trojan War was proven.
Archeologists now believe this to have taken place in about 1200 BC.

The war began
after Paris, son of
King Priam,
kidnapped Helen, the
wife of Menelaus and
took her back to
Troy. Menelaus's elder
brother gathered a
fleet of 50 ships, and
an army which
included the great
warrior Achilles and
Odysseus, King of
Ithaca, and sailed to Troy to get Helen back. A 10-year siege ensued,
ending only when the Trojans were tricked into taking a wooden horse
into their city. Soldiers hidden inside opened the gates for the Greek
army and in the desperate battle that followed, Troy was destroyed.

The *Odyssey*, sequel to the *Iliad*, describes Odysseus's subsequent
journey home to Ithaca. On the way, Odysseus encountered the one-
eyed Cyclops, the enchantress Circe, the monsters Scylla and
Charibdis, and the seductive Sirens. Arriving home after a voyage of
20 years, Odysseus wreaks revenge on the suitors who have pursued
his wife Penelope.

▲ *The city of Troy is destroyed by flames during the Trojan War.*

The Legacy of Ancient Greece

THE ROLE OF ANCIENT GREECE as the crucible of modern Western civilisation cannot be underestimated. Modern science, astronomy, mathematics, medicine and architecture are all rooted in Greek ideas. When the Renaissance began in about 1450, artists, scientists, physicians, politicians and many others looked back to Greece and Ancient Rome for their inspiration.

Modern theatre, too, began with the Greeks, and plays written by Greek dramatists, such as *Oedipus* by Sophocles or *The Frogs* by Aristophanes are still performed today. The proscenium arch that frames the action on modern stages developed from the *proskenion*, the columns that supported the stage in Ancient Greek open-air theatres.

The ancient Olympic Games, held every four years and revived in modern form in 1896, perpetuate Ancient Greek ideas about healthy competition and the unity it can create. In Greece, the warring city-states declared a truce so that athletes could compete on Mount Olympus, the home of the gods. Pierre de Fredi, Baron de Coubertin (1863–1937), who revived the Games just over 1,500 years after they were abolished by the Romans in AD 394, was inspired by a similar idea, that an unsettled, warlike world could benefit from a period of co-operation.

◄ Trompe l'oeil *from the Sala dei Giganti, showing the gods of Olympus.*

Islam

Origins

ISLAM, WHICH MEANS 'Submission to God' and is the faith of the Muslims, began with the preachings of Muhammed (AD 570–632) who was born in Mecca, now in Saudi Arabia. The Arabs of Mecca were idol-worshippers and much given to disputes, quarrels and violence. Muhammed, however, came to believe that if only his people would worship one God, like the Jews and Christians, their behaviour might be curbed.

In AD 610, according to Islamic tradition, Muhammed was meditating on this problem in a cave on Mount Hira, when he had a vision. Afterwards, Muhammed claimed that the Archangel Gabriel had appeared and told him he had been chosen as the prophet of Allah, the one God.

However, after Muhammed began preaching his new religion in Mecca, the enraged inhabitants plotted to murder him. Muhammed escaped with a friend, Abu Bakr and, eluding the soldiers sent to capture him, made his way to friendly territory in Yathrib, where there were already many Muslims. Subsequently, Muhammed renamed Yathrib Medinat un Nabie, or Medina, city of the Prophet. His flight from Mecca to Medina was later called the Hegira and the Muslim calendar is counted from the day his journey began – 16 July AD 622.

The Angel Gabriel who appeared to the Prophet Muhammad. ▶

The Spread of Islam

THE MECCANS, EVEN MORE INFURIATED by Muhammed's escape, sent an army, apparently 1,000 strong, to attack Medina, but were defeated by Muhammed's 313 Muslims, who leapt into battle with the war cry 'Allahu Akbar' ('God is Great'). This was the start of many years during which the armies of Islam fought for their faith against the infidels, or unbelievers. In AD 630, Mecca fell to Muhammed's forces and afterwards a majority of Meccans agreed to become Muslims.

From then on, Islam began to gather hundreds of converts, and by the time Muhammed died in AD 632, the new faith had spread through Arabia from the Persian Gulf to the Red Sea, and from Yemen in the south to the frontiers of Syria in the north. All the people of this vast region now lived under the laws of the Qur'an, the holy book of Islam, which were gathered by his followers from Muhammed's own writings. The Qur'an was completed by AD 650.

After this, Islam spread beyond Arabia with amazing speed. By AD 750, the Muslim armies had won an empire which stretched from the borders of Afghanistan in the east to Spain in the west. It included Egypt and the whole of the North African coast.

▲ *The Qu'ran, the Holy Book of the Islamic faith.*

The Bedouins

MUHAMMAD'S MILITARY SUCCESS WAS NOT SURPRISING, since the Bedouin tribesmen of Arabia, the earliest converts to Islam, were an extremely warlike people. They were fierce fighters who could do battle on horseback or on foot with equal skill and ferocity. The rigours of long, punishing campaigns and successive battles against the infidels were well within their aggressive scope.

Bedouins lived by strict rules of behaviour and honour, and had an extraordinary talent for 'navigating' the outwardly featureless desert sands, seeking out the oases and the water they needed for themselves and their camels, sheep or goats. The name 'Bedouin' came from *badawi*, the Arabic word for 'desert dweller', and even after Islam gave rise to great cities and sophisticated cultures, they refused to give up the independence that went with the nomadic life. It was not forbidden, however, to do battle with non-Muslims and to judge by the results, this was something the Bedouins did with gusto.

Their lifestyle had effects, though, on the formulation of their faith. Although beautiful mosques were later built all over the Islamic world, daily practice was largely conceived in the context of the vast sandy desert. There, Muslims turned towards Mecca to pray five times a day.

▲ *The Bedouin people managed to survive in the hostile desert environment and to encourage the spread of the Muslim faith.*

Christianity vs Islam

MUSLIMS BELIEVED THAT THE PROPHET Muhammad rose to heaven from a place in Jerusalem on which they built the mosque the Dome of the Rock. This made Jerusalem very important to Islam, just as it was to the Jews and Christians. Christian pilgrims were allowed to visit Jerusalem on pilgrimage, but when some of them were attacked, Pope Urban II (1042–99), in 1095 called on Christian Europe to undertake a crusade to retrieve the Holy Land from Muslim rule. A force 30,000 strong set out and in the first and most successful of the eight crusades, they captured Edessa, Antioch, Tripoli and Jerusalem and there set up Christian kingdoms.

Crusading motives were not entirely pure, though. There were, of course, exemplary leaders like Geoffrey de Bouillon (d. 1100), first ruler of the Kingdom of Jerusalem, who refused to accept a crown where Jesus had worn a crown of thorns and Richard I 'the Lionheart' (1157–99) who led the Third Crusade (1189–92), who was admired as a valiant warrior. Even so, many crusaders went to the Holy Land for riches, land and power. Consequently, crusading had lost it lustre by the mid-thirteenth century and was regarded in Europe as an ignoble venture.

▲ *Stone carvings showing three knights being blessed as they leave for the crusades in the eleventh century.*

Islam Pushed Back in Europe

THE BATTLE OF LEPANTO in 1571 was afterwards called the 'Last Crusade', since many Europeans came to believe that it had saved Europe from Islamic domination. Lepanto was not, in fact, the last struggle for power in Europe between Christians and Muslims. The siege of Vienna by the Ottomans, from which they were forced to retire, occurred over a century later, in 1683, and Ottoman rule survived in parts of south-east Europe until 1908. Only with the collapse of the Ottoman Empire after the First World War was the proximity of a large and powerful Muslim state finally removed from the environs of Europe.

What the Christian victory at Lepanto did do, however, was to destroy Ottoman naval supremacy in the Mediterr-anean and so diminish the danger to the security of Europe which had threatened the continent for many years. In the battle, which was fought on 7 October 1571 off Lepanto near the Gulf of Corinth in Greece, 280 Christian ships and 50,000 seamen faced 310 Muslim vessels and 25,000 fighting men. The Ottoman centre and right were destroyed, with the loss of around 200 ships and 30,000 soldiers and sailors. The Christians lost 10 galleys and 8,000 men.

▲ *Timur the Lame was one of the militant Islamic conquerors, worthy of comparison with Genghis Khan. He created a savage empire, inhospitable to all Christians.*

Dazzling Damascus

DAMASCUS IN SYRIA was one of the first towns to be captured by the Muslim armies, in AD 635. Under Muslim rule, it became a magnificent city with elegant mosques, minarets, gardens, fountains and houses decorated with elaborate mosaics. Damascus also became a great trading centre, famous for damask, the elaborate embroidered cloth in which the beautiful patterns could be seen from both sides, and for fine steel 'damascening', in which gold and silver were etched or inlaid onto the metal or decorated with a watery pattern which was welded on. Because of its many beauties, Damascus was given many admiring names, such as 'pearl of the east' or 'city of many pillars'.

Damascus was the political and cultural focus of Islam for almost a century, and the capital of the Caliphate – the territories conquered by the Arab Muslims and ruled by the immediate successors of Muhammad. It was from Damascus that the Umayyad sultans, who ruled there from AD 661 to 750, made further conquests for Islam. They spread their faith as far as Afghanistan in the east and in the west, conquered all of North Africa and Spain, and afterwards invaded the Visigoth Kingdom of Aquitaine in south-west France.

◄ *The mosque of Muhammad Ali in Egypt.*

Beautiful Baghdad

AFTER AD 750, WHEN THE Umayyads were supplanted by the Abbasid caliphs, the focus of the Islamic world shifted to the Abbasid city of Baghdad. In Abbasid times, this was known as the 'Round City of Mansur' – after Al-Mansur, the second Caliph, who built Baghdad on the west bank of the River Tigris after AD 762, on the site of a Sassanian village of the same name. Also called Madinat-al-Salaam, 'City of Peace', Abbasid Baghdad was surrounded by a stout wall with four gates, each of them defended by 1,000 men. Baghdad later became a centre of culture and learning, and this status was typified by the most famous of its Caliphs, Harun al-Raschid (AD 766–809) who possessed a library containing some 600,000 books. Harun aimed to gather the learning and riches of the known world in Baghdad. The splendour of this period, the zenith of Baghdad's glory, was reflected in the tales of the famous 'Thousand and One Nights'.

The Abbasid dynasty, which lasted in Baghdad until 1258, when the city was sacked by the Mongols, set up libraries through their empire, and built hospitals in every city as part of their initiative to encourage the study and practice of medicine.

▲ *The Mongols put an end to the Abbasid dynasty.*

Safavid Persia

IN 1501, THE SUFAVIDS, who originated in southern Russia, challenged the power of the Turkmen confederation in Persia, known as Ak-Koyunlu, or the 'White Sheep'. The Safavid Ismai'il I (1487–1524) defeated the Turkmen at Sharur in that year and proclaimed himself Shah. Before long, the Sufavids began threatening the territory of the neighbouring Muslim Ottoman Empire, but in 1514 they were confined to the Iranian plateau after suffering a series of heavy defeats.

The Sufavids were not inward-looking. They encouraged contacts with western Europeans who, like themselves, were enemies of the Ottomans. Diplomatic and commercial relations with the Sufavids were therefore a bonus for Europeans, all the more so later, when Shah Abbas I (1571–1629) encouraged the manufacture and export of beautiful silks.

Shah Abbas, known as Abbas the Great, was a consummate politician. He created a standing army to control the feuding Turkmen chiefs and after 1598, also used it to seize Azerbaijan and parts of Armenia from the Ottoman Empire. Abbas's astute rule left a legacy of stability which enabled his dynasty to survive a succession of mediocre shahs, as well as pressure from the Ottomans until the Sufavid state was overthrown in 1722 by the Afghans.

▼ *Architecturally, the Taj Mahal stands as a tribute to Muslim-style architecture (see p. 140).*

Other Islamic Empires

THE RICHES AND MAGNIFICENCE of some Islamic rulers were possible because, unlike Christianity with its emphasis on the virtues of humility, the Muslims were not forbidden material wealth as a condition of their faith. In this context, the Ottoman Empire established after the capture of Constantinople, capital of the Byzantine Empire in 1453, or the Mogul dynasty of northern India, established in 1526, were celebrating Islam by their own lustre.

The Ottoman sultan Suleiman I 'the Magnificent' (1494–1566) added to his domains by conquest and penetrated into Europe to capture Belgrade, Budapest and the island of Rhodes as well as Baghdad, Aden and Algiers. Suleiman's navy was dominant in the Mediterranean, and Suleiman, whose reign was regarded as a 'golden age' was himself an enthusiastic patron of the arts and architecture.

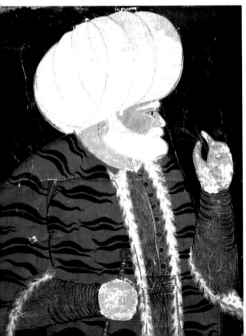

The riches of the extensive Mogul Empire and the palpable wealth of its emperors astounded the first British emissaries to visit them in the eighteenth century. Muslim-style architecture, with its curved domes and finely detailed decorations, was a particular glory of the Moguls, and today is typified most by the magical Taj Mahal at Agra, near Delhi, which has been described as 'a poem in stone' and 'a dream in marble'.

◄ *Suleiman the Magnificent, one of the greatest Ottoman emperors of the sixteenth century.*

Islam Teaches Europe

ISLAMIC EMPHASIS ON CULTURE AND LEARNING put the Muslims far ahead of contemporary Europeans in several ways. Muslim seamen, for instance, used the triangular lateen sail which made better and faster use of the wind at sea than the square sails on European vessels. The Europeans soon adopted the lateen and had much to learn, too, from Muslim geographers who had a more accurate and comprehensive view of the layout of the earth. This made Muslim maps preferable to the European 'plane' charts, since they were better guides for vessels venturing out of sight of land. Even the Scandinavian Vikings, the greatest of all European seamen, benefited from the map-making and navigational skills of the Muslims.

A similar process took place in medicine, where the crusaders were among the first to learn of the more gentle and more effective treatments practised by Muslim physicians. Astronomy, too, was well advanced in the world of Islam and Muslim astronomers had a much better understanding of the heavens at a time when many Europeans still believed the world was flat and that the sun moved round the earth.

▲ *Muslim explorers not only imparted the Islamic faith to the rest of the world, they brought, amongst others, new ideas on medicine, astronomy and geography.*

The Muslims as Traders

THE CLOSE ACQUAINTANCE ARAB MUSLIMS had with living in the desert stood them in good stead when it came organising the trading caravans which crossed the sandy wastes of the Sahara in Africa or the Gobi desert in central Asia. The camel, with its stamina, endurance and ability to keep going for days on end without fresh supplies of water, was an ideal animal for Muslim purposes. By this means, the Muslims built up a rich land-borne trade, not only in staple goods such as grain or cloth, but in luxuries such as wines, ivory, sweet-smelling woods, perfumes, silks, brocades, silverware, gold objects and jewellery. Slaves, too, were trade goods for the Muslims who transported them both by land and by sea.

The success of Muslim sea-borne commerce owed a great deal to their superior navigational and map-making skills, and Muslim trading vessels were able to reach as far as East Africa; by 1600, their commerce was dominating the eastern Mediterranean and the Indian Ocean. They acquired a distinct edge over their principal rivals, the Spaniards and the Portuguese, although the latter admitted Muslim vessels to their ports because they needed the revenue this brought in from harbour tolls.

◀ *African slave gangs were led across the desert by Arabs who knew how to navigate and survive the hostile plains.*

Muslim Medicine and Science

IN MEDIEVAL EUROPE, GANGRENOUS LEGS were amputed, often leaving the patient to die of shock; wounds were cauterised with boiling oil; deep crosses were cut in patients' foreheads to drive out 'devils'. Later on, patients were 'bled' to expel 'evil humours'. The experience often killed them. Muslim physicians proceeded quite differently. They used acupuncture or drugs and ointments to cure diseases or heal wounds. They prescribed poultices to treat inflammations and curative diets for stomach complaints.

The studies of Muslim botanists were allied to medicine, since they tapped liquid from balsam trees to make healing ointments. Muslim botanists also wrote books, mainly in Persian but also in Arabic and Urdu, about how plants grew and the effect the weather had on them. Zoologists made a special study of horses, made drawings of both their internal as well as their external anatomy and passed on their knowledge to veterinary surgeons. Geometry was another specialisation and played an important part in Muslim artistic design, especially as Islam, like Judaism, forbade the making of images, obliging the artist to use only flowers and abstract or geometric shapes.

Muslim medical practice relied on the use of herbal remedies and holistic medicines rather than the barbaric surgery practised in Europe. ▲

Avicenna

ABU-ALI AL-HUSAIN IBN ABDULLAH IBN SINA (AD 980–1037), or Avicenna, was a Persian philosopher and physician of very great influence both in the Islamic world and in medieval Europe. Born in Bukhara in Turkistan, Avicenna was already an accomplished physician by the time he was 18, and had acquired an enormous amount of philosophical knowledge. He later became the author of many weighty encyclopedias that contained his distillation of Ancient Greek thought.

Avicenna regarded the Islamic way of life as the highest and most perfect that could be achieved, and regarded the gift of prophecy as the greatest attribute of the intellect rather than a product of the imagination. Avicenna's concept of God was of a being in whom essence and existence were identical.

His great contribution to medicine was his *Al-Qana fi'l Tibb* ('The Canon of Medicine'), an encyclopedia of medical knowledge taken from his own experience and from the theories of Greek physicians. The Canon of Medicine became popular not only in the Islamic world, but in European universities where it was studied from the twelfth century. Before 1500, the Canon was reprinted 15 times and was only the second text to be printed in Arabic in 1593.

▲ *It would be many centuries before men would begin to understand the most intricate workings of the human body, but the foundations for modern medical science were partly laid by Islamic physicians.*

Averroës

THE ARABIAN PHILOSOPHER IBN RUSHD (1126–98), known as Averroës, came from Cordoba, in Muslim-ruled Spain. He trained as a doctor and became physician to the Caliph as well as a judge in Seville and Cordoba. Averroës believed that matter was eternal and that the individual soul was not immortal. Like Avicenna, he studied the Ancient Greek philosophers and wrote learned commentaries on the thought of Aristotle and on Plato's Republic. Also like Avicenna, his work became well known in Europe after it was translated into Latin.

Averroës believed, like the Ancient Greeks, that philosophical truth comes about through reasoning, a view opposed by some Christian thinkers such as the Italian philosopher and theologian St Thomas Aquinas (1225–74).

Unfortunately for him, Christians were not the only ones to reject Averroës's teachings. The Muslim authorities regarded them as heretical and he was banished from Spain in 1195. Later, however, Averroës was allowed to return, but eventually left Spain again and died in Marakkesh in Morocco in 1195.

His philosophy, known as Averroism, gained adherents in Europe and was taught in Paris and elsewhere in the thirteenth century. Its supporters, the Averroists, maintained the distinction between philosophical truth and revealed religion.

Italian philosopher and theologian, St Thomas Aquinas, whose thought was very much in opposition to that of Averroës. ▶

Allahu Akbar

IN ISLAM, THE ONE TRUE GOD IS ALLAH, though this name is neither feminine, masculine or neuter. Muslims believe that Muhammad was only the last of the prophets, who also included Noah, Abraham, Moses and Jesus Christ. It was Muhammad's task, one given him by Allah, to complete the divine religious law, and through him, they believe, Allah sends messages to the people of the earth.

For Muslims, the Islamic code of conduct, based on the Qur'an and the Sunnah, is known as the Shari'ah and because it is the law of Allah, it is immutable. The major source of Islamic law is the Hadith, in which the practices of Muhammad's life, the Sunnah, are recorded. The Sunni Muslims, who are a majority of 80 per cent of all Muslims, represent the orthodox tendency in Islam and base their Sunnah or 'path' of the Prophet Muhammad firmly upon the Qur'an.

The Shi'ite Muslims, who live mainly in Iran and Iraq, believe that Ali, the nephew and son-in-law of Muhammad was the rightful inheritor of the Muslim caliphate but was prevented from taking up his inheritance by his murder in AD 661. The Arabic name for Shi'ite, Shi'at Ali, means 'partisans of Ali'.

▼ *The Islamic code of conduct in the Qur'an informs Muslims how to live every aspect of their lives, including how they dress, correctly.*

The Practice of Islam

ISLAM LAYS ON ITS followers five obligatory duties or 'pillars'. The first is to recite the profession of faith, the *shahada*, in which Muslims state 'There is no God but God, and Muhammad is his prophet'. The second consists of prayers, the third the payment of *zakat* (purification) tax. The fourth is fasting and the fifth is the *hajj*, or pilgrimage to Mecca. There is no priestly hierarchy, but a muezzin calls the faithful to prayer from the minaret of a mosque with the announcement 'Allahu akbar' – 'God is great' – and there are imams who lead prayers. There are also five articles of the Islamic faith: belief in Allah, the one God; in the angels; in the Qur'an; the prophets; and the Day of Judgment.

There is no such thing as secular Islam. Muslims do not recognise a division between faith and state. Ramadan, one of the main festivals, takes place in the ninth month of the Islamic year and requires Muslims to refrain from food and drink between sunrise and sunset. According to Muslim tradition, the month of fasting commemorates the night, believed to be the 27th of Ramadan, when the first revelation of Islam occurred.

▲ *The Saint Sophia Mosque in Istanbul. Every day, imams lead the faithful to prayer in mosques around the world.*

Israel

The Israelites and the Bible

THE ORIGINS OF THE PEOPLE OF ANCIENT ISRAEL are bound up with the Biblical account of the escape of the Israelites or Hebrews from Egypt, led by Moses, their 40 years of wandering in the desert and their arrival in the 'Promised Land' of Canaan in about 1265 BC. Modern research, however, has cast some doubt on this Exodus as the dramatic event described in the Bible, even though it remains fundamental to Judaism, the religion of Jews in modern Israel and throughout the world. There is one theory that the Israelites were never slaves in Egypt but that they emigrated there at a time of famine in Canaan and later returned home of their own accord.

They first came to Canaan sometime between 2300 and 1750 BC, when the religious leader Abraham is reputed to have led his tribe there from the city of Ur, in Sumer. Abraham's own ancestry was said to derive from Shem, the son of the biblical and quite possibly mythical Noah. This is why the two family strains – the Jews, descended from Abraham and his wife Sarah, and the Arabs, descended from Abraham and Sarah's maidservant Hagar – are both termed 'Semitic' peoples.

Illustrations of biblical stories conveyed the faith to the illiterate and spread the faith around the world. ▶

Prehistoric Peoples

ARCHEOLOGICAL EVIDENCE SUGGESTS that Canaan was already settled in Paleolithic or Old Stone Age times (3.5 million–8500 BC). From about 9000 BC, wild cereals were being harvested with flint sickles, some cattle and sheep were being domesticated and wheat, barley and pulses were farmed in Jericho 2,000 years later.

Excavations on Mount Carmel have led to the conclusion that the Stone Age inhabitants had cultural connections with Europe and belonged to the same group as the Neanderthals. In Canaan, as elsewhere, people called Natufians lived in caves, experimented with farming, produced carefully carved hafts for sickles and made utensils for grinding. Flint and bone industries existed in the area of Jericho.

Solidly built homes made of mud appeared in Jericho in the Neolithic or New Stone Age period, and by 6750 BC, a strong wall, covering about four hectares, was built to surround the settlement, doubtless as a defence against attack.

In time, however, the population of the

area changed, absorbing immigrants called Ghassulian, who probably came from Syria, and various other newcomers, to form the thriving Bronze Age society that began in around 5000 BC and which, in its later stages, also received the people who came to be known as Israelites.

▲ *Early flint and stone tools and weapons, used by prehistoric peoples.*

Conquering Canaan

THE CANAANITES, KNOWN TO THE Greeks as Phoenicians, were a semitic people who had created a large empire covering Syria, Canaan and part of Mesopotamia some time before the Israelites began arriving in appreciable numbers between 1300 and 1200 BC. This was a time when Canaan was coming under fierce attack from the Sea Peoples, who may have been Achaeans from Greece, Etruscans from Italy or the Philistines from the Aegean who later conquered the whole Canaan region. Meanwhile, Moabites, Ammonites and Edomites settled in what is now southern Jordan.

The Israelites who had preceded them became firmly established in Canaan by about 1130 BC, and in their strong monotheistic faith and strict code of ethics had the moral weapons that suited them for conquest in their own right. The 12 tribes into which the Israelites were divided were disputatious and sometimes waged civil war against each other. However, when attacked by their neighbours in Canaan they, like the city-states of Greece, united and became a formidable force.

In around 1020 BC, the tribes found a leader, Saul, whom all supported, and after becoming king, he defeated both the Ammonites and the Philistines and set up the first kingdom in Israel.

Saul, David and Solomon

THOUGH DEFEATED, THE PHILISTINES WERE not crushed, and war with Israel continued. In one battle with the Philistines, King Saul's three sons were killed and their father, who appears to have suffered some form of mental depression, committed suicide. However, his successors, King David (1060–970 BC) and David's son King Solomon (974–937 BC) built on Saul's success and between them created an empire that stretched from Elath on the Red Sea in the south, into present-day Syria in the north.

David, King of Israel ▶

Solomon's kingdom had the strength and stability given it by an efficient bureaucracy, and a fully professional army that included an élite corps of charioteers, comprising 4,000 horses and 1,400 vehicles. An economic boom got under way, with rich copper mines at Wadi Araba, healthy trade with neighbouring Phoenician states and an extensive programme of public building. Among the new structures was the Temple of Jerusalem on Mount Moriah, which housed the Ark of the Covenant, the covenant between Israel and its one God.

The fame of Solomon's kingdom and its wealth spread to neighbouring countries, and the famous Queen of Sheba (Yemen) travelled some 2,414 km (1,500 miles) to establish trade links with Israel and witness the great wisdom for which its king was renowned.

Captivity and Conquest

DESPITE THE STRENGTH AND POWER of the kingdom of Israel, the region where it flourished continued to be restless and prone to fighting and disputes. The worst uprising followed Solomon's death, when a dispute over the succession split his kingdom and the new, though smaller, realm of Judah was formed in the south. The mutual antipathy of the two kingdoms was expressed by intermittent war. Now truncated, Israel also faced ongoing hostilities with neighbouring Syria which lasted until 732 BC.

Meanwhile, the ferocious Assyrians, seizing the chance to exploit the weakness of the two contestants, had intervened, thrashing the Syrians, capturing Damascus and annexing Israel into their empire in AD 721. Within a century, the glories of Solomon's kingdom had disappeared, and only tiny Judah remained as its heir. There followed mass deportations of captured Israelites, some 27,290 of whom were taken to Babylon where they were used as slaves in forced labour camps. Even Judah, though technically independent, was tied to Assyria for all religious and political purposes. The Judean king, Manasseh (d. 642 BC) had to allow the pagan Assyrian gods to be honoured in the temple at Jerusalem. As for the exiled Israelites, they were not allowed to return home until 538 BC.

▲ *Mosaic of the Royal Standard from the royal graves of Ur, early Dynastic period, 2750 BC.*

Alexander Invades

WHILE THE JEWS OF ISRAEL had been kept in their Babylonian captivity, the mighty Assyrian Empire had been vanquished, in about 609 BC, and the great power in the area was now Persia. It was, in fact, a Persian king, Cyrus II 'the Great' (d. 530 BC), who ordered the restoration of Judah and the rebuilding of the Temple at Jerusalem. This did not, however, mean that Israel had regained independence, and the Persians did not hesitate to interfere in religious as well as political affairs. Israel also suffered as the killing ground of others when, in 343 BC, the Persian king, Artaxerxes III Ochus (d. 338 BC), reputedly caused devastation in parts of Israel on his way to conquer Egypt.

A conqueror far more powerful than Artaxerxes arrived in Israel in 333 BC when Alexander the Great used the country just as the Persian king had done, as a corridor leading to Egypt. As he moved southwards down the Mediterranean coast, he destroyed city after city to prevent their being used as bases for the Persian fleet. Alexander left the Israelites strictly alone to observe their religion and their customs, but his intrusion was nonetheless devastating.

▲ *Illuminated manuscript depicting Alexander the Great on horseback in battle against the Persians.*

The Romans and After

FOLLOWING ALEXANDER'S DEATH, the area once covered by Israel and Judah fell into the hands of one of his generals, Seleucius I Nicator (358–280 BC). Seleucid's attempts at Hellenisation later provoked the rebellion led by the priest Judas Maccabaeus (d. 161 BC) which, in 165 BC, restored independence to Judah.

Independence lasted for only a century. In 63 BC, the Romans became involved in a dispute over the throne of Judah. Within a relatively short time, by 44 BC, the Romans had added Judah to their already extensive empire and were imposing their own choice of king. Revolts and uprisings ensued, all put down with great brutality until, in AD 66, a massive rebellion led by the Zealots required a powerful Roman army to suppress it. The subsequent punishment was appalling. The Temple was destroyed, captives were sent as slaves to Rome and in AD 70, hundreds were forced to leave the country. This was the start of what Jews call the 'Diaspora', the dispersion, and although many of them remained in Palestine, it did not officially end for nearly 19 centuries until the slaughter of Jews in the Holocaust during the Second World War (1939–45) prompted the creation of the modern state of Israel.

▲ *The mighty Roman army conquered Judah and caused mass destruction and bloodshed throughout Israel.*

The Phoenicians

THE TRADE OF ANCIENT Israel, such as trading with Yemen in gold, incense and spices, had long relied on land transport, often in the form of caravans which travelled over great distances to reach their destinations. However, the Phoenicians – or Canaanites – were the first people to open up different opportunities by making commerce by sea a feasible proposition. The Phoenicians were well placed for such an enterprise, with the long Mediterranean coastline and its cities and ports at their disposal. These ports were within reach of Egypt and Mesopotamia, but in about 1200 BC, Phoenician ships, manned by skilled sailors, began to be able to range much further, right across the Mediterranean, in fact, to Spain.

Along their way, they established bases in Cyprus, Sicily and on the north African coast where their most famous settlement was Carthage, near modern Tunis, founded in 814 BC. Always seeking new markets, Phoenician fleets ventured through the Straits of Gibraltar and out into the Atlantic, no mean feat for the ships of the time which were not built for the exigencies of ocean sailing. By these means, the Phoenicians were able to exchange exotic spices and textiles from Asia for Spanish copper and tin from Britain and Brittany.

▲ *The fall of Carthage at the hands of the Arabs.*

Hanno Sails South

IN ABOUT 460 BC, A NAVIGATOR NAMED HANNO, from the Phoenician colony of Carthage, sailed with a fleet of 60 ships beyond the Straits of Gibraltar and turned south down the African coast. The ships, made from cedar or cypress wood, with one large square sail and measuring some 36 m (118 ft) long and 9 m (30 ft) wide, were transporting some 30,000 settlers for the five new colonies Hanno intended to found.

However, Hanno did not turn back after disembarking his settlers. He sailed southwards for several days, hoping to locate a people who possessed gold. He had taken rich trade goods with him, including carpets, pieces of cloth and glass jars. Unsure of the temper of the inhabitants, Hanno and his crews placed their goods on the shore, then retired to their ships and waited. Before long, people wearing animal skins came onto the beach and placed pieces of gold in the sand.

The explorers also experienced some of the wonders of Africa – thick forests down to the water's edge, a volcano, possibly Mount Kakoulima, in Guinea, which appeared to be erupting, crocodiles, hippopotami and elephants. In all, Hanno's fleet sailed some 9,656 km (5,996 miles) on a voyage lasting four years.

Writing for Commerce

THE NAME OF CANAAN APPEARED IN CUNEIFORM from about the fifteenth century BC, but this wedge-shaped writing, impressed on clay, was largely impractical when it came to making complex records or the manifests of trading ships. However, a suitable alphabet, and one which allowed the sounds of the local language to be written down, was devised by scribes at Ugarit in about 1400 BC. This offered traders a much more flexible form of writing for commercial purposes.

It was no accident that Ugarit, or Ras Shamra, a wealthy, busy port

Cuneiform symbols carved into stone. ▶

along the Levantine coast in Syria, was the site of this development. Weapons were produced and exported from Ugarit, together with luxury metal objects and bronze vessels. The Ugarit alphabet had the advantage of simplicity over cuneiform or hieroglyphics. The number of signs used was reduced to only 30.

The Ugarit system, however, had a rival. Further south, in Phoenicia and the area which was to become the Kingdom of Israel, a linear script was being developed that involved carved or straight lines rather than wedges. This form of writing could be applied to parchment, paper or animal hides, obviating the need for the cumbersome clay tablets that had formerly been used.

Christianity in Israel

THE FIRST CHRISTIANS WERE JEWS who created a sect in response to the formal nature of Jewish priestly tradition, and the decadence and materialism of city life in ancient Israel. The Christians and sects like them sought a more direct spiritual connection with God. They advocated simple living, non-violence and prayer. To them, God was not a distant king on high who spoke only to priests, but a Father who cared for his children. Like a father, God, they believed, would provide for all material needs so that the pursuit of wealth was unnecessary.

This early Christian worship centred around Jesus Christ, the son of carpenter born in Galilee, who was regarded as the Son of God, and the Messiah whose return Jews had awaited for centuries. This, however, was where the Christians differed radically from Orthodox Jews, who did not recognise Jesus as the Messiah.

Christianity attracted many non-Jews, including Roman soldiers. As a religion, now the most widespread in the world, Christian principles were largely formulated by Paul of Tarsus (AD 3–68), originally an orthodox Jew strongly opposed to the new faith, but dramatically converted by a vision which he saw on the road to Damascus in Syria.

◀ *Jesus, the Son of God, dies on the cross.*

Judaism

JUDAISM, WHICH INFLUENCED BOTH its offspring religion, Christianity, and later, Islam, was unusual in its devotion to one God. Whereas pagan faiths with many deities were more common, Abraham, founder of the Hebrew nation, was preaching monotheism in the twenty-fourth century BC. The central teaching of Judaism is that the one God created the world and all the life it contained. God designated the Jews as His 'Chosen People' and promised them a fertile land of their own. In the Bible, this fertile land turned out to be Canaan or Israel.

Jews, however, have paid dearly for adherence to their faith. The seminal event in their later suffering was their expulsion by the Romans from their land in about AD 70 and their subsequent homelessness as a people. For centuries, exile meant persecution, especially in Christian Europe, where Jews collectively were

considered to have 'killed Christ'. The Jews, however, never lost their longing to return to their ancient land, a quest fulfilled in 1948 when the modern State of Israel was created. Tragically, however, this was accomplished in blood during the Second World War, when the greatest of all persecutions took place at the hands of the Nazis.

▲ *A young boy reads the Torah with a Rabbi.*

The Dead Sea Scrolls

IN 1947, A REMARKABLE FIND WAS MADE when Muhammad Dib, a young Bedouin shepherd, came upon jars containing ancient scrolls in caves at Qumran, close by the Dead Sea, west of the River Jordan. More scrolls and fragments of scrolls were uncovered by 1956, and were found to contain copies of Old Testament books predating those previously known by as much as 1,000 years. The scrolls were written some time between 150 BC and AD 68, at a time when the Essene scribes might have been living in a monastic community in the area. The Romans destroyed the monastery after the Essenes supported the Zealot rebellion against their rule in Palestine.

There were 800 manuscripts in all, and except for the Book of Esther, they contain the entire Old Testament. In many cases, tiny fragments had to be carefully pieced together by scholars so that they could be read. The scholars believed that the Scrolls have meaning both for ancient Judaism and early Christianity.

Thirty years passed before they became available to the public in 1986, although half the scrolls had been published prior to this date. Ten years later, the Dead Sea Scrolls became the first ancient writings to feature on the Internet.

The Bible

THE BIBLE, THE SACRED BOOK of both the Jewish and Christian religions, contains the Old Testament, comprising the Hebrew Bible, and the New Testament, which includes the Gospels, the teachings of St Paul and mystical texts. The New Testament, written in the first and second centuries AD, was not recognised as sacred doctrine by the Church until the fourth century AD. The Roman Catholic Bible also contains the Apocrypha, 14 books that were not included in the Hebrew Bible. Another Apocrypha, which comes from the Greek *apokryptein*, meaning 'hidden away', comprise disputed New Testament texts. The Hebrew Bible is regarded, variously, as the history book of the Jewish nation and as a sacred testament written by God. Bible scholars, however, have recently been attempting to identify human writers who may have been responsible for the texts.

The Bible is the most frequently published and most widely translated book in the world. The first single-volume Bible was printed after 1200 and the first translation into English, published in 1535, was the work of the priest Miles Coverdale (1488–1568). The best-loved translation in English was the King James Bible or Authorised Version, published in 1611 during the reign of king James I (1567–1625).

Decorative page from an illustrated Bible. ▲

The Prophets

THE MOST STRIKING PERSONALITIES of the Old Testament were the fearless, outspoken Prophets, the most prominent of whom were Eliah, Amos, Hosea and Isaiah.

Isaiah (eighth century BC) was the son of Amos, who was possibly a high-ranking priest, and lived largely in Jerusalem. Life in Israel had never been entirely without its fierce disputes, either among the Israelites themselves or with neighbouring states and empires. In Isaiah's lifetime, great conflict and danger loomed especially large over the country due to threats of invasion from the warlike Assyrians. Isaiah prophesied that unless the people of Israel had faith in God and lived honestly, the land would become desert and the nation would be destroyed. He depicted God as the judge of the nation, punishing sinfulness through drought and plague and rewarding virtue through rain and harvest. If only the people would mend their ways, the desert would blossom and the gardens of paradise appear on earth. Unfortunately, the disaster Isaiah had prophesied came true in 721 BC.

Isaiah is believed to be one of the authors of the Biblical book named after him. In Jewish belief, he did not die, but was taken up to heaven in a fiery chariot.

▼ *It was believed that the great deserts of the world would expand to punish the people if they did not adhere to the teachings of God.*

David and Solomon

BOTH THE GREAT KINGS OF ISRAEL, David and his son and successor Solomon, became legendary figures and both are thought to have made contributions to the Bible – David with the authorship of several Psalms, Solomon with the Songs of Solomon.

Among the stories told about David, who became the second king of Israel, the most famous concerns his confrontation with the Philistine giant Goliath. The reputedly invincible Goliath, seemingly an impossible challenge for his youthful opponent, was killed by a stone from David's sling. In both Jewish and Christian belief, the Messiah, the saviour who could solve all troubles and herald an age of peace, would be a descendant of David.

Solomon, the son of David and Bathsheba, was renowned throughout the then-known world for his wisdom. One story frequently told of him recounts how each of two women claimed a child to be hers. Solomon, called upon to choose between them, ordered that the infant should be cut in half. At this, the true mother made herself known by offering to let the other woman keep the child rather than let it die.

Solomon later gave his name to the famed King Solomon's Mines at Aqaba, Jordan, which produced copper and iron.

▲ *King David of Israel.*

Japan

Origins

THE FOUR MAIN ISLANDS OF THE JAPANESE archipelago have been inhabited for at least 50,000 years. Until around 12,000 BC there were land bridges between Japan and both mainland China and Korea and it is likely that these routes enabled early migrants to settle in Japan.

According to archeological evidence, the original wave of settlers arrived in Japan during the Palaeolithic Age (50,000–12,000 BC). More came during the eras of the Jomon culture (11,000–300 BC) and the Yayoi culture (300 BC–AD 300), whose people are thought to be the main cultural and racial ancestors of the present-day population.

Traces of the Jomon culture, possibly represented today by the 20,000–25,000 Ainu people centred on Hokkaido, can be found throughout Japan, but there is a distinct concentration in the northern half of the main island of Honshu. The later Yayoi people – named after the Tokyo street where their traces were discovered – originally centred

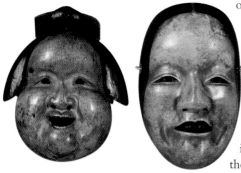

on Kyushu, Shokoku and the Kii peninsula south of present-day Osaka and Nara. Racial connections between the Japanese and the Koreans are likely, due to the narrow La Perouse Strait between Sakhalin in Korea and the north of Hokkaido island, the route by which they came about.

▲ *Japanese Noh masks.*

Life in Early Japan

IN AROUND 12000 BC, THE EARLY JAPANESE were living by gathering food and fishing. They used crude pottery vessels impressed with cord, an indication that they were leading settled lives in permanent communities. This way of life continued for thousands of years. As long afterwards as 6500 BC, stone and bone objects connected with hunting, gathering and fishing were being used in Japan, together with pottery decorated with geometric motifs.

The arrival of the Yayoi in Japan saw the beginnings of rice cultivation and wheel-made pottery. Later, around AD 250, copper and bronze casting was introduced. Iron weapons and tools were subsequently being used and by around AD 560, the Japanese had acquired horses.

By 660 BC, Japanese society had developed to the point where a royal family emerged to unify the country and institute an imperial throne. According to tradition, Prince Jimmu Tenno, who was reputedly born in Kyushu, founded an empire after defeating the Kingdom of Yamato and conquering eastern Japan in about 667 BC. Jimmu was believed to be descended form the sun goddess Amaterasu-Omikami, which accounts for the native name of the island country, Nippon. Nippon means 'Land of the Rising Sun' or, in Chinese, *jhi-pin*, from which the name 'Japan' derives.

Ancient Yayoi terracotta vase. ▶

Copying China

CHINA, MEANWHILE, WAS MAKING rapid progress administratively, technologically and artistically. As early as 600 BC, for example, the Chinese had smelting works and metal-working factories. The advances in China became of great interest to the Japanese, who were relatively isolated in their islands and were anxious to acquire superior tools and weapons. Their interest did not end there and when, eventually after the second century AD, they began acquiring ideas from China, they imported the Chinese calendar and system of writing, the Buddhist – and later the Confucian religions – and the harsh, strictly disciplined Chinese form of government which required absolute obedience to authority.

There was also a marked change in the technology the Japanese used, to judge from the more effective iron implements that replaced the bronze tools formerly used in Japan. Archeological finds have indicated that the Japanese had become adept at forging, and excavated tombs revealed decorative clay figures known as *haniwa*. The 'clothing' of the *haniwa* indicated that the mounted warrior on horseback had become an important figure in Japan. This, in its turn, attested to the fact that the Japanese were extremely warlike from their earliest times, a development fully confirmed by their later history.

The Chinese used their metallurgy skills to fabricate magnificent works of art, such as this Buddha, as well as for making weapons and tools. ▶

The Struggle for Power

THE CLANS, OR *UJI*, AROSE IN JAPAN before the seventh century AD as powerful, ambitious groups which vied for power and challenged the authority of the emperor. In AD 604, the Yamato clan, from whom later Japanese emperors were descended, began a long endeavour to create a centralised government which would emphasise imperial power. For example, a new constitution introduced by the Yamato Prince Shotokou (AD 593–622) declared the power of the emperor over the aristocracy. During the so-called Taika reforms, all land came into imperial ownership. Buddhism was used as a means of strengthening imperial authority. So was the permanent administrative capital established at Nara in AD 710.

None of this, however, achieved its prime objective. The emperors were never able to consolidate their authority and were always at the mercy of the clans. One of them, the Soga, acquired great power over the imperial court and manipulated state affairs for their own benefit. Their power faded in AD 645, when Soga no Iruka was murdered in the crowded audience hall of the imperial palace. Another clan, the Fujiwara, who were major landowners, bolstered their political influence by marrying into the imperial family and after AD 794 reduced the emperor to a mere figurehead.

◀ *A Bronze statue of a Japanese god.*

Enter the Samurai

AS TIME WENT ON, THE GREAT LANDOWNERS, or *daimyos*, emerged as the real rulers of Japan. They possessed private armies of samurai warriors and in 1185, the Minamoto clan overthrew the Fujiwara, seized power and established military rule. Seven years later, the emperor named the head of the clan, Yorimoto, as shogun, or general, and in that capacity, he ruled in the emperor's name. The Minamoto shogunate, however, was overthrown in its turn by the warlord Takauji Ashikaga in 1336. Ashikaga primacy declined in time, to usher in – and not for the first time in Japan – a long period of civil war.

The pattern of clan rivalry and warfare, punctuated by regular coup d'états with the emperor sitting on the sidelines as little more than a puppet, repeated itself over and over again. The constant thread that ran through the centuries of upheaval and persisted until the late nineteenth century was the influence of the samurai military caste which, over time, imposed its character on the Japanese at large. A particularly dominating influence was the samurai code of Bushido which made death preferable to dishonour and required the loss of honour to be assuaged by *seppuku*, or ritual suicide.

▲ *The Japanese shogun, Yorimito with his armed guard.*

Samurai Japan

THE SAMURAI WARRIORS WERE FEARSOME masters in Japan, even though only eight in every hundred Japanese belonged to samurai families. Highly privileged, and well-versed through centuries of almost constant internecine warfare, they believed total respect and subservience was their due. Instant execution could await those who failed to fall to their knees and bow deeply whenever a samurai passed by.

The distinguishing equipment carried by the samurai consisted of two swords, and they wore battle cosmetics to make themselves appear fierce and menacing.

Swordsmanship was an important skill for them, and they spent much time and effort perfecting their technique. Nevertheless, the chief samurai weapon was the bow and they were also adept at unarmed combat. Kung fu, jujitsu and kendo are martial sports today, but in samurai times, they were important adjuncts to war. The samurai rode into battle on sturdy ponies, but actual fighting often meant a series of single combats as each samurai strove to defeated another hand-to-hand. The higher class of samurai would fight on horseback, but for all of them, defeat was regarded as a deep disgrace. The samurai preferred to kill themselves rather than face the contempt they would earn from their colleagues for failing to do so.

▲ *The Samurai warriors fought with beautifully decorated, ornate swords. They were the true masters of swordsmanship.*

The Arrival of Western Civilisation

IN 1636, IN RESPONSE TO FEARS of Western and, in particular, Christian missionary influence, an Isolation Decree was issued, cutting off Japan from the rest of the world. During the next two centuries, while Western nations progressed technologically, politically, socially and culturally, Japan remained caught in its medieval time-warp. To keep Japan in this stasis, no one was allowed to build ocean-going ships, and European sailors washed up on Japanese shores were treated with great brutality.

By the mid-nineteenth century, however, some Western powers were building lucrative empires and setting up trading stations in Southeast Asia. The chauvanistic Japanese posed a danger to both trade and trade routes and in 1853, US president Millard Filmore (1780–1874) dispatched Commodore Matthew Perry (1794–1858) to demand that the Japanese open up their ports to international trade. For all their isolation, Japanese rulers were not unaware of the progress the outside world had made, and they knew, too, that unless they agreed to Perry's demands, they could be punished by war, humiliation and exploitation just as China had been after the Opium War of 1840. They therefore had no option but to agree and with that, Japan stood on the threshold of rapid and fundamental change.

The British and the Chinese meet face to face in Nanking during the Opium War. ▶

Resisting Change

DESPITE THE LOGIC OF THE WESTERNISATION demanded of the Japanese in 1853, some fierce resistance arose to the idea that Japan should so drastically alter its traditional ways. There were violent protests and cries of 'Sonno joi! Revere the Emperor! Drive out the foreign barbarians!', and as late as 1877, the uprising attempted not only to turn back the Western tide, but to overthrow the government.

The Rebellion was promptly crushed, but despite the protests, the prospect of fundamental change was not all that daunting for the Japanese. Their long isolation had left unaffected, or perhaps had prompted, a great curiosity in foreign innovations and the Japanese themselves were ingenious and accustomed to copying from outside. After all, much of their culture, even including 'bonsai', the practice of dwarfing trees, had been borrowed from China in the past.

Nevertheless, upending an entire culture rather than following the more usual course of gradually changing it was no small task, but the Japanese possessed what amounted to a secret weapon. The emperor, though a figurehead for so long, was regarded as divine and his command incontrovertible, and a new emperor, Matsuhito (Meiji) (1852–1912) who came to the throne in 1867, was willing to follow modernising advice.

Emperor Matsuhito of Japan, the first emperor to consider the modernisation of Japan. ▶

Making Treaties

THE EMPEROR'S COMMANDS, for modernisation or anything else, had to be obeyed and this provided a hidden assurance that the treaties that the Japanese made with foreign powers were going to be observed. The first treaty of co-operation was concluded with the United States in 1854, and the next with Britain, Russia and the Netherlands in 1856. Later, in 1871, Japan signed the Treaty of Tienstin with China and a treaty with Korea in 1876.

With this, Japan was ready for its root-and-branch conversion which went forward with such phenomenal speed that, ultimately, Japan leapt from medieval to modern in only about 40 years, a tenth of the time the same process had taken in Europe.

Any other nation but the ultra-obedient Japanese might have suffered cultural collapse at the pace and extent of the advances. However, by 1899, railways, factories, electric power, telephones and cinema had been introduced into a country which in 1853 had had no steam engine, no industry and no telegraph. A modern of system of education (1872), local government elections (1878), a cabinet of ministers and a parliament (1890) were accepted by a people who had for generations known only feudal authoritarian rule.

▲ *Commodore Perry of the United States Navy negotiates the trade agreement between America and Japan in 1853.*

Modernisation vs Samurai

THE BANK OF JAPAN was established by 1882, and by 1890, government paper-making and cotton-spinning plants were in operation, with steam-power introduced into some 200 factories. Railways, steamships and electric power plants were constructed and the Japanese were soon catching up so fast that they absorbed new innovations, such as aircraft, not long after they appeared in the West.

By 1896, the Japanese were operating steamships on international routes and had a modern army, trained by the Germans, and a modern navy trained by the British. Ironically, it was the new Japanese army equipped with modern weapons and modern tactics that suppressed the Satsuma Rebellion in 1877.

Despite the advances, though, the samurai that had provoked the Rebellion remained for some time the last bastion of the old traditional Japan. It remained, therefore, to expunge their influence. The samurai were forbidden to wear battle cosmetics or carry their characteristic two swords. Their pensions, previously awarded, were taken from them. Now quite emasculated, the samurai warrior class virtually ceased to exist. Nearly 1,000 years of samurai influence, however, could not be so easily set aside, and their warlike spirit lived in beneath the crust of newly-acquired modernity.

▲ *Early illustration of Japanese Samurai warriors guarding the coast of Japan against Mongol invasion in 1281.*

The Last Flourish of the Samurai

WITH THEIR WARLIKE PAST, the Japanese found little difficulty in emulating the Western taste for imperialist conquest. They attacked China in 1891, thrashed Russia in 1904–05 and committed later aggressions which, ultimately, led them into the Second World War in 1941. It was then that chilling aspects of samurai Japan surfaced.

The Japanese, who conquered a vast swathe of territory in Southeast Asia and in Burma (Mayanmar) in 1941–42 showed utter contempt for prisoners-of-war who, in their eyes, had disgraced themselves by surrender and so deserved the ill-treatment they received.

Yet the Japanese were also willing to sacrifice themselves for their

'divine' emperor. In battles on the Pacific islands, American GIs were shocked and astounded when their enemies made massed *banzai* charges which were tantamount to suicide, directly into the barrage of guns and other weapons being used against them. Likewise, the Japanese kamikaze pilots who flew one-way missions crashed their aircraft onto the decks of American ships, hoping to sink them or at least kill as many Americans as they could. When defeat or capture was inevitable, the Japanese would ask permission to commit *seppuku*, leaving the Americans aghast at the gruesome spectacle of mass self-slaughter.

▲ *Kamikaze pilots sacrificed their own lives as they deliberately crashed their aircraft into ships, hoping to cause maximum damage to the enemy.*

An Isolated Society

EVEN BEFORE THE ISOLATION DECREE of 1636 shut out the rest of the world, Japanese society evinced a form of 'ghetto' mentality. The Japanese came late to developments such as writing and printing, philosophy or mathematics, and even then it arrived largely through borrowings from the neighbouring China. The great ingenuity and inventiveness that has made present-day Japan a giant of the industrial world was confined by isolation to improving and adapting such imported cultural elements to make them fit Japanese patterns. In fact, for a long time, and well into the twentieth century, the Japanese were considered to be mere copyists of other peoples' cultures, rather than constituting a culture in their own right.

After acquiring writing from the Chinese, they invented characters and an alphabet to incorporate the Chinese style into the Japanese language. Likewise, the Japanese adjusted Chinese or Korean drama, poetry, art, literature and architecture to create variations that accorded with their own traditions.

Once they had adopted the Buddhist religion, imported through Korea from China, in AD 552, the Japanese explored new avenues of faith and thought, such as Zen, and modified it to take into account their own reverence for ancestors.

▼ *This Japanese painting, showing the goddess Amaterasu emerging from the earth, is similar in style to Chinese art.*

Japanese Artistry

MINUTE, SOMETIMES PETTY, ATTENTION TO DETAIL in artistic pursuits was another indication of isolated Japanese society. For example, the complexity and precision of Japanese traditional paintings and prints revealed the Japanese concept of appreciating the outside world from within, intuitively.

In Japanese hands, gardens became 'living paintings' in which flowers, trees, rocks, pools and bushes were arranged to resemble beautiful pictures. There were strict rules of arrangement. The complete garden picture required several 'mountains' which framed the central lake – distant mountains, mountains at the side and in the middle- and near-distance, together with a small hill for a cascade and a mountain spur. The shores of the lake were given beaches, and there were several islands, a worshipping stone and, as a centrepiece, a 'guardian' stone.

The overall effect of Japanese artistry, as also seen in sculpture, architecture and arts such as origami (paper folding) or flower arranging, is both exquisite and delicate, features which appear to run counter to the violence and upheaval that characterised so much of Japanese history. Yet even the samurai had their artistic leanings, and thought nothing of joining the parties which gathered in gardens to view and admire the blossom on the trees.

▲ *This minute Japanese carving with inlay stands only 3 cm (1.2 in) high, yet the artist has paid extraordinary attention to detail.*

Shinto

SHINTO, NAMED FROM THE CHINESE SHIN TAO, the 'Way of the Gods' was the native religion of Japan and one that combined empathy with natural forces and with loyalty to the emperor as the 'divine' descendant of the sun goddess Amaterasu-Omikami. In time, Buddhist and Confucian influences became entwined with Shinto, the first providing sacred written scriptures, personal morality and the means of salvation, and the second, social ethics including ideas such as purity.

Traditional Shinto, however, was quite different from either of these spiritual faiths. In Shinto, the Kami-no-Michi stood as the mysterious force of Nature present in mountains, stones, springs, caves or trees. Invoking the *kami* was at the heart of Shinto ceremonies and purification rituals were necessary before a worshipper was presentable enough to

make requests of it. Similar rituals are required if contraventions of the purity, devotion and sincerity required by Shinto are to be cleansed.

Shinto was, however, disestablished by the American occupiers after Japan's defeat in the Second World War in 1945. Since the reign of Meiji, the religion had taken an unacceptably aggressive 'state' form. At the same time, the emperor, Hirohito (1901–89) renounced his divinity, but a worshipful attitude towards Japanese royalty persisted.

◀ *Shinto priests in traditional dress at the Gion festival in Japan.*

The Creation Myth

THE MYTH OF WORLD CREATION was primarily linked to the Yayoi people. In their concept of the Creation, the universe originally existed as an unformed, oily jelly-like lump from which, eventually, there rose a god named Amanominakanushi-no-kami. Four other gods appeared after him, and subsequently a further seven generations of gods and goddesses who inhabited Takama-gahara, the High Plains of Heaven. At that time, there was no firm land, until the youngest of the gods, a male and female known as Izanagi and Izanami, took on the task of creating it. This was achieved when the young gods stood on the Floating Bridge of Heaven and stirred

the murky depths below with a sacred spear. When they lifted the spear out, the drop which fell from it formed the first land, an island called Onogoro.

That done, Izanagi and Izanami descended from heaven to the newly formed land and built a palace for themselves. They invented the ceremony of marriage and Izanami later gave birth to the islands of the Japanese archipelago, several gods and goddesses linked with the wind, the mountains and other natural phenomena and finally, to Kagutsuchi, the god of fire who burned her to death as he was being born.

▲ *Amongst the gods of the natural world that the Japanese worshipped, was Raijin, the god of thunder.*

Japanese Philosophies

WHEN BUDDHISM CAME TO JAPAN, it came with many different ideas about the ways in which religious observance could lead to enlightenment. The Chan school, traditionally brought to China by an Indian monk, taught that the direct realisation of reality came through meditation. The Southern School of Chan believed that enlightenment was immediate, the Northern School, that it came about gradually. Zen, the form of Chan which became established in Japan came from the Southern School, but itself took two forms. One was Soto Zen, taught by Dogen (1200–53), which emphasised zazen meditation and the Rinzai Zen expounded by Hakuin (1686–1769) which used *koans* or unanswerable riddles to force the human mind out the delusions created by the world of words.

Pure Land Buddhism in Japan emanated from the Hua-Yen school of Fu Tsang (AD 643–712) and his interpretation of the Avatamsaka or 'Flower Ornament Sutra'. This stresses the total interdependence of all things. Those who chant the mantra 'Nam-Amida-Butsu' ('I take refuge in the name of the Amida Buddha') will be reborn in the Pure Land of Sukhavati. Another form of Pure Land Buddhism, developed by Nichiren (1222–85) states that salvation can be acquired by chanting Nam-Myoho-Rene-Kyo, the name of the Lotus Sutra.

A Buddha sat in a traditional pose, seated between two other Japanese divinities. ▲

Mesoamerica

The First Americans

BETWEEN 30,000 AND 20,000 YEARS AGO, humans began making their way across a land bridge which then connected Siberia and Alaska and now lies beneath the Bering Strait. Over time, they gradually spread throughout North, Central and South America until some 15,000 years ago, they reached the southernmost point, Mont Verde in Chile.

These first Americans were Asians, but inhabiting the Americas meant cutting themselves off from the social, cultural and technological influences in the outside world. Consequently, their societies developed in isolation.

For environmental reasons, however, considerable differences appeared between them. The Americas contain startling contrasts – vast plains and pampa, soaring mountains, mighty rivers, swamps and forests. Lifestyles developed accordingly. The great plains of what is now the United States offered its early inhabitants copious opportunities for hunting and gathering, a lifestyle which was so satisfactory that it remained more or less unchanged into modern times. The high sierras – and especially the Andes mountains which form a western 'spine' in

South America – were less yielding and here, civilisations developed in which humans pitted their ingenuity against Nature and succeeded in making a life for themselves.

◄ *The people who inhabit the high snow-capped mountainous regions of America lead a very different lifestyle to the peoples of the warmer plains.*

The Europeans Arrive

ONCE THE SPANIARDS begin to settle in the Americas in the wake of the discoveries of Christopher Columbus (1451–1506) after 1492, a fundamental and tragic change ensued for the first Americans. Most importantly, they had no more resistance to European diseases than the Spaniards had to theirs, but their numbers were far greater and they died in their thousands from 'new' infections such as smallpox.

Secondly, the Spaniards, together with the Portuguese, were intent on conquest and exploitation of the massive mineral resources of America, its gold and silver in particular. This eventually led to the enslavement of the first Americans to Spanish and Portuguese masters and also to the British, French, Dutch and Danish colonists who followed them from the seventeenth century onwards. Of these more modern intruders into America, the Spaniards were the most active in marrying 'native' wives in what has been called a 'biological invasion'. The result was a race of mestizos, people of mixed blood who account for a large portion of, for instance, the present-day population of Mexico. In 1921, in fact, 60.5 per cent of Mexicans were classed as mestizos in that year's census, with only 29.2 per cent classed as 'Indian' or first American.

▲ *Natives watch as Christopher Columbus arrives on the shores of Watling Island.*

The First Mesoamerican Civilisations

THE OLMECS, WHO LIVED AROUND THE Gulf of Mexico, created the first civilisation established in the Americas, in around 1200 BC. Their most spectacular archaeological legacy is in huge heads over three metres high and with markedly Chinese facial characteristics, which were carved from basalt and probably represent Olmec rulers.

The Olmecs had a form of picture writing and were skilled mathematicians. They devised a 'dot and bar' system of arithmetic, dots representing the figure 1, the bar representing 5 and a shell representing zero. Though simple, this system enabled the Olmecs to make quite complex calculations.

The Mayan civilisation, almost as ancient the Olmec, was established in the Yucatan peninsula, southern Mexico and Guatemala in about 1000 BC and afterwards created a culture of high achievement, possibly the highest in all Mesoamerica.

▲ *Ancient Olmec carved head.*

Mayans, Toltecs and Teotihuacan

BY 300 AD, THE MAYANS were using hieroglyphics and setting down their history on large stone slabs. Mayan astronomers knew how to estimate the length of a year, predict solar eclipses and chart the orbit of Venus.

Mayan sculptors created beautiful statues and carvings and their architects built cities such as Tikal, Chichén Itza and Uxmal with their pyramids which had steep-sided staircases leading up to richly decorated temples at the top.

Then, in about 900 AD, this civilisation seemed to collapse possibly through disease, possibly through war. The culprits were probably the ferocious Toltecs who later, in about 930 AD, occupied Chichén Itza and later founded their own capital of Tollan, or Tula, the 'city of reeds' about 80 km (50 miles). from present-day Mexico City. For the next two centuries the Toltecs were the dominant power in central Mexico.

Another of their depredations may have been the destruction, in about 600 AD, of the great ceremonial centre of Teotihuacan, 32 km (20 miles) north of Mexico City, which was dedicated to Tlaloc, lord of all the waters. Later rebuilt together with its imposing pyramid temples to the sun and the moon and its temple to Quetzalcoatl, the 'feathered serpent', this sacred city was originally founded in about 300 BC.

▲ *A Mayan pyramid remains as a testament to the architectural skill of this now-vanished civilisation.*

The Aztecs Conquer Mexico

THE AZTECS, ALSO CALLED THE MEXICA or Tenochca, provided the rags to riches story of Mesoamerica. They probably originated in Aztlan, the 'white land', in north-west Mexico and before 1168, when they overcame the Toltecs, they were poor nomads who lived by hiring themselves out to other tribes as mercenaries. All too often they disgusted their employers by their savagery and their proclivity for human sacrifice. Once, they presented the Lord of Calhuacan with the ears of 8,000 captives they had taken on his behalf.

Spurned and moved on by other tribes, the Aztecs eventually arrived at the shores of Lake Texcoco in the Valley of Mexico. It was an unhealthy and undesirable place but here, nevertheless, they built their great city of Tenochtitlan which meant 'stone rising in the water.'

Tenochtitlan later grew into the magnificent city which astounded the Spaniards when they reached it in 1519. It was, by then, the capital of a great empire. By 1440, the Aztecs had overrun the entire Valley of Mexico. Ultimately, they ruled a vast empire, Anahuac, 250,000 sq. km (96,525 sq. miles) in size containing some 12 million people and 38 provinces from the Gulf of Mexico to the shores of the Pacific Ocean.

▲ *The wall and entrance gate to the Aztec city of Tenochtitlan.*

The Aztecs as Warriors

IN WARLIKE AZTEC MEXICO, military virtues were inculcated very early on. Boys were sent to military schools where they were trained to fight in the difficult mountain country of central Mexico. They learned endurance by going on long marches outside Tenochtitlan carrying heavy packages and supplies, and fought each other with wooden clubs and spears from which the obsidian blades and spikes had been removed. Real Aztec weapons could have horrific effects. The *maquihuitl*, a cross between a sword and a club, had pieces of razor-sharp obsidian set in it and could shred flesh or sever a horse's head from its neck.

Aztec war expeditions began operations by sending out spies and reconnaissance parties to discover the enemy's positions and the best place for an attack. These advance groups were made up of 'Ocelot' warriors. The 'Eagle' warriors, the best fighters, actually led an attack. Aztec strategy in hand-to-hand fighting consisted of pushing against the shields of their opponents while attacking their faces and shoulders with swords or clubs. It was ferocious combat, and the Aztecs had to stamp their sandalled feet continually on the ground to prevent themselves from slipping in the blood which soon covered it.

▲ *The Aztecs defending the temple at Tenochtitlan.*

The Spanish Conquest

IN MEXICAN TERMS, THE AZTECS WERE FORMIDABLE, even irresistible, enemies, but their style of warfare was primitive at a time when Europeans were using firearms and guns. This the Aztecs soon discovered after the conquistador Hernan Cortés (1485–1547) arrived in Tenochtitlan on 8 November 1519 with about 400 Spaniards and 1,000 native troops.

The Spaniards rode in across one of the causeways connecting it to the shore, and the sight of their horses, an animal never before seen in America, gave notice that here was a superior force, despite is limited numbers. The Aztecs, it seems, came to believe that horse and rider were a single animal. Later, when it came to fighting for Tenochtitlan, the terror of the Spaniards' guns spoke for themselves.

The Aztecs managed to drive Cortés and his men from Tenochtitlan, but he returned with an army greatly augmented by forces recruited from the Aztecs' subject tribes who were thirsting for revenge against their cruel masters. In the battle for Tenochtitlan which followed, almost the entire Aztec population fought to expel the invaders. The end came on 23 August 1521 when the Aztecs' great city, now pulverised into ruin, fell, and with it their Empire of Anahuac.

▲ *The Battle of the Platform at Tenochtitlan in Mexico.*

An Agricultural Society

SOCIETY IN MESOAMERICA WAS basically agricultural. The practice of cultivating plants developed in Mesoamerica in about 2500 BC and after about AD 250 the Mayas and Toltecs as well as the Aztecs were using hybridised corn to increase yields. They cultivated beans, squashes, chilli peppers, avocados and potatoes and grew both tobacco and cotton. Irrigation channels were constructed to encourage crops and the Mesoamericans also built artificial gardens.

The Aztecs made maximum use of the waters of Lake Texcoco, on which Tenochtitlan was built, by constructing *chinampas*, floating garden islands where vegetables and other plants grew in profusion. A *chinampa* could be as large as 92 metres (302 ft) long and 10 metres (33 ft) wide, big enough for Aztec farmers to build their homes on them. They were made by heaping up a tangled mass of water-plants and covering them with the extremely fertile mud from the bottom of the lake. Almost anything could be grown on the *chinampas* – maize, flowers, chillis, tomatoes. The gardens were anchored to the bed of the lake by the roots of willow trees which were specially planted for this purpose.

Model temple used as a household shrine to the god Quetzalcoatl. ▲

Market Day in Tenochtitlan

MARKETS WERE HELD IN TENOCHTITLAN every five days, and there was a vast variety of goods on sale – paper, paint, glue, feathers, rubber, salt, obsidian blades and mirrors, pottery, jewellery, baskets, lengths of cloth, herbs and potions for curing illnesses and specially fattened puppies which were sold as delicacies for banquets and feasts. It was also possible to buy slaves at the market.

Strict rules prevailed about giving proper measures and selling goods of the right quality. Traders sold maize and grins in measures of about 90 kg (198 lb) called *troje* or measures of 60 kg (132 lb) called tlacopontli.

▲ *Statues to the gods worshipped by the ancient American civilisations would be made by local craftsmen and sold at the markets.*

Anyone failing to give the full measure had his measuring instruments smashed by the market supervisor. Sometimes, they might confiscate a trader's entire stock of goods if these were considered to be of poor standard. Customers who stole were flogged to death.

No money was used in the market. Trade was done by barter, but there were some fixed prices in which the currency was a number of cloaks or mantles. A canoe, for instance, cost one mantle. So did 20 lumps of rubber. A gold lip-plug cost 25 mantles and a military costume with a feathered shield cost 64.

Trading in Aztec Mexico

THE AZTEC TRADING CARAVANS which wound out of Tenochtitlan, usually at night, used no pack animals or carts. They consisted of merchants, their slaves and other porters walking in file and carrying their trade goods on their backs. Wheeled vehicles had no practical use in the high mountain terrain.

An attempt was made to assuage the perils faced by travelling merchants as they traversed dangerous mountain passes or crossed fast-flowing rivers by consulting the stars to make sure the date of departure was a lucky one. However, it might be years before the merchants would come home and their families observed careful rituals in hopes of a safe return. Wives and children ceremonially washed their heads and cut their hair, things none of them would do until the merchants were home again.

Goods coming into Tenochtitlan from the 38 subject provinces of the Aztec Empire were, of course, a form of tribute to their masters. The tribute book of the Great Speaker of the Aztecs Moteçuçoma II (1466-1520) better known as Montezuma contained, on one page, gifts of a war costume and shield, 400 mantles, 5 bags of cochineal, 400 handsful of green feathers and 20 bowls of gold dust.

Religion in Mesoamerica

THERE WERE MANY DIFFERENCES in language, politics and art styles between the various peoples of Mesoamerica, but a surprising unity when it came to religious beliefs and mythologies. The use of the 260-day calendar, originally developed by the Maya, was also widespread. This linked a ritual 260-day cycle with the solar year of 365 days, each day being connected to a specific patron deity.

The Olmecs, the first Mesoamerican civilisation, introduced a pantheon of half-human, half-animal gods, together with the principle of human sacrifice. Along with the building of pyramid temples, ancestor worship and the divine status of emperors and rulers, these ideas and practices were emulated by all the subsequent Mesoamerican cultures.

In addition, throughout Mesoamerica, individual myths and groups of related myths, served to integrate and make sense of the political, spiritual and natural worlds of the creators. They did this by placing society a the centre of the universe and by bestowing a sacred legitimacy on the social hierarchy and the activities of the élite. In the Mesoamerican worldview, the spiritual boundaries between life an death were indistinct, and humans, animals, ancestors and gods could live in spirit form and change their outward appearance.

▲ *This figure represents both life and death, and as such is half man, half skeleton.*

The Creation According to the Aztecs

LIKE MANY MESOAMERICAN PEOPLES, the Aztecs believed that the universe was conceived in a struggle between the powers of light and darkness. In the beginning were Ometeotl and Omechihuatl, the male and female lords duality. Their cosmic children were the four Tezcatlipocas: Red Tezcatlipoca or Xipe Totec, the flayed lord, associated with the east; Blue Tezcatlipoca or Huitzilopochtli, the sun god, with the south; White Tezcatlipoca or Quetzalcoatl, the feathered serpent with the west; and Black Tezcatlipoca, with the north. Tlaloc, the rain god and Chalchiuhtlicue, his consort and goddess of water, were the lords of fertility.

The series of cosmic struggles between these gods led to the Creation and also the destruction of successive worlds, which is a regular feature of Mesoamerican creation myths and may be used to explain the frequent incidence of earthquakes in the volcanic Valley of Mexico. The Aztecs believed that there were five creations or 'Suns', each of them identified by the cataclysm which finally engulfed it.

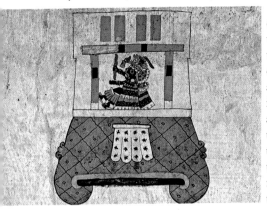

After the first four creations, all imperfect worlds which ended when the earth was engulfed by floods and humans turned into fish, Tezcatlipoca and Quetzalcoatl transformed themselves into two great trees and raised the sky above the earth.

▲ *Tlaloc, the god of rain, pictured here in his mountain temple.*

The Creation of Human Beings

QUETZALCOATL THEN DESCENDED into the Underworld and retrieved the bones of those drowned in the flood, after which the bones were ground into power and mixed with the penitential blood of the gods to create human flesh. This was how the earth became inhabited, but even so it remained in darkness.

The gods therefore met at Teotihuacan in order to bring about the fifth creation, the creation of the Aztec world. The god Nanahuatzin hurled himself into a blazing fire, and is magically transformed into the rising sun. The sun, however, does not move and so the other gods sacrifice their blood to give him the energy required for his daily journey across the Heavens.

This part of the Aztec creation myth was the source of their practice of human sacrifice, in which the hearts of victims were cut out with obsidian knives and offered, apparently still beating, to the sun. As disgusting as this was to other, less savage Mesoamericans and to the Spaniards, the Aztecs believed that if their sun god, Huitzilopochtli, failed to receive sufficient hearts, then he would not have the strength to rise again next day. As many as 50,000 human sacrifices were made each year.

▲ *The Toltec god, Quetzalcoatl.*

The Aztec Calendar Stone

THE AZTEC CREATION MYTHS are vividly portrayed in the huge and impressive Calendar Stone which was discovered in 1790 near to the place where the Great Aztec Temple of Tenochtitlan stood before it was destroyed in the wake of their defeat by the Spaniards. The disc is 4 metres (13 ft) wide and is less a true calendar than a monumental vision of Aztecs creations carved in stone.

At the centre of the Stone is the face of the sun god Tonatiuh, flanked by two giant claws and four boxed figures representing the four previous Suns: these had been dedicated to the jaguar, wind, fire and water. Surrounding these are *da* signs from the sacred calendar and symbolic representations of Tezcatlipoca, Quetzalcoatl and Tlaloc. Art and myth were closely entwined in ancient Mesoamerica, and the Calendar Stone is a dramatic reminder of it.

The Stone itself is a thing of fearsome beauty in the reconstruction with original colours created in 1939 and presented at the XXVII International Congress of Americanists held in Mexico City. A vivid brick red dominates the colour scheme. The design is a series of concentric circles edged with feather motifs and including ferocious images of a jaguar and a serpent, among others.

▲ *The Calendar Stone.*

The *Popul Voh*

THE *POPOL VUH*, OR 'BOOK OF COUNSEL', preserves the ancient myths relating the creation of the earth of the Quiché Maya of Guatemala. It tells how Gugumatz and Huracan, the creator gods, shaped the earth, and made trees, bushes, jaguars, deer, birds and serpents.

This first creation, however, did not satisfy, since the animals could not speak and praise their work. In a second creation, the gods fashioned humans who, however, proved no better when the mud from which they were made crumbled and dissolved.

For their third attempt, Gugumatz and Huracan invoked aid from ancestral diviners, sorcerers and spirit animals. Humans were then carved from wood, but they had no memories. They failed to speak their creators' names. and the gods destroyed them.

In the fourth, successful creation, the gods used maize to fashion human flesh and make the first four men, the mythical founders of the Quiché Maya. They praised their creators, but Gugumatz and Huracan grew jealous of them, fearing they might become as great as the gods. They therefore made the men fallible and limited in their under-standing; with this the Quiché nation was founded and the first dawn broke, spreading light across the earth.

Terracotta head of the Mayan fire god. ▶

Myth, Magic and Sorcery

THE AZTECS WERE INTENSELY SUPERSTITIOUS and believe in all sorts of spirits, magic, witchcraft and sorcery. The Aztecs used all possible methods to calm the cruel and furious forces of Nature and nothing they did – getting married, going on a journey or naming a child – could proceed until the astrologer-priests had consulted the stars and found if the time was favourable.

Good-luck rituals had to be strictly observed, such as rubbing ashes into knees and joints before visiting a newborn child. This preserved the infant against lameness and rheumatism. Later on, when the infant lost a tooth it had to be dropped into a mousehole, otherwise the permanent adult tooth would not grown its place.

The Aztec healers or *ticitl* mixed magic spells and incantations with some knowledge of healing herbs and a great deal of trickery. To the Aztecs, sickness was a divine punishment or the result of a curse from a wicked spirit. Some gods were thought to be responsible for certain types of illness. Tlaloc caused dropsy, gout, leprosy, swellings and ulcers. Xipe Totec caused skin diseases and eye troubles. These were regarded as punishments for failing to observe religious ritual or offer the proper sacrifices to the gods.

▲ *Aztec superstitions were recorded pictorially. The meaning of these pictures was translated into Latin script by visiting scholars in the sixteenth century.*

Mesopotamia

Origins

MESOPOTAMIA, THE 'LAND BETWEEN THE TWO RIVERS' Tigris and Euphrates, was probably the site of the earliest human civilisation, Sumer, founded in about 3500 BC. This, however, was fairly recent history in the area later called the 'Fertile Crescent'. Archaeologists have uncovered a Neanderthal grave dating from about 50,000 BC at Shanidar Cave in the Zagros Mountains of present-day Iraq, in which a man was ceremoniously buried surrounded by brightly coloured garlands of sweet-scented flowers.

The whole area, which stretched from the Persian Gulf in the south to the eastern Mediterranean in the north, was open to wandering nomads who may have settled there long after Neanderthal times, in around 6500 BC. This is the earliest date for known cultures in the area, beginning with the Hassuna culture (6500 BC and 6000 BC.) where pottery was fired in kilns.

In the Samarran and Halafan cultures which followed between 6000 BC and 5400 BC, canals were built and other irrigation techniques developed. Fine pottery was produced, together with jewellery, sculpture and tools made of flint and obsidian. These early Mesopotamian cultures were probably based in villages, where subsistence was the main occupation of their few hundred inhabitants. The later Ubaid culture (5900-4300 BC) in southern Mesopotamia advanced several steps further.

▲ *Pottery female statuette. This figurine has been dated to the sixth millennium* BC.

Substantial Settlements

AT TEPE GAWRA, NORTH-EAST OF MOSUL in present-day Iraq, the Ubaid culture left behind a temple with walls decorated by pilasters and recesses which is the oldest known building in the world. This region, which received very little rain, was a difficult place in which to live and the first inhabitants probably survived by fishing, hunting and herding goats, sheep and cattle. Irrigation transformed their parched land. Some time in the fifth century BC, the plough was introduced and large farming villages, such as Eridu, began to grow into small towns.

A temple found at Eridu set the standard for later temples in Mesopotamia, with its ornamented façade, offering table and an altar to contain the statue of a deity. Trade links had been established with neighbouring lands, prompted by the need to import vital materials lacking at home – timbers, metals, stone and semi-precious stone. The goods offered by the Ubaid culture appear to have been beautifully decorated pottery which has been discovered throughout the area around the Persian Gulf.

With these developments, the stage was set for the founding of the first civilisation in the Fertile Crescent. Important basic requirements were present: the proximity of rivers, farming, religion, industry and trade.

The Sumerian goddess of fertility. ▶

Sumeria

THE OLDEST AND LARGEST CITY of the Sumerian civilisation was Uruk which had a population numbering about 10,000. Founded in around 3500 BC, Uruk's population quintupled over the next eight centuries. The majority occupation in Uruk was farming, and this was so rich and fruitful that before long, surpluses were being produced. This encouraged specialist occupations which thrived on a food supply furnished by others and Uruk became a centre for sculpture, pottery, bronze-casting, bakeries, breweries, weaving and stone-masonry.

This in its turn produced a supply of goods and manufactures for trade and in Uruk and other Sumerian cities, the temples were the storehouses and entrepots. This was, in its way, big business which required accurate account and record-keeping. The Ubaid culture had already developed a system of clay tokens to keep track of goods and materials. In Sumeria, by around 3400 BC, this progressed to a system of pictographic writing.

All, however, was not well in Sumeria. An early sign of trouble appeared in about 2900 BC when huge defensive walls were constructed around the cities. Bronze weapons were produced in increasing quantities and pictographs were used to record the mighty deeds of the priest-kings in casting down and trampling on their enemies.

Uruk craftsmen were skilled artists and stonemasons portraying mythological people such as this, the Goddess Ninsun, mother of Gilgamesh, in their work. ▲

Sargon the Great

SOCIETY IN UBAID TIMES had been largely egalitarian, but this arrangement gave way in Sumeria to a hierarchy better suited to the creation of complex government and military forces. At its apex were the new secular kings who first appeared in around 2750 BC and ruled by strict codes of law, and the charisma that came from splendid palaces, an opulent life style and a reputation for military conquest. Such a reputation was very necessary at a time when the city-states of Sumeria were becoming overcrowded and were vying with each other for land and resources. The rivalries eventually led to war, with first one city predominating, then falling to another which replaced it. Ultimately, a ruler able to overtake all others came on to the scene: Sargon of Agade who conquered Mesopotamia in around 2334 BC and set up the Akkadian empire.

Sargon's origins were apparently humble. He maintained he was the son of a date-grower and that he himself had been an official at the court of the King of Kish. He seems to have usurped the throne of Kish, and once in power proceeded to crush his rivals in Mesopotamia, conquer Sumeria and then extend his empire to the Mediterranean and Anatolia.

▲ *Bronze mask of Sargon the Great.*

Empire and Instability

SARGON'S AKKADIAN EMPIRE had all the appearance of overwhelming power, but within only three generations, it met the fate of all empires. Undermined by invasions, probably from the Gutian people, it fell in 2193 BC and in its wake, the former rivalries between city-states resumed. Another, Sumerian, empire arose under Ur-Nammu (2112-2095 BC) but like its predecessor collapsed under pressure from the Elamites who sacked the city of Ur in 2004 BC. The next imperial conqueror was the Amorite Hammurabi (d. 1750 BC) Hammurabi, known as the great law-giver of the ancient world, died only five years after completing his conquests and once his empire came under attack from outside, it, too, disintegrated in time. Even worse, the great city of Babylon was sacked in 1595 BC, heralding a 'dark age' two centuries long.

This dismally recurrent pattern revealed an inherent weakness in the early empires of Mesopotamia. There was no central government and no garrisoning of conquered states who were required only to pay tribute to their imperial masters. This was a ready made formula for rebellion as a means of regaining independence and whereas a strong emperor like Sargon or Hammurabi was able to impose his will on his vassals, a less dominant ruler was easier to defy.

▼ *Part of the impression made by a cylinder seal.*

The Assyrian Empire

TO JUDGE BY THE FAR GREATER length of time their empire survived, from 2500–612 BC, the Assyrians seemed to have resolved the cycle of conquest soon followed by decline and fall. Despite periods of setback and difficulty, they were able to revive and reclaim their former power and dominate once again. At its greatest extent, the spread of the Assyrian Empire was vast, encompassing not only Mesopotamia but Israel, Judah and Egypt as far down the River Nile as Thebes and beyond.

Assyrian rule was of a very different order from the relatively light-handed ruling system of previous empires. This was a stern and brutal military state which acquired a terrifying reputation for blood-thirstiness and cruelty in war. No region or city they conquered could expect any mercy from them. For instance, the Assyrian king Sargon II (d. 705 BC) prevented uprisings by deporting entire populations. In 689 BC, Sennacherib (d. 681 BC) devastated Babylon and turned it into a wasteland of rubble and ruin. Nor were conquered peoples left to their own devices and their plots against the central power. Officials who were directly under royal command were sent out to the provinces and inspectors were appointed to check on their performance.

Assyrian relief depicting the imperial guard, Nineveh. ▶

Fighting Men of Mesopotamia

WAR WAS AN EARLY RECOURSE in Mesopotamia. Soldiers carrying spears and shields were fighting in close order before 3500 BC, and in 2334 BC, a new weapon – the chariot – was introduced.

Drawn by four asses, the two- or four-wheeled chariot revolutionised warfare with previously unknown mobility, carrying a charioteer and a soldier armed with spear and javelin. A line of charging chariots could throw an enemy into disorder while foot soldiers armed with spears and shields followed behind. In time, chariots acquired lighter bodies, spoked wheels, axles placed further back to give better balance and manoeuvrability and horses instead of asses to draw them.

The Assyrians fielded as many as 120,000 soldiers, together with large numbers of horsemen who rode bareback into battle carrying long lances. An array of archers accompanied them, each with his own shield-bearer to protect him. Assyrian chariots were made of heavily panelled, metal-covered brilliantly-painted wood and carried a driver, an archer and a shield bearer. The Assyrian infantry rode into battle, but dismounted to fight and were protected by conical helmets and metal breastplates. Assyrian siege engines, some made of iron, battered down walls, showered opponents with missiles and generally created havoc and terror among all who encountered them.

▲ *The hero Marduk, shown here in his chariot, defeats Tiamat, goddess of the Deep, personification of evil.*

The Last Empires of Mesopotamia

IN 612 BC, AFTER NEARLY 19 CENTURIES, the Assyrian empire was conquered and divided between Babylonia and Media. This far, Mesopotamian empires had been empires in their own right. The end of Assyria, however, heralded a new phase in which the area was conquered from outside and became part of 'foreign' empires.

The first was the Persian which ruled for some two centuries before Alexander the Great (356-323 BC), the Macedonian king of Greece vanquished the Persian emperor Darius III (d. 330 BC) in 331 BC. After Alexander's death, Mesopotamia fell to his general Seleucius I (358-280 BC). whose dynasty ruled until the Parthians overran the area in about 140 BC.

Next came the Romans, who added Mesopotamia to their Empire after AD 165, then the Sassanids from Persia who retained it until the

spread of Islam swept it into the Muslim orbit in AD 637. Subsequently, Mesopotamia was occupied by the Mongols, and, for the third time, the Persians until in 1534 the Ottoman Sultan Suleiman I, the Magnificent (1494–1566) occupied the Crescent. Mesopotamia remained under Ottoman rule until the end of the First World War (1914–18); when it emerged it was no longer a unit, but was separated into the states which cover the area today.

◄ *Suleiman the Magnificent, one of the greatest Ottoman emperors of the sixteenth century.*

203

Trade in Mesopotamia

THE LARGELY LOCAL TRADE LINKS of pre-Sumerian Mesopotamia expanded enormously once the civilisation was established. Sumerians traded as far away as Afghanistan and Egypt and in around 3400 BC, a merchant colony was established at Habuba Kabira in northern Syria.

By around 1800 BC, Ashur on the River Tigris had developed as a major trading centre, and had links with Persia, Anatolia and the Persian Gulf. At about the same time, a major Assyrian merchant colony was founded at Kultepe in south-east Turkey and formed part of an extensive trading network which reached as far as the Black Sea in southern Russia. Metals such as copper formed a substantial part of this trade together with pottery, ironwork and bronze-cast luxury goods.

The commercial economy of Mesopotamia was well organised fairly early on. A system of trading based on market prices and rules for buying and selling existed there from about 2500 BC. This, though, was not a money economy, nor was its alternative, barter, universally used by merchants. Barter was normally confined to exchanging goods on a personal basis, between peasant farmers. To start with, merchants' prices were calculated in barley; later, silver bars served the same purpose, especially where larger amounts were involved.

◀ *Ornate Sumerian harp decorated with a golden bull's head.*

Technology in Mesopotamia

IRON WAS THE SECOND MAJOR METAL, after copper, to be discovered by humans. The first known man-made iron object, a wrought-iron dagger dating from about 2800 BC, was found in Mesopotamia. Mesopotamia was also the scene of several other innovations. One of them was glass, another was casting in bronze, which evolved in around 3000 BC. At this time, too, wheels were being used for transport in and the town of Hit, in west-central Mesopotamia, was the source of bitumen for bonding courses of bricks.

In Mesopotamia, where stone was lacking, bricks were first made from reed plastered in mud. Later, brick-making became so skilful that large, strong defensive city walls were constructed. So were huge buildings, the greatest of which was the Ziggurat at Ur, a step pyramid containing a shrine where the sun-dried bricks were faced with glazed bricks or tiles. One important discovery at Ur was the earliest surviving potter's wheel, and the first known to use a rotary motion.

Later, in about 2200 BC, during the Akkadian empire in Mesopotamia, metal-working reached a high standard of artistry. metal was hammered into relief, gold and silver filigree was produced, and engraving, granulation, cloisonné or inlaid cavities were developed.

▲ *The Mesopotamians became so skilled at brick-making that they made tiles and created works such as this ceramic art depicting a lion.*

A Cautionary Tale

THE ADVANCE OF TECHNOLOGY in Mesopotamia, and the development of sophisticated farming did not always have a happy ending. In the case of Sumerian agriculture, Nature connived with humans to bring about disaster.

Once the problem of irrigating the land had been solved, farming techniques developed rapidly. There was, however, a natural limit to how far farmland could be extended. At first, Sumerian farmers moved into new land whenever old farmland became degraded or their harvests began to diminish. The limits of expansion, however, were reached in about 2400 BC and farmers were faced with making their existing land work for them or, alternatively, go under.

They went under over the next six centuries; farmland gradually accumulated salt, the by-product of evaporating irrigation water. The salt, in its turn, poisoned the soil and harvests began to decline. Eventually, much farmland was completely barren. The salts continued to depress crop yields more than 40 per cent and as a result, food reserves were reduced and the prosperity of Sumeria suffered. The end came in around 1800 BC, when the agriculture system collapsed and with that, the great days of the world's first civilisation were over.

Carving of Baal, Lord and Master, the generic name given to the weather gods of the Fertile Crescent of Mesopotamia. ▶

The Myths of Sumeria

SUMERIAN MYTHS ARE KNOWN from often fragmentary cuneiform tablets dating from between 2600 BC and 1900 BC which were found in temple archives. Reflected in their myths is the Sumerian concept of a coherent cosmic order represented by various deities, each of which fulfils an essential role in bringing divine harmony to both heaven and earth. The creation and maintenance of this harmony and the need to protect it against the forces of chaos or rival claims among equal contenders is a constant theme of Sumerian mythology. In addition Sumerian myths of origin outline the inauguration of Sumerian institutions, practices and rituals.

The myths reflect the socio-political background of a bureaucratic and hierarchical society and project the image of a well-managed universe, while also addressing general human concerns and the ambiguities of life and death. The style in which Sumerian myths were expressed varied widely, from a solemn liturgy and litany-like repetition to lyrical sentiment and even to raunchy dialogue.

However, Sumerian myths have to be approached with caution. Important passages are missing from the cuneiform records, and knowledge of the Sumerian language is still developing. Sumerian grammar still remains something of a mystery.

▲ *Cuneiform symbols carved into stone.*

The Gods of Sumeria

THE SUMERIAN GODS lived within the temples dedicated to them where they were represented by their images or statues. The most important was An, the sky god. Other major deities were Enlil of Nippur, Enki of Eridu and Inanna of Uruk. Inanna, representing Venus, was also an astral deity along with Utu, the sun and Nannar the moon. Female deities, often the tutelary goddesses of cities included Baba of Lagash, Nammu of Eridu and Ninhursaga of Kesh, all of them mother-goddesses.

As in many other pantheons, deities were assigned specific functions. For instance, Nisaba was the patroness of scribes and Nanshe the goddess of fish and magic. Ninisana was goddess of healing.

Enlil's cult centre and temple at Nippur in southern Mesopotamia made it the most important of Sumerian religious sites. Enlil was the son of An and the bestower of kingship, while also acting as a weather-god whose rains ensured good harvests. Like the weather, though, he possessed an unpredictable temperament which caused him to punish the world with floods and plagues.

Demons and evil spirits were also the offspring of An, but they were not all-powerful: they were to some extent vulnerable to magic spells and rituals of banishment.

▲ *The goddess Innana seeking to seduce Gilgamesh.*

Babylonian Deities and Myths

THE BABYLONIANS WERE ORIGINALLY Amorite tribes who came to prominence in Mesopatamia under their leader Hammurabi, whose capital was at Babylon. Although they introduced new deities, they also adopted many Sumerian deities, renaming them in their own Semitic language. By this means, An became Anu, Enki became Ea, Enlil became Ellil, Utu became Shamash, Nannar became Sin and Inanna became Ishtar, the goddess of love and war. When the Assyrians assumed power in Mesopotamia, Ishtar was personified as the legendary queen Sammuramat, or Semiramis in Greek, who lived in the ninth century BC. The adoption of the Sumerian pantheon was hardly surprising since the Babylonians inherited the culture and religious institutions of Sumer.

Several Sumerian myths were translated into Babylonian, but their emphasis was changed to reflect a more pessimistic outlook which was in keeping with the social and political upheavals that occurred after about 1000 BC. In the Babylon version, the setting is a more unpredictable world in which capricious gods uphold, yet also threaten, the universal order. The Babylonian myths also reveal a growing consciousness of national identity and ideology as exemplified by the rise of Marduk, the god who created both the earth and the human race.

▲ *Relief depicting the Babylonian sun-god Shamash.*

Gilgamesh

GILGAMESH WAS THE HERO of an ancient story said to be the oldest ever written and one which featured in Sumerian, Assyrian and Hittite legend. The Epic of Gilgamesh, which included an account of the Flood, was recorded on 12 cuneiform tablets by the scholars of the last Assyrian king Ashurbanipal (d. 626 BC).

The Epic tells how Gilgamesh the Mighty Warrior, was created as a perfectly formed man by the gods, who gave him both beauty and courage. However, as king in Uruk, he was a tyrant who so terrified his subjects that the gods sent down to earth another man, Enkidu, who equalled Gilgamesh in power and looks.

A first Gilgamesh and Enkidu fought savagely. Gilgamesh won but

impressed by Enkidu's power, he offered friendship and asked to learn Enkidu's gentler ways. Under Enkidu's influence, Gilgamesh calmed down and was no longer a tyrant. Later, when Enkidu fell ill, Gilgamesh cared for him personally and wept for seven days and nights after Enkidu died. This experience made Gilgamesh afraid of death and he sought some way to become immortal. The gods, however, refused him and he resigned himself to his own mortality, spending his remaining days glorifying and beautifying his city.

◀ *Stone relief of the hero Gilgamesh with captured lion.*

Baal

BAAL MEANT LORD OR MASTER and it was one commonly given to western Semitic deities. Most of them were weather-gods associated with rainfall, which was an important preoccupation in the Fertile Crescent of Mesopotamia. There were local manifestations of this weather god who was usually named after a mountain peak, the habitual domain of storm deities.

The Baal featured in the texts from Ugarit, an ancient city on the Syrian coast near Lattakia was Baal-Zaphon, the present-day Jebel el-Aqra who was identified with the ancient Syrian deity Hadad. Baal-Zaphon was called 'ride on the cloud' and was thought to be manifest in the storms which herald the autumn season in the Levant with displays of thunder and lightning.

In the Ugarit myths, Baal-Zaphon battles with the unruly waters of the sea, which made him the protector of Ugarit which depended on maritime traffic for its prosperity. Unfortunately Baal-Zaphon was not particularly successful, since he was regularly overcome by his foes. However, he was destined to rise gain in a cyclical waning and waxing of power. Baal-Zaphon represented fertility and the renewal life, so he is often associated with the Bull, an ancient symbol of vitality and sexual vigour.

◀ *Bronze statue of the Ugaritic god Baal.*

North America

Origins

THE SIBERIAN HUNTER-GATHERERS who moved across the land
bridge leading from east Asia into Alaska after about 22,000 BC, were
probably following the herds of mastodon, mammoth, musk-ox and
caribou on which they depended to live. What they found once they had
filtered down from the icy north into what is now Canada and the
United States was a land of plenty, blessed by Nature. Here, there was
ample wildlife, fertile soil, rivers full of fish, all of it offering a simple but
bounteous semi-nomadic lifestyle in which hunting, gathering, fishing
and small farming, gave them all they needed.

This, ultimately, was to be their downfall when more technologically
advanced Europeans arrived after the Genoese navigator Christopher
Columbus (1451–1506) happened upon the Americas in 1492 while
searching for a way west to the riches of China and Japan. Native
American weaponry was no match for European swords and guns, and
the European quest for settlement and riches no respecter of age-old
rights to the land nor a way of life completely different from their own.
Nevertheless, for as long it lasted the continent belonged to the first
Americans to develop their cultures, customs and religious beliefs.

The New Americans

EUROPEANS AND SOME ASIANS, such as the Chinese or Japanese,
came to the Americas with tremendous expectations. Ever since the
Spaniards became the first Europeans to colonise the Caribbean islands
of Hispaniola in 1496 and Cuba in 1511 and, in 1517, cross to
mainland Mexico. America had been seen as the land of wondrous

A Quaker meeting; such meetings would have helped to establish communities as newcomers
arrived in America. ▶

opportunity and wealth, free from the poverty, tyranny and restrictions suffered at home.

Settlement from Europe left North America relatively untouched at first until, in 1607, English emigrants came out to set up home in what is now Virginia. They were followed by the so-called 'Pilgrim Fathers', non-conformists from England escaping religious persecution at home. They were the first among many including Quakers and Dutch protestants, to regard America as a place where they could practise their faith in peace. These were small beginnings, but the major influx when it came, transformed the face of North America. In the nineteenth century, North America received thousands of Irish, Scots, Welsh, Jews, Germans, Swedes, Danes, Norwegians, Italians, Greeks, Poles, Russians and many others, all of them seeking to make a new life in the New World and a better one for their children than the 'old country' could offer.

Native Life in North America

THE ENVIRONMENTAL CONTRASTS of North America were so great that several patterns of living developed across its enormous land mass. In the southern desert regions, for instance, the people lived on plant seeds and small game. To the east of the Great Lakes, acorns, seeds, berries and tubers became an important part of the diet. Native Americans living by the coasts looked to the sea for food, in the form of shellfish, sea mammals and fish.

Lifestyles varied widely. The Anasazi of the south-west built villages called pueblos consisting of several houses joined together. They grew crops until about 1100 when the climate became too dry. The Sioux followed buffalo herds as they migrated across the plains. and like other tribes similarly engaged, lived in temporary villages featuring as 'houses' the characteristic teepee.

In the north-east, the Mohawk hunted deer, bear and caribou for meat and skins. They also trapped rabbits and beaver. Mohawk women cultivated the fields with hoes and digging sticks, planted seeds and tended crops. The most important of these crops were the 'three sisters': maize, beans and squash. Mohawk villages consisted of perhaps 50 longhouses each up to 45 m (148 ft) long and housing 20 families.

▼ *Sioux Indians were skilled hunters, killing buffalo for food and for their hides, from which they made shelter and clothes.*

The Caribbean

THE SOUTHWARD MIGRATION OF THE first Americans eventually covered the whole continent, but in around 5000 BC, some doubled back, leaving the tropical rainforests and savannahs of South America to settle in the Caribbean islands. The first to receive them was Trinidad but they soon moved north by canoe to Tobago, Grenada, Martinique and beyond.

Many centuries later, in around 300 BC, a new wave of settlers arrived from the mouth of the Orinoco river in Venezuela. Unlike their predecessors, who were hunter-gatherers, the newcomers lived a settled village life centred around the cultivation of manioc or cassava and sweet potato. They felled trees with sharp stone axes in order to clear areas for fields and villages, and by AD 300 had spread throughout the Caribbean.

The Caribs, who gave the area and its sea their name, seem to have been late arrivals. They sailed to the islands from South America in large sea-going canoes in about 1000, around the time, in fact, when far to the north, Vikings from Greenland were said to have reached Labrador in Canada. The Caribs set about colonising Dominica, St Vincent and Guadeloupe and there, ruled by war-chiefs, they lived in villages centred around the mens' meeting houses.

▲ *The landscapes of the comparatively small Caribbean islands must have seemed very far removed from the vast American plains.*

The Coming of Columbus

CHRISTOPHER COLUMBUS MADE LANDFALL in America on the Bahamian island called Guanahani by the natives and San Salvador by the Spaniards on 12 October 1492. During this and his three subsequent voyages Columbus discovered Cuba, Hispaniola, Guadeloupe, Montserrat, Antigua, Puerto Rico, Jamaica, Trinidad, the South American mainland, Honduras and Nicaragua.

At this time, the Caribbean was occupied by the Taino or Arawak in the Greater Antilles and the Carib in the Lesser Antilles. Arawak society had evolved out of previous migrations from South America, and was based on the cultivation of manioc which supported large villages ruled by chiefs. The Arawak religion was based on ancestor worship and their shamans contacted the spirits by sniffing the hallucinogenic powder *cohaba*. The Caribs, on the other hand, practised cannibalism, which was important in their religion and mythology, and usually involved the ritual consumption of a relative's powdered bones mixed with liquid in a ceremonial drink.

It did not take long for those who followed in the wake of Columbus to conclude that the islands were inhabited by godless savages with disgusting habits and so the stage was set for an era of exploitation and annihilation which ultimately destroyed the native cultures of America.

▲ *Columbus is greeted by the* caciques, *or chiefs.*

The Thirteen States

IN THE AREA NOW COVERED BY the eastern United States, native attitudes to the European settlers varied between outright hostility and willingness to help the new settlers survive. In Virginia, for instance, 800 settlers were massacred in two native uprisings, in 1622 and 1644. Yet in the Pilgrim Fathers' settlement in New England, the natives showed the newcomers woodcraft, trapping, hunting and other skills necessary for survival.

Either way, though, natives and newcomers were bound to be incompatible if only because their use of the land was different. The natives were hunters; the newcomers, farmers. In addition, many Europeans in America were ruthless and intolerant. The English Quaker, William Penn (1644–1718) was extraordinary in his approach when in 1682, he concluded the friendship Treaty of Shackamaxon with the Delaware tribe, which neither side ever broke. Afterwards, Penn paid the Delaware for the land he needed in his colony of Pennsylvania. This, though, was virtually unique in European-native relations and that was something the first Americans were to discover not long after the 13 colonies established by 1773 fought their War of Independence (1773–81) against Britain and became the United States of America.

▲ *Battle of Bunker Hill during the American War of Independence.*

The Way West

GEOGRAPHICALLY, THE NEW UNITED STATES was confined to the area east of the Appalachian Mountains. The 'Cumberland Gap', the way through the mountains, was discovered in 1750 by Daniel Boone (1734–1820). This opened up the fertile vastnesses of the American 'West' and by 1774, settlers were making their way through the Appalachians to settle in Kentucky. Over the next century, thousands more followed them, including new immigrants who headed west within days of arriving in America.

While the British ruled, they had warned that the West should not be colonised until the natives had been 'pacified'. Just how right they were became clear as the natives fought ferociously to preserve their ancestral lands. They attacked wagon trains, raided the coast-to-coast railway which was nevertheless completed in 1869, burned settler camps, towns and farms, stole crops and cattle, killed and captured men, women and children and created havoc and terror wherever they appeared.

It was all in vain. Gradually, the newcomers pushed the 'frontier' further and further westwards while the might of the US Army was used

to subdue the natives. Eventually, the first Americans were herded into 'reservations'. In 1890, after settlement reached the Pacific coast, the 'frontier' was declared closed.

◀ *The settlers crossed America in wagon trains, which were frequently attacked by native Indians who were forced to defend their lands.*

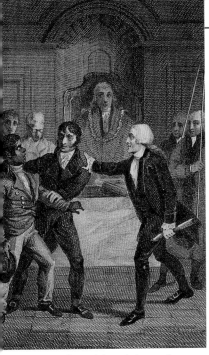

Slavery and the Civil War

SINCE 1563, BLACK SLAVES had been transported in fearful conditions from West Africa to labour in the American plantations, most of which were in the south. There, they were often ill-treated and sometimes murdered by their masters. Slaves who attempted to escape had their toes amputated after recapture to prevent them escaping again.

By around 1860, there was a clear division within the USA between the industrialised North and the slave-owning economy of the South. Abolitionists who wanted an end to slavery had become influential and the upshot was that the southern states seceded from the 'union' in 1861, virtually declaring themselves independent.

This was the start of the tragic and damaging Civil War (1861–65) in which the 'Federal' North fought to preserve the union of the American states and the 'Confederate' South fought to retain the slaves and free themselves from centralised rule. Over 600,000 Americans died in the War and deep and long-lasting hatreds were forged between the two sides before the South was defeated in 1865. After the War, the US Congress passed the 13th Amendment to the Constitution, abolishing slavery and so legalising the Emancipation Proclamation issued in 1863 by President Abraham Lincoln (1809–65).

▲ *Abolitionists, such as Granville Sharp, fought for the abolition of the cruel and inhumane slave trade.*

Trade Links Across North America

DESPITE THE COPIOUS BOUNTY of North America, where the traditional life of hunting and gathering was so well supplied that the first Americans never entirely abandoned it, the various native tribes developed a vigorous trading network.

By about 1000 BC, communities were established in the eastern woodlands of North America, the most prominent being the Adena people who settled in the Ohio Valley after about 700 BC, and the Hopewell people who had lived in the Mississippi basin since around 100 BC. They were hunter-gatherers but also small farmers, manufacturers and traders. In fact, they set up trading links right across North America.

The Adena and Hopewell used stone obtained from various areas to make tools, weapons and pipes. They also acquired copper and silver from the area around the Great Lakes and turned it into jewellery and musical instruments. Mica from the Appalachian Mountains was manufactured into models, badges and decorations. Obsidian, the volcanic glass which could be given wickedly sharp cutting edges went to make knives and spearheads. There was a good trade to be had, too, in pottery from south of the Appalachian Mountains, and shells and alligator teeth from the Gulf of Mexico which were fashioned into necklaces.

▲ *Decorative North American burial bowl, punctured at the base to let the spirits out, painted with a male and female figure.*

The Ingenious Inuit

THE ANCESTORS OF TODAY'S ESKIMOS, more correctly known as Inuit, were relative latecomers in the great migrations from eastern Asia into North America. They did not arrive until about 4000 BC and either remained in the Arctic regions of North America or spread eastwards, reaching the vast ice-bound island of Greenland by about 2500 BC.

The Inuit lived in the only feasible way their demanding environment allowed: they were nomadic hunters and fishermen, but great ingenuity was required of them if they were to survive in the sub-zero temperatures and endless snow and ice of the homeland they had chosen. They used kayaks, light canoes made of wooden frames with a covering of skins, for hunting seal, walrus and caribou as well as larger open boats, called *umiaks*, and sledges.

For hunting, the Inuit employed a range of tools and implements, including harpoons, bows and arrows and spears. Other ingenious tools invented by the Inuit comprised the bow drill, which was used to make holes in walrus tusk or other hard materials.

With only the arctic ice from which to make homes, the Inuit constructed igloos from large blocks of it, so skilfully put together that they were remarkably warm inside.

▼ *Today's inhabitants of Greenland and the Arctic still use traditional sledges pulled by teams of Huskies to cross the frozen landscape.*

Industrial America

NATIVE AMERICAN TECHNOLOGY differed radically from that of the European and other immigrants, some of whom ultimately turned the United States into the world's greatest industrial superpower. The natives only use for technology was as an aid to survival and to this end, they produced spears, bows and arrows, knives, choppers, scrapers and other 'primitive' implements.

The new Americans from Europe and elsewhere in the world had a different agenda. They came, first of all, from societies which were already technologically advanced and which did not live with Nature, like the natives, but challenged it with machines that provided facilities

▲ _Native Americans used simple yet effective weapons to hunt; they celebrated their kills with dances, such as the one shown here – a post-hunt buffalo dance._

the natural world did not afford. They were already strongly driven by scientific curiosity, the success ethic and the desire for wealth.

This more adventurous mind-set led Americans to discover the electrical charge in lightning, invent the cotton gin for cleaning cotton, devise the production line in motor car manufacture, a tabulating machine, conveyor cables for moving carcasses in meat-processing factories, invent the first liquid fuel rocket, apply robots to industrial production, invent the electric light bulb, the telephone, telephone transmitter and the phonograph and, of course, construct the first heavier-than-air flying machine which fulfilled man's most enduring dream.

Native American Creation Myths

THE MOST WIDESPREAD CREATION MYTH among the native Americans concerned a bird – often a duck – which dived into the sea and brought up mud from the seabed in its beak. The mud grew to form the earth. In a Cheyenne myth, the earth rested on the back of Grandmother Turtle.

In most of these myths, men and women were created out of clay, or *hopi*, grass, feathers, sticks or ears of corn. Humans could also emerge from the bones of the dead. Other sources of creation were the Earthmaker's sweat or the act of making a wish.

In some tribes, the belief was that the gods mated to produce human beings. Mother Earth, for instance, mated with Father Sky, the Sun with the Moon, the Morning Star with Evening Star. According to the Iroquois and Huron of the north-east, and the Navaho of the south-west, the first human being was a woman.

By contrast, the Micmac of eastern Canada saw creation as a constant state of flux. Their universe consisted of six worlds: the World Beneath the Earth; the World Beneath the Water; the Earth World; the Ghost World; the World Above the Earth; and the World Above the Sky.

The Trickster

THE MOST POPULAR PROTAGONIST in North American mythology was the trickster, who combined both animal and human features. He was regarded as a figure of fun, a joker, a fool, and, perhaps curiously, also as creator of the universe.

The trickster could take many different forms. One was the Great Hare of the Winnabago people of Wisconsin, Nanabush or Glooskap in northern and eastern North American woodlands. In the south-east, he was seen as a Rabbit, a Spider in parts of the Great Plains and Mink or Blue Jay among the peoples of the north-east coast.

The trickster-god was best shown in the Raven stories of the North Pacific coast and the Coyote cycles of the Great Plains. In the Raven cycle, Raven was a transformer, part-god and part-clown. He had an insatiable appetite which drove him to a perennial search for something to eat, which included tricking animals out of their food supply. The Raven was also an incurable womaniser, though frequently frustrated in his quests. Like Coyote, the Raven was creative and invaluable to the tribe. The Haida called the Raven 'He-Who-Must-Be-Obeyed', which evidenced his power. However, many trickster tales were quite rude and not meant for sensitive ears.

◀ *Knife hilt shaped as a raven. Ravens were believed to have brought fire from the sky and were blackened as punishment.*

The Supreme Being and the Gods

MOST NATIVE AMERICANS HAD A supreme god or spirit. The supreme being was Awonawilona or the 'One Who Contains All' for the Pueblo peoples of Arizona and New Mexico, Tirawa or 'Heavenly Arch' for the Pawnee of Oklahoma, Sagalie Tyee for the Coast Salish in British Columbia, Gitchi Manitou for the Algonquians of north-east Canada, and the twin brothers Tobats and Shinoh among the Pahutes of Utah. However, the Supreme God normally delegated the everyday affairs of the world other gods.

The stars personified heroes who hunted through the sky. The thunder, wind and storm lived in human form and could also take the shape of an animal. The beating of the Thunderbird's wings created the noise of thunder as well as the storm below as it flew through the sky.

Anything struck by the Thunderbird's lightning exerted a spiritual power which was to be either avoided or venerated.

Heroes able to overcome seemingly impossible obstacles may be demigods or ordinary mortals who had to endure certain ordeals, like going to the sky world or down to the land of the dead to rescue a maiden who had died. In mythical times, the demigods banished primeval monsters from the earth.

◀ *Thunderbird head-dress identified by its hook beak and feathered horns.*

The Ghost Dance

AFTER MORE THAN A CENTURY of attempting to stem the unstoppable tide of settlement and halt the urge of the United States to spread its territory from the Atlantic to the Pacific coast, the Plains 'Indians' resorted to a desperate, but ultimately doomed measure. They revived the Ghost Dance movement, which had originated in Nevada in 1870 and now spread rapidly.

This revival followed a vision which came to a Paiute native American named Wovoka in which he was told that the hated white man would disappear, the herds of bison – massacred by the whites – would come back and the old traditional native ways would return. The rituals and ceremonies of the Ghost Dance sought to conjure up aid from long-dead ancestors and, in particular, from the dead braves of the past who, the natives believed, could be persuaded to come back to life and by their efforts and their courage make all as it was before. The focus of the Movement was the Ghost Dance, which involved dancing frenzied enough to induce trances and so put the dancers in touch with the mystical spirit world. There, its adherents believed, they could be reunited with dead friends and relatives.

Caribbean Mythology

THE MYTHOLOGIES OF THE INDIGENOUS peoples of the Caribbean were similar in many ways to those of their better-known neighbours in Mesoamerica and South America. In particular, they shared the same ideas of successive creations of the cosmos, and of the spiritual animacy of the physical world. What sets these myths apart is fragmentary modern knowledge of them, and the social and physical settings of the Caribbean island landscapes in which they were set. Metamorphosis, the ability to change outward appearance from animal to human forms or vice versa, is central to understanding of the Taino myth.

Wolf head-dress used in ritual dances. Animals were believed to have certain human traits. ▶

Behaviour and feelings could also alter, with mythical figures possessing superhuman animal strength, and animals possessing human sensibilities. Some animals could be tribal ancestors. Some trees were the spirits or souls of dead chiefs. The souls of the dead were believed to hide themselves during daylight hours, only to emerge at night to seek out and eat the guava fruit. Taino myths, like all myths, are philosophical statements of how people regarded and made sense of their uniquely fragmented natural world. The events of Taino myth take place not in linear, but in mythic time, where movement, nearness and distance have little meaning.

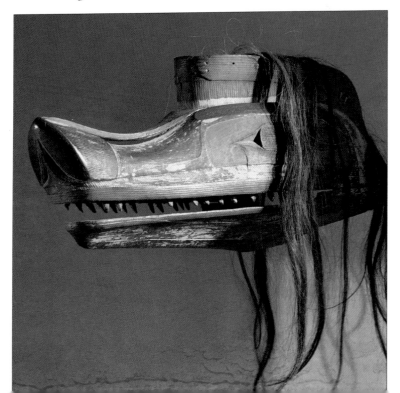

Northern, Central and Eastern Europe

The First Europeans

EUROPE WAS POPULATED FROM VERY EARLY TIMES, and traces have been found for habitation in both the Old and the New Stone Age. Neanderthal Man was there during the last Ice Age up to 1,800 million years ago, but was supplanted or absorbed after about 40,000 BC by Homo Sapiens, the immediate ancestor of humans today.

In the Mediterranean area of Europe, immigrants came from Asia Minor during the New Stone Age when they cultivated cereals and raised pigs and cattle. In central Europe, settlers lived in large villages with long rectangular timber houses and lived mostly by agriculture and animal herding.

The origins of these early Europeans appear to have been in the east, in Anatolia or Russia, though the Celts who spread into the present-day Czech Republic and Slovakia, western Hungary, Austria and Italy came the other way, from western Europe.

The first known Bronze Age culture – the Unetice culture of central Europe – appeared after 2500 BC and working with bronze was under way two centuries later. However, the disputatious nature of the continent's early communities became clear by about 2000 BC, with the building of hill-forts for defence.

◄ *The wealth of Celtic artefacts, such as this bronze statue, give an insight into this ancient civilisation.*

The Slavs

THE MOST INFLUENTIAL STRAIN among the early Europeans was Slavic, and the ancestry of the Slavs lay much further east, in Central Asia. The Scythians from the Black Sea and Sarmatian nomads from India are thought to have been among the ancestors of the Slavs, who first came west between 3000–2000 BC, and settled in east and south-east Europe.

In time, the Slavs spread all over this part of Europe, up to the Baltic Sea in the north, down to the Adriatic in the south and into Russia to populate that vast territory all the way to the Pacific Ocean. They encountered many different terrains – the treeless steppe of feather grass in the present-day Czech Republic and Slovakia, and a mild climate in Serbia, Croatia, Slovenia, Macedonia and Bulgaria in a region ringed by snow-capped mountains.

Wherever they settled, their environment left deep imprints on Slav civilisation and mythology. The steppe gave a feeling of vast horizons and distant dreams. Where there was forest, the Slavs learned caution, but found fantasy kindling in the imagination. Slavs who encountered rivers and seas made their homes on the banks and shores, but became wary of the demons and gods who lived in the water.

▲ *The Slavic divinity, Vodianoï, was believed to favour stretches of water near mills.*

Scandinavia

WHILE THE EARLY EUROPEANS WERE ARRIVING and settling down in other parts of the continent, the slow retreat of the ice at the close of the last Ice Age ensured that Scandinavia, in the far north-east, remained closed to human habitation for many centuries. It was, in fact, only by about 10000 BC, or possibly after that by 6000 BC that Scandinavia became a proposition for peoples looking for a viable home.

With this, settlers who lived by fishing established themselves on the shores of the Baltic sea in present-day Denmark, where barbed harpoons made of bone or horn have been found, together with chipped flint axes

▼ *The Ice Age retreated across most of Europe leaving the exposed land habitable, however Scandinavia remained impenetrable, covered by ice.*

and bone, horn and stone tools. Pottery came into use, in the form of a wide-bodied jar with a tipped base.

However, further north in the much harsher terrain of Norway and Sweden, a more primitive Old Stone Age-style life prevailed unaffected for some time by the technological advances being made to the south. The early Norwegians and Swedes did not yet practice agriculture, and their only domesticated animal was the dog. This indicates that they lived at the most primitive level of human life, by hunting and gathering and possibly fishing as well.

The Germanic Peoples

THE ORIGIN OF THE GERMANIC PEOPLES has long been a mystery, although their language is clearly Indo-European, which suggests ancestry in Persia or further east in the Aryan peoples of India.

In around 400 BC, they were living in southern Sweden, Denmark and northern Germany while the so-called 'barbarian' tribes the Vandals and the Goths occupied the south Baltic coast. Tracing the early history of the Germanic tribes has proved difficult, since they had no written language or at least none that was suited to making records and setting down events.

The first detailed accounts of these people came from the Romans, whose empire in the first century BC was close, in fact, uncomfortably close, to Germanic tribes who had settled west of the River Rhine and by the River Danube. Julius Caesar observed that the Germans were not generally farmers, but lived on the produce of their cattle and sheep. There was no right to land as private property: available land was distributed on a yearly basis by 'magistrates'. Government among the Germanic tribes was non-autocratic, and in fact barely existed in times of peace. In times of war, however, a council of chieftains was elected to conduct the necessary campaigns.

Into the Roman Empire

FOR A LONG TIME, THE GERMANIC PEOPLES clamoured to be allowed to settle inside the Roman Empire and so savour the sophisticated benefits of its civilisation. Easier said than done, for the mighty Roman army stood in the way, guarding the Empire's borders against intruders. The annihilation of Germanic forces which attempted to invade southern Gaul and northern Italy in 102 BC showed them what to expect from the greatest military power in the then known world.

However, by AD 376, Rome was in decline and the army with it. There was now very little to hold back mass incursions and Germans, together with other tribes, swarmed across the border in large numbers. The Romans attempted to mollify them by allowing Visigoths from the Danube area to settle inside the Empire, but they proved ungrateful guests. In AD 410, the Visigoths sacked Rome, robbing, burning, plundering and spreading terror for three days. This,

though, was only the start. In AD 455, Rome was pillaged again, this time by Vandals, and they were followed by wave upon wave of Germanic and barbarian invaders who swarmed across the frontiers and settled in Spain, North Africa, Gaul and Italy. It was the end of the Roman Empire.

◀ *Stone relief showing Roman soldiers in combat.*

The Vikings Strike West

THE WEST PROVED TO BE of more interest to other Germanic peoples, such as the Angles, Jutes and Saxons, who began invading England in the third century AD. Raiding was followed by settlement, a course also followed by the Vikings or Norsemen of Scandinavia. The Vikings also invaded and later settled in France, where they were given the Duchy of Normandy in about AD 911.

The Vikings, however, were nothing if not adventurous. Consequently, in the great movement of peoples which boiled across Europe after the fall of the Roman Empire, it was the Vikings who went furthest and most successfully into the unknown. They were magnificent seamen and navigators and, in AD 874, one of them, Ingolfr Arnarson sailed halfway across the Atlantic Ocean and landed in Iceland where he founded a colony at Rekyavik. The Viking settlers who followed him came mainly from Norway.

About a century later, in AD 982, Greenland was colonised from Iceland by Erik Thorvaldsson, known as Erik the Red (AD 950–1010) and a few years afterwards, Greenland apparently served as the springboard for the Viking discovery of America. There, they established the short-lived colony of Vinland somewhere on the coast of Nova Scotia or New England in about 1000.

▲ *Viking helmet and mask found amongst the treasures discovered at Sutton Hoo.*

The Slavs in Europe

THE MIGRATIONS OF GERMANIC TRIBES reached into south-east Europe where they occupied present-day Hungary after the fall of the Roman Empire. There, they were overcome by the Huns who entered Europe from Central Asia in about AD 372. Later, the famous Attila (AD 406–453) set up a kingdom in Hungary which did not, however, outlast his death. A further kingdom, set up in AD 567 by the Avars, another nomadic people from central Asia, also declined in its time and west and north Hungary attained its independence under Slavic rulers.

The Slavs also predominated in parts of Poland. However, early Slavic history in central Europe was, however, marked by frequent subordination to other peoples. Their masters included the Goths, who brought many Germanic words into the Slavic languages, and then the Huns, who probably used Slavic troops for their campaigns.

Eventually, the Slavs arrived in the Balkans some time before the start of the sixth century where they overran Greece by AD 584 and afterwards appear to have terrorised the Byzantine Empire. By the end of the eighth century AD, Slavs had spread throughout the Balkan peninsula, though they suffered regular incursions from other peoples, such as a further influx of Germans and the Magyars of Hungary.

Attila, king of the Huns, whose attacks in Italy contributed to the fall of Rome. ▶

The Holy Roman Empire

THE FALL OF THE ROMAN EMPIRE meant the disappearance of the one strong, centralised and powerful force which had kept most of Europe together as a unit. The constant movements, invasions, settlements and rivalries that marked Europe for centuries afterwards were, therefore, inevitable. In AD 800, however, an attempt was made to revive if not the Roman Empire itself, then at least the power to unify which it had exercised.

On Christmas Day, AD 800, Charles I, king of the Franks, known as Charlemagne (AD 742–814) was crowned as Holy Roman Emperor and the ruler of almost all the European territory once ruled by the Romans. The Empire was 'holy' because it was Christian and 'Roman' because of its revivalist nature.

At first, the formula was brilliantly successful. Charlemagne was not only able to restore a semblance of law and order to Europe, he also ushered in a revival of learning and provided a seedbed for the development of Christian culture. Above all, Charlemagne maintained peace in Europe. This, however, lasted only for his lifetime, and after his death, history began to repeat itself as his Empire broke up into separate kingdoms and large areas fell prey to new waves of savage invaders, like the Norsemen.

▲ *Charles I, king of the Franks, also known as Charlemagne.*

The Nation States of Europe

THE ULTIMATE FAILURE OF THE Holy Roman Empire was a disappointment, but also a benefit. A monolithic power at the heart of Europe was an obstacle to the natural development of separate states in which independent peoples could express their own cultures, languages and traditions. It accorded far more with human nature and the nature of the various tribes which made Europe for nations to have a country to call their own, even if they had to fight to obtain and retain their territory, rather than simply be an anonymous part of a greater whole.

The states of Europe emerged gradually, some much later than

others. At first the city-state as in Italy or small duchy as in Germany was more common on the map of the continent, but a spirit of national unity was nevertheless aroused and eventually both countries became unified in the same year, 1870. France emerged much earlier, in 1558, when the French retrieved Calais, the last English possession on their soil. By contrast, Hungary and Poland became individual countries only after centuries of struggle against foreign occupation and for a time, absorption into empires, the Austro-Hungarian and the Russian respectively.

Achievements of the Dark Ages

THE 'DARK AGES' IS A NAME GIVEN to the centuries after the fall of the Roman Empire when Europe was in a state of flux, with constantly migrating peoples, local wars, and 'barbarians' spreading terror, destruction and instability. This picture is not entirely inaccurate and this era was certainly 'dark' for historians, with its paucity of information and records. However, this did not mean that these centuries saw no advance or progress, especially in the scientific field.

For instance, in around 1000, German cultivators invented a new type of heavy mouldboard plough, capable of draining wet, low-lying lands and strong enough to work the heavy clay soils which covered much of northern Europe. Here, the light scratch ploughs known in the Mediterranean and the Middle East had proved useless.

Other developments included the construction of windmills and watermills; not new inventions but now greatly improved in design. Further innovations were the horse collar and horseshoes, which allowed horses to be used as work animals instead of oxen. Trading settlements also grew up at this time. In all these senses, the 'Dark Ages' in Europe were not as dark as may be supposed. They were, in fact, very productive times.

◀ *Bridge across the River Danube, Hungary. Hungary only became independent after the Second World War.*

The Invention of Printing

WHILE PRACTICAL SKILLS WERE MORE important for men and women to possess, literacy was not always highly regarded. For centuries, in fact, it was the preserve of church clerks who made records, wrote letters and histories and also produced the beautiful illuminated manuscripts, all of it done painstakingly by hand.

The invention that changed all this was printing. In 1450, Johannes Gutenberg (1398–1468) set up a printing business in Mainz, Germany, which employed his own system for using individual type characters, cast in moulds from an alloy of lead, tin and antimony. These were interchangeable within a frame.

The phonetic nature of writing in Europe, with its relatively few characters, gave it a distinct advantage over other writing systems such as Chinese which comprised thousands of different characters.

With European languages, however, it was quick and easy to assemble whole pages of type which could all be used time and time again for successive jobs. As a result, printing took off rapidly. Within 30 years most of the western European countries had printing works and by the early sixteenth century, most classical manuscripts were made available in print. The year 1609 saw the first newspaper go on sale in Germany.

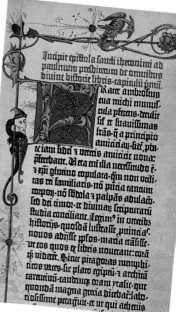

▲ *A page from one of the first books printed by Johannes Gutenberg.*

The Myths of Central Europe

UNLIKE THE SUMERIANS, EGYPTIANS AND Ancient Greeks, the Slavs left no written record of their myths. Only after they adopted Christianity in the late tenth century did the relevant literature appear.

Although the names of the Slavic pagan gods have been preserved, little is known of their cults and stories. However, like other peoples in pre-Christian times, Slavs believed that some mysterious and fantastic power controlled the sun, sky, stars, rivers and seas, but that mighty heroes were able to overcome their depredations.

In one Slavic mythical tale, Ivan's three bird brothers-in-law are really the Rain, Wind and Thunder. The three princesses they wed are the Sky, Moon and Stars. Marya Morlvna which means 'Daughter of the Sea' is the Sun which at dawn and dusk 'bathes' in the ocean. Old Bones is the storm cloud chained by winter frosts. He gains strength when he drinks his fill of melting spring waters, tears himself free and carries off Marya, so clouding over the Sun. Winds bring rain clouds that pour the water of life upon the earth. Prince Ivan is Perun, the pagan god of Thunder, who smashes the storm cloud and saves the Sun, leading her out of darkness.

▲ *Illustration of Bilibine's tale showing Prince Ivan fleeing with his beautiful wife, Queen Marya Morevna.*

Rome

Origins

TRADITIONALLY, ROME WAS FOUNDED IN ABOUT 753 BC by the semi-mythical twins Romulus and Remus. According to archeological finds, however, Roman origins went further back than that. People were living in Italy in Neolithic and Bronze Age times, mostly along the coast, in the hills and near the River Tiber, on which Rome later stood. They appear to have filtered south from the River Danube region and central Europe, had links with with people in Aeolian Islands and Sicily and established settlements along the entire length of the peninsula and in the hills, with a few in the forests.

▲ *A she-wolf suckles the abandoned Romulus and Remus.*

The area round Rome was probably settled during the Bronze Age (5000–1200 BC) when there was a small settlement possibly on the Aventine Hill, one of the seven hills of Rome. Later, in the early Iron Age (900–500 BC) new migrants appear to have taken over the site. Traces of the huts, utensils and pottery they left behind have been found on the Palatine Hill and the remnants of other contemporary peoples on the Esquiline and Quirinal Hills. This was the small and primitive nucleus from which mighty Rome later grew, to become the military superpower of the ancient world.

The First Romans

THE FIRST ROMANS LIVED A hard and demanding life in their original farming villages. They lived in wood and wickerwork huts plastered with clay and thatched with straw. Like the Spartans, they had no place for weak or sickly infants who might grow up to be a liability on the community; those were considered to weak were left on the hillsides to die. Later Romans disapproved of this practice, although historically they admired their hardy, disciplined and courageous forebears.

Even in these very early days, the Romans appeared to be extraordinary people. They were proud and fierce and always ready to fight to protect their land, their property and their freedom. At first, they were ruled by kings, the first of whom was the legendary and semi-divine Romulus, the founder who gave Rome his name. After 616 BC, however, an Etruscan dynasty, the Tarquinians from Tuscany to the north occupied the throne. Rome grew and prospered under their rule, but the immoral behaviour of the seventh and last of them, Tarquinius Superbus, greatly offended the strong Roman sense of justice and honour. Tarquinius was ejected in 509 BC and Rome was declared a republic. Afterwards, the Romans detested the very idea of kingship.

Rome the Republic

WITH THE HELP OF LARS PORSENNA, the Etruscan king, Tarquinius attempted to retrieve his throne, but their siege of Rome failed when Porsenna, fearing an attempt on his life, withdrew and went home. After their experience of rule by royal dictators, the Romans determined that no one man should ever be able to gain complete power in the city. They therefore created a complex system of controls on all officers of state. Power was exercised by two consuls, who were elected every year. There were also elected officials in charge of the treasury, the police and of the city itself. The ruling class in Rome was, however, predominantly patrician, or aristocratic, until a revolt in 494 BC by the plebaeians – the ordinary working people – managed to secure some popular power, in the tribunes elected to speak for them.

The plebaeian victory was hard won. A century of argument and fighting ensued before popular rights were recognised, with enraged patricians struggling hard to prevent it. In 486 BC, in fact, one patrician who supported the plebaeians was executed for his efforts. Ultimately, though, it became clear that Rome could not afford this in-fighting. Threats from outside were endangering its very survival.

◀ *Busts of a Roman official and his wife.* ▶

The Roman Army

THE ROMAN ARMY MAY HAVE LOST BATTLES, but it never lost a war. Highly trained, strictly disciplined and innovative, Roman soldiers fought mainly with the *gladius*, or short sword, iron-tipped javelins and with a variety of siege machines, although they later adopted cavalry tactics from some of their defeated enemies. Soldiers lived in stone or wooden barracks in a camp surrounded by strong walls and defensive ditches, all of which they had themselves constructed. The soldiers also acted as smiths, toolmakers, carpenters, stonemasons, engineers and architects. They were even capable of building ships cannibalised from the wreckage of other vessels.

The organisation of the Roman Army and its tactics inevitably made it superior to enemies who tended to rush wildly into battle in an unformed mass. In the testudo, or tortoise, for example, Roman infantry turned themselves into a virtually impenetrable armoured column by placing their wood, hemp and leather shields over their heads and backs.

Life in the Roman Army was, however, rough and dangerous, especially in those areas bordering barbarian territory. Those who survived the statutory twenty years' service were given about £600 as retirement pay and sometimes a plot of land on which to live.

▲ *Roman soldiers were forced to be brutal and bloodthirsty. They are shown here massacring Druids at Anglesey.*

The Republic and its Enemies

REPUBLICAN ROME, SURROUNDED BY ENEMIES, was an aggressive city-state which was almost constantly at war. One of these wars brought them to the brink of disaster when the Gauls who had occupied the Po Valley in northern Italy began advancing southward and in 390 BC, assaulted Rome. The Gauls sacked Rome, and had to be bought off with a large ransom. Rome, largely destroyed, had to be rebuilt.

Next came the Samnites, a mountain people from central Italy, who in 321 BC starved two Roman armies into surrender and force the soldiers to crawl beneath a 'yoke of spears'. Then, in 280 BC, King Phyrrhus (319–272 BC) of Epirus in Greece invaded Italy and twice thrashed the Roman army. Each defeat, however, had its revenge. The Romans thrashed the Samnites in 295 BC, and vanquished Pyrrhus 20 years later.

The Romans, however, developed a wise policy of making allies of defeated enemies and turning their territory into Roman colonies. Consequently, by 275 BC, Rome's power had spread until it covered almost all of Italy from Rimini in the north to the Straits of Messina in the south. It was here, across the straits, that the Romans came face to face with the people their most deadly enemies: the Carthaginians.

▲ *Roman coins can be found throughout their former empire.*

Rome vs Carthage

CARTHAGE, NEAR PRESENT-DAY TUNIS, had also spread its power by war and conquest. and a trial of strength with the Romans was inevitable. The three Punic Wars, the first of which began in 264 BC, proved to be struggles to the death and the combatant which died was Carthage.

The first Punic War (264–241 BC) was fought at sea, where the Carthaginians were superior, but nevertheless suffered three heavy defeats from a nascent Roman navy. The Carthaginians sued for peace. Then, in 218 BC, the Carthaginians, now led by a brilliant general, Hannibal (247–182 BC) invaded Italy by way of the Alps, and inflicted three heavy and humiliating defeats on the Romans. The Romans, however, wore Hannibal down with guerrilla attacks, while in 204 BC, another force landed in Africa to assault on Carthage, forcing Hannibal to sail home to help defend it in 203 BC.

The defence of Carthage was in vain. The Romans prevailed in 201 BC and the Carthaginians were forced to hand over all their colonies. around the Mediterranean. Not content with that, the Romans went to war with Carthage again, in 149 BC, and this time destroyed it utterly. The site of Carthage was ploughed over, and its surviving inhabitants were sold into slavery.

The Romans instigated the total destruction of Carthage. ▶

Julius Caesar

THE TRAGIC END OF CARTHAGE LEFT ROME the mightiest power in the Mediterranean. Sicily, Corsica, Sardinia, Spain and large parts of North Africa were now under Roman domination and Roman power also extended a far as Macedonia and into Asia. Yet, there was a lot wrong with Rome itself. The city was rich, but also corrupt. Politicians surrounded themselves with bodyguards who beat up their opponents. There was civil war in 88 BC between two generals contesting power, a slave rebellion in 73–71 BC and another uprising among Rome's Italian allies.

The need for a strong man to restore order and discipline was evident and the man in question was at hand: Julius Caesar, a brilliant general who added Gaul to the Roman empire (58–51 BC), and a force greatly feared by the Senate. Dictators had been appointed before in times of danger and unrest, and in 48 BC, Caesar took up the title and its powers. Order was duly restored and conditions in Rome improved.

Caesar, however, was too powerful for some Romans, who feared he intended to make himself king. This was something the Romans would not endure. In 44 BC, Caesar was murdered, stabbed 35 times, in full view of the Senate.

▼ *Classical painting showing Roman Emperor, Julius Caesar.*

The City of Rome

BY THE SIXTH CENTURY BC, Rome was already becoming a very fine city. The most important improvement took place in about 575 BC, when the Cloaca Maxima, or Great Sewer, was built to drain the marshland between the Palatine and Capitoline hills. With this, Rome gained a heart, a centre for it most important activities. Here, the Romans built a paved forum, with shops and colonnades. Later, temples were erected in the area round the forum, as well as many impressive public buildings such as the basilica or law courts or the libraries.

As time went on, Rome grew, and grew more beautiful, acquiring magnificent statues, fountains, arches and monuments and as well as a plethora of shops – furriers, chandlers, stonemasons, locksmiths, blacksmiths, silver-smiths, cobblers, wine shops, bakeries and cookshops.

Once every nine days, there was market day in Rome, including a slave market, where visitors came to buy labourers for their country farms or villas, teachers, usually Greeks, for their children, or scribes to deal with their correspondence. The slaves came from all over the Empire, including Celts from Britain, Iberians from Spain, blonde, brawny Germans, Numidians and Egyptians from North Africa, and Parthians, Bithnyans and Phoenicians from Turkey and Palestine.

▲ *The remains of a Roman villa still hint at its former magnificence, with its mosaic floors, door arches and pillars.*

The Roman Empire

ROME HAD AN EMPIRE BEFORE it had an emperor, but one was soon forthcoming in the coldly ambitious person of Caesar's great-nephew, Gaius Octavius (63 BC–AD 14) In 31 BC, Octavius disposed of Caesar's friend and champion, Marcus Antonius (AD 82–14), and four years later, in 27 BC became known as Imperator Caesar Augustus.

Eventually Augustus, a commendable ruler, unlike many of his successors, became master of a huge empire which later stretched from Britannia in the north to the deserts of Arabia in the south. Yet at various times, this vast swathe of territory was in the hands of degenerates such as Tiberius (42 BC–AD 37), or madmen like Caligula (AD 12–41) or Nero (AD 37–68). Between ad 98 and 180, 'Five Good Emperors', men of

▲ *Bust of the Roman Emperor Julius Caesar.*

integrity and enterprise, occupied the throne, but several who followed were murdered and in AD 193, the throne was won by an emperor who gambled for it.

Meanwhile, corruption, rivalry and struggles for power weakened the Roman army on whom the security of the Empire depended. When the army became unable to hold back the tide of barbarian invaders, they swarmed in to sack Rome in AD 410 and AD 455 and occupy the Empire's territories. In this way, by AD 476, the once mighty power of Rome was extinguished.

Pax Romana

THE NAME AUGUSTUS MEANT 'worthy of trust and respect' and in many ways he lived up to it. He established what came to be known as Pax Romana, the Roman peace, which made the empire a vastly safer place in which to live, and a vastly more efficient one. Augustus created a civil service more honourable and honest than the greedy administrators who had once taxed the provinces so harshly. Although he largely controlled the Senate, the army and the colonial service, he at least gave opportunities to men of worth to become senators, consuls, magistrates and administrators. He made Rome cleaner, better run and more beautiful, with a new forum, new temples, new theatres, new colonnades and new statues. Augustus' saying that he 'found Rome built of brick and left it built of marble' was quite literally true.

Pax Romana also meant that opportunities opened up which had not been available before. Architects, engineers, artists, writers, silver- and gold-smiths were able to produce fine work. Some of the greatest Roman poets and prose-writers lived in this 'Augustan Age' including Publius Virgilius Maro known as Virgil (70–19 BC), Quintus Horatius Flaccus or Horace (65–68 BC) and Titus Livius or Livy (59 BC–AD 17).

The Roman Roads

PAX ROMANA ALSO SAW SOME of the greatest feats of Roman engineering, including aqueducts, bridges and the magnificent empire-wide network of Roman roads. Built by the army, the roads were constructed solidly, systematically and with the intention that they should last. The first great road, the Via Appia, or Appian Way, had been started in 321 BC, but more roads were constructed in the time of the emperors than ever before. By the second century AD, in fact, the Roman Empire was covered by over 80,450 km (49,960 miles) of first class roads and 321,800 km (199,838 miles) of secondary roads.

The soldiers chose the best routes, then dug down until they struck the rock or gravel which would form the roadbed. After filling in with

rubble, stones and flints, a layer of smaller stones and pebbles was laid on top and covered with a layer of sand and crushed stone. Next, pentagonal stone paving blocks were laid, each cut so precisely that they interlocked. Finally, the blocks were packed with finely-ground gravel for a smooth surface.

These roads were cambered and furnished with drainage ditches. The Romans spanned river valleys with bridges, viaducts and aqueducts which featured the use of their own invention, the arch.

▲ *The Old Appian Way, one of the finest surviving examples of a Roman road.*

Soldiers and Merchants

APART FROM THE BENEFIT TO CIVILIAN travellers, the Roman roads enabled the army to move quickly from place to place, an ability vital for a force with an empire to patrol.

Columns of troops could move rapidly and easily over these roads, and so could the couriers of the Imperial postal service. There were posting stations placed about 17 km (11 miles) apart, where fresh horses were kept and mansiones or resting places were built every 40 km (25 miles).

Roman roads were also very important for trade and in the age of Pax Romana, merchants were able to travel along them freer than they had ever been from the fear of being waylaid and robbed or murdered. The merchants of Imperial Rome traded in a huge range of goods, including corn from Egypt, cosmetics from Judea, spices from Asia, glassware and pottery from the Rhine, oil from Spain, Gaul and North Africa and enamelled crockery from Belgium. Most of these were luxury goods, of course, but then one result of Pax Romana was a widespread demand for luxuries of all sorts to go with the leisurely, pampered and pleasure-loving life of the rich who enjoyed a standard of comfort which was not known again until the nineteenth century.

The Romans were expert potters, making vessels from red clay which they fired in kilns such as this. ▶

Homes and Hypocausts

LIFE COULD BE SWEET FOR THE RICH in ancient Rome. As excavations at Pompeii, 22 km (14 miles) south-east of Naples, have revealed, careful craftsmanship was lavished on the wealthier villas and houses, which featured delicately made mosaic floors, beautiful wall paintings and frieze decorations, bronze statuettes, fountains and gardens skilfully laid out in courtyards surrounded by colonnades of pillars.

Several villas in Pompeii had their own private baths, where the water was warmed by hypocausts. The hypocausts also provided central heating, in which heat radiating from fires in the basement permeated the walls of the rooms above. These rooms were scattered with silken cushions, statues of gods and goddesses, carved lamps and candelabra and beautifully figured tables.

▲ *Roman text carved in stone, detailing the sacred law.*

The insulae, or 'islands', the apartment blocks in which the plebaeians lived were a complete contrast. Built of concrete, a Roman invention, they were nevertheless unsafe, unhealthy, always over-crowded and always susceptible to fire or collapse. Only those who lived on the ground floor had running water or heating. Everyone else had to fetch water from taps in the street or buy it from water carriers. There was only one toilet, on the ground floor, so most people living had to use the *forica*, or public toilets.

Roman Baths

ROMAN BATHS, A RARE EXERCISE in the ancient world into mass hygiene, were not only the great washing places of Rome, but next to the forum, they were the regular meeting places for the men. Here, they met to discuss business, sign contracts, exchange news and generally enjoy the company of their friends.

Meanwhile, bathing attendants rubbed their bodies with a mixture of oil and sand to loosen the dirt and scraped the dirt off with a curved metal spoon called a *strigil*. Either that or the Romans talked and joked together while sweating it out in the hot room or lying on couches whilst being massaged and anointed with sweet-smelling oils.

The public baths were 'exported' to places all over the Roman Empire, including far-north Britannia. At Aquae Sulis, or Bath in Somerset, the bathing pool was 24 m (79 ft) long, 12 m (40 ft) wide and nearly 2 m (6.5 ft) deep. Hot water entered through a lead conduit. Its temperature was about 49°C (120°F), and the three springs which fed the baths could produce nearly 25 litres (5.5 gallons) of water a day. There was a *calidarium* or warm room, under-floor heating and a circular bath for women and children which was 10 m wide.

The Byzantine Empire

AFTER THE FALL OF ROME IN ABOUT AD 476, Roman power
persisted in the eastern Byzantine Empire created in AD 293 when
Emperor Diocletian (AD 245–313) divided his territories to make them
easier to govern.

Constantinople, the Byzantine capital, was built between AD 324 and
330 by the first Christian emperor, Constantine I (AD 265–337) and was a
veritable storehouse of fine art and architecture, with buildings featuring
carved marble, scented woods, colourful mosaics and gold finishings.

By the thirteenth century, the Byzantine Empire was the greatest
commercial power in the world. Throughout Europe and Asia, there was
enormous demand for Byzantine textiles, leatherwork, armour, silver-
and gold-work, ivories, mosaics, porcelains and embroidered silks.

As in Rome, however, Byzantine security depended on its army with
its heavy cavalry and mail-shirted soldiers who carried broadsword,
dagger, short bow, axe and lance. This army,
forged among others by the brilliant
general Belisarius (AD 505–565) was
so successful that in AD 543, the
Persians vowed not to wage
another full-scale war against
Byzantium as long as
Belisarius lived. However,
enemies could not be resisted
for ever and in 1453,
Constantinople and the
Byzantine Empire succumbed
to the Ottoman Turks, so
bringing an end to over 2,200
years of Roman power.

◀ *The first Christian emperor of Rome, Constantine I.*

Paterfamilias

AS MIGHT BE EXPECTED OF A MILITARY POWER, the social structure of Ancient Rome was hierarchical, with the paterfamilias or father exerting complete power over his family. The paterfamilias was able to demand total obedience from his children. If he wished, he could sell them into slavery and flog or even kill them for some misdemeanour if he so decided.

The principle of the paterfamilias developed early on in Roman history, a time when weaklings who could not fulfil the demands of a tough society were left in the mountains to die. This meant that the first duty of a paterfamilias was to decide which children should live and be reared and which should not.

The paterfamilias had the duty to see that his children were named according to tradition, and consecrated to the Roman state and its gods. He also had the responsibility of educating his family and bringing them up as good citizens, worthy of Roman traditions and virtues.

The power of a paterfamilias extended beyond his own children to his younger siblings, so that even when adults, with children of their own, they lived their entire lives under his domination. This was not power without responsibility, though.

▲ *Classical art depicting a young bride and groom (centre), surrounded by other members of the Roman family.*

Entertainments

ROMAN EMPERORS WERE ALWAYS CONSCIOUS that they had to keep the people happy to retain their loyalty, and this they did by providing exciting distractions. As the satirical poet Juvenal (AD 60–140) put it, 'Duas tantum res anxius optat – panem et circenses' ('he limits the anxieties of the Romans to two things – bread and circuses').

At the circus – the Circus Maximus in Rome – charioteers, who were often slaves, raced around the circuit at break-neck speeds. Accidents and death were common. The best-known 'sport' was gladiatorial combat, in which two men fought each other to the death, death often being decided by popular vote among the audience.

The gladiators took their name from *gladius*, the short Roman sword and originally fought at funeral ceremonies. Whoever was killed

accompanied the deceased into the world of the dead. In the arena, some gladiators wore helmets and carried shields an swords. Others were *retiarii* or net men who entangled their opponents in nets. There was also the *andabatae* who fought blindfold on horseback, *dimachaeri*, who were armed with two swords and men who fought from chariots. The *hoplomachi* wore full suits of armour. Others, the *laquerarii*, carried only lassos as weapons.

◀ *Gladiators fought each other to the death for the entertainment of the emperor and his subjects.*

The Roman Gods

THE ROMANS BORROWED A GREAT DEAL from the Greeks, including their pantheon of gods, whose names they altered. They also added gods of their own.

As in the Greek, the Roman pantheon was headed by a 'father' and 'mother' – Jupiter, the Greek Zeus, and Juno, the Greek Hera. Jupiter was also god of rain, thunder and lightning, and with Mars, god of war and Quirinus, who was Romulus, founder and first king deified, was a special protector of Rome. Mars' remit also covered agriculture and the protection of cattle. Romulus, together with his twin Remus, were believed to be sons of Mars, who also bore the name Quirinus.

Juno was worshipped by the Romans as the Queen of Heaven and was goddess of marriage, childbirth and of newborn infants. At the shrine in the forum in Rome dedicated to Vesta, the Roman goddess of the hearth, the Greek Hestia, a sacred flame was tended by six Vestal Virgins each of whom served her for 30 years. Ceres, the Greek Demeter was the Roman earth goddess and producer of corn, and Venus, the Greek Aphrodite, was the goddess of love and fertility. Julius Caesar used to boast that he was descended from Venus.

The voluptuous goddess of desire, Venus. ▶

Roman Mythology

THE EXTENT OF THE ROMAN EMPIRE, which contained some 50 million people, explains much about its mythology. The Roman state was too large for a single set of mythological traditions to suffice. As Rome expanded its territories, it incorporated the mythology of conquered peoples into its own. By this means, Roman mythology became a strange hotch-potch of Greek, Egyptian, Celtic and other myths.

For example, at the end of the second century BC, the Egyptian goddess Isis was introduced into Italy. A mother goddess, associated with fertility, Isis was sometimes linked to the Roman Fortuna, spirit of fertility, agriculture and love, and was known as Isis-Fortuna. Another Egyptian deity, the ram-horned god Amon, became Ammon in Greek mythology and in Rome became incorporated into the imperial cult. He was a protector of the Roman armies and his image appeared on breastplates and medallions. The cult of the Phrygian goddess Cybele, Great Mother of the Gods, named Magna Mater by the Romans, came to Rome in 204 BC from Pessinus in Galatia as the result of a prophecy. A temple was erected on the Palatine Hill, containing the sacred symbol of the goddess, a meteorite believed to have fallen from heaven.

▼ *A Parthenon Frieze of Artemis, Apollo and Poseidon.*
The names, characters and powers of the Roman gods are echoed in other mythologies.

The Legacy of Rome

ROME IS OFTEN THOUGHT OF as an ancient civilisation which fell and became dust, with its language, Latin, a dead tongue. This is by no means the case. Roman ideas still permeate Europe today, and Latin is still alive and well. For example, the Romance languages French, Spanish, Italian and Portuguese are direct descendants of Latin. Though English does not belong to this category, it uses many words derived

from Latin and some phrases, unchanged from Roman times, such as et cetera, 'and the rest', are part of its vocabulary. The alphabet used in western Europe is the Latin alphabet. Most months of the year were originally named by the Romans. Sciences such as botany, ornithology or astronomy use Latin phraseology.

Roman law is still has its place in the British and other legal systems. The routes the Romans chose for their roads are still used, and in some cases, the roads themselves remain usable. In Britain, the names of towns such as Manchester or Cirencester reveal that a castrum, a Roman fort once stood there.

Ancient Rome, therefore, is far from being a piece of dead and buried history. It led straight into the world we know today.

One of the most impressive and longest lasting legacies of the Roman empire is the aqueduct, such as this one, at Pont du Gard, France. ▲

Russia

Early Origins

GEOGRAPHICALLY, RUSSIA IS TWO COUNTRIES. The great forests covering the north, full of lakes and rivers, and freed late from the prehistoric Ice Age, was difficult territory in which to survive. Homo Sapiens was here some time after 98,000 BC, but widespread settlement did not follow. In the scattered, isolated prehistoric settlements, people lived by fishing the rivers, hunting fur-bearing animals in the forests and keeping bees. The forests of Russia were also the home of the Slavs who came from the marshland between the rivers Vistula and Dneiper, where the Antae formed the first federation of eastern Slavonic tribes in the third and fourth centuries AD. Two and three centuries earlier, the Slavs had migrated

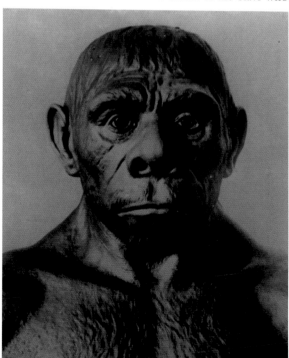

to the area round the River Danube.

In southern Russia, however, the level, grassy plains of the steppe provided many more opportunities. Archeologists have found evidence of settlement in both Palaeolithic and Neolithic times, together with the early, primitive culture which later moved west to the Aegean Sea between Greece and Turkey. The presence of the Greek culture was not coincidental. There were ancient Greek colonies on the northern shores of the Black Sea. Other settlers had Persian origins, but there were many more to come.

The Making of the Russians

THE RUSSIAN STEPPES ATTRACTED NOMADIC TRIBES, including the Avars, who overcame the Antae in the sixth century AD. The pattern in which newcomers displaced established populations continued from there, with the Khazars dominating the steppe from the sixth century, only to be overcome in the tenth century by Turkic Hungarians and Pecheneg tribes.

New invaders, however, arrived from the north in the early ninth century: the Rus whom ancient writers believed were related to the Swedes; the Angles of Germany; and the Norse of Scandinavia. The Norse came first as pirates, warriors and leaders of trading caravans which called each year at Constantinople. The Norse required all their brilliant skills at seafaring and navigation, bringing their caravans south by way of the dangerous Dnieper cataracts.

When the Rus settled, they settled near water at Lake Ilmen, near Novgorod, Lake Ladoga, the mainspring of the River Neva and later at the confluence of the Neva, Volga, Dnieper and Western Dvina rivers. It was in this area that the Norse founded settlements, of which Kiev, later known as the 'mother of Russian cities', became the centre of the first Russian state in about AD 862.

◀ *A scientific reconstruction of a prehistoric Neanderthal Man.*

A Time of War

THE RICH TRADE AND PROSPERITY enjoyed by Kiev made it the target for almost ceaseless attacks from outside. The activities of the nomadic tribes of the steppe – Khazars, Pechenegs and Polovtsy – put Kiev on an almost constant war footing. However, when the Russian princes took to quarrelling among themselves, the power and prestige of Kiev, already damaged, declined even further. In this weakened state, the city was an easy target for Tatar armies of the Golden Horde, a feudal state in the western sector of the Mongol Empire, who attacked in 1240 and totally destroyed the city.

With this disaster, the Grand Princes of Kiev, members of a dynasty founded in 1019 by Yaroslav, Prince of Novgorod, were neutralised. The unified state Kiev had created collapsed into a mass of small principalities which proceeded to wage ongoing war against each other.

The clouds of chaos did not begin to clear until the fourteenth century when Halicz, Novgorod and Moscow emerged as three centres where some semblance of government could be established, with a princely class, an aristocracy or *boyars*, and a *veche*, or popular assembly. Of these centres, Moscow was going to be by far the most important.

Ivan the Terrible

THE GRAND PRINCES OF MOSCOW were vassals of the Tatars, but ingratiated themselves so well with their masters that they were appointed their tax collectors. This gave the princes the power and the means to expand their own territory which they did by a mixture of land purchase and war. Tatar power declined, towards the end of the fourteenth century, and in 1547, when Ivan IV (1530–84) later nicknamed 'the Terrible' came to the throne, he took the title of Tsar or 'Caesar', with power over a huge integrated state which before long stretched into Siberia.

Ivan aimed to be an absolute ruler and early on, became convinced that he had a divine right to rule. First though, Ivan had to neutralise his rivals. His first target was the boyar aristocracy which had once advised the Grand Princes on important matters of state. Ivan lost little time in breaking *boyar* power and sent them into a decline which ended when Tsar Peter III (1672–1725) the Great abolished them as a class. The Russian Orthodox Church, too, was stripped of its political influence and the way was open for despotic tsarist rule which persisted to its violent and bloody end in 1918.

◄ *The Kremlin by night, Red Square, Moscow.*

Under Tsarist Rule

THE ARBITRARY NATURE OF THE MONARCHY manifested itself in predictable ways during the 370 years the tsars ruled Russia. Individual tsars, like Ivan IV or Catherine II the Great (1729–96) were enthusiastic patrons of the arts. Some, like Alexander II (1818–81) who freed the Russian serfs in 1861, had the welfare of their subjects at heart. Nevertheless, the basic barbarity of Russia seemed to require the iron fist without the velvet glove, and many tsarist policies were implemented by brute force while protest was met with repression.

The Romanovs, who succeeded to the throne in 1613, introduced serfdom into Russia in 1649 and tied city-dwellers to their homes. Peter the Great imposed a crippling burden of taxes on the peasantry while

compelling them to do military service and provide labour for construction work. The liberalising influence of the French Revolution (1789) was seen as both wicked and dangerous by Russian tsars such as Nicholas I (1796–1855) who believed himself infallible and savagely persecuted intellectuals and anyone else suspected of free thought.

Free thought and its handmaiden, revolution, came to Russia nevertheless with the Bolshevik takeover in 1917 when Tsarist Russia went down in an outburst of violence, blood and slaughter that shocked the world.

▲ *Tsar Nicolas II (1868–1918), Russian monarch.*

Trade in Russia

AS THE NORSE VIKINGS FROM SCANDINAVIA discovered, the direction of the ancient trade routes into Russia was determined by its four chief waterways: the Neva basin and the Volga, Dnieper and Western Dvina rivers. Their convergence formed an outlet to the Baltic, the Caspian and Black Sea. Here, archeologists have discovered clear evidence of a rich and longstanding trade, in the Arabian, Byzantine and Anglo-Saxon coins dating from the ninth and tenth centuries which have been found at several sites.

However, after Ivan IV became the first tsar in 1547, he looked not south, but west, to Europe and in particular to Britain after Sir Hugh Willoughby (d. 1554) set out to find a passage along the north Russian coast to China. Tragically, Willoughby's ships became trapped in the Arctic ice and he and his crews froze to death. However, his chief pilot, Richard Chancellor (d. 1556) managed to reach safe harbour at Archangel. From there, he travelled the 2,414 km (1,499 miles) to the court in Moscow where Ivan received him with great interest. The result was the first trading treaty between Britain and Russia, and the formation in Britain of the Muscovy Company which did a lucrative trade for many years.

▼ *The undisturbed wrecks of Viking ships that sank carrying gold coins and other treasures provide some of the best clues to ancient civilisations.*

Peter the Great Modernises Russia

PETER THE GREAT, WHO BECAME TSAR of Russia in 1682, was determined that Russia, until then a largely backward country, should be brought into the modern world and be reorganised along western European lines. This was why, in 1703, he moved his capital from Moscow to St Petersburg, which he called his 'window on the west'. He established a school of navigation (1701), a naval academy (1715) and a school of engineering (1719), invited foreigners to bring their technological skills to Russia and sent Russians abroad.

Accompanied by an 'embassy' of 250, including bodyguards, Peter himself travelled around Europe, learning industrial and other techniques, and acquiring the knowledge he needed on shipbuilding, guns, machines such as lathes and also coinage. In England, in 1698 he was employed in the shipyard at Deptford, London wielding saw, hammer and adze alongside ordinary workers. He also acquired experience as a carpenter in Dutch shipyards.

An early result of these new links was a vast increase in trade. Russia imported wine, sugar, woollen and silk goods and dyestuffs through St. Petersburg and Archangel and exported hemp, flax, sailcloth, linen, leather, tallow and pig iron. This export trade was valued at some 2.5 million roubles by 1726.

▲ *Peter the Great, Tsar of Russia, studying ship building at Deptford, London.*

More Modernisation

THE REFORMS OF PETER THE GREAT were very much of the root-and-branch variety. His basic aim was to transform Russia into a great European power and he did not stop at forming a modern army of some 200,000 men and building a fleet which made his country a sea power.

In some 30 years of radical change, Peter concentrated on the fine detail as well as the broader issues. He introduced a new, better organised military and civil service and opened their ranks to commoners. He set up some 200 textile and metallurgical factories, most of them located in a new industrial estate built near St Petersburg on the River Svir as well as around Moscow, at Tula on the River Don and near Ekaterinburg in the Ural Mountains.

However, Peter also banned the wearing of the long Russian robe and the bushy beard which characterised the *boyars*. Anyone found wearing a long coat was made to kneel while it was cut to the short length worn in western Europe. The big beards had to go, too, in favour of the European-style shaven chin. Peter also reformed the Russian calender, simplified the cyrillic alphabet and founded the first Russian newspaper.

▲ *Peter the Great forbade the wearing of the traditional long Russian robe shown here, and beards were no longer acceptable.*

Christianity in Russia

ACCORDING TO BYZANTINE RECORDS, Christianity was introduced
into Russia from Constantinople between AD 860 and 867. It was not,
however, accepted as a state religion until after Vladimir, Prince of Kiev
(AD 956–1015), was baptised in about AD 989. After that, the Russian
Orthodox Church grew to be a strong influence in the state centred
round Moscow and in 1448, its bishops severed connections with
Constantinople.

The seventeenth century, however, saw a serious ideological upheaval
when a sect known as Raskolniki, or the Old Believers, resisted minor
liturgical changes in Orthodox traditions which reflected the reforming
influence of the Catholic and Greek Orthodox churches. Instituted by

the Patriarch of Moscow, Nikon (1605–81), the changes had the support of the tsar, Alexis (1629–76) The leader of the Old Believers Avvakum Petrovich (1621–82) was exiled to Siberia in 1653 and thousands of his followers were hanged. In 1682, after further persecutions which involved some 15 years' incarceration in an underground prison in northern Russia, Avvakum was burned at the stake. Some 2,500 Raskolniki burned themselves to death rather than abandon their beliefs. The sect nevertheless survived as an active, if persecuted, dissident group in Russia until an edict of toleration was issued in 1905.

Rasputin

THE STARETS, A SPIRITUAL LEADER in the Orthodox Church, was regarded by many Russians as a blend of holy man, seer and saint. However, the deeply superstitious nature of Russian society ensured that his powers were thought to go beyond mere guidance. In this context, a peasant starets, like Grigori Efimovich Novykh (1871–1916), known as Rasputin, was an object of particular fascination among the aristocracy and noble families would retain them in their households to serve as 'oracles' and good-luck insurance.

Rasputin attached himself to the most illustrious household of all, the Romanov royal family. The key that opened the way for him was the haemophilia which afflicted Alexei (1904–18), heir to Tsar Nicholas II (1868–1918). Haemophilia in which blood fails to clot normally, was incurable. Nevertheless, Alexei's desperate mother, the Tsarina Alexandra (1872–1918), believed Rasputin could cure her son and by this means, the starets acquired enormous political power within the royal court and was able to appoint officials to positions of influence. The scandal led to his murder in St Petersburg on 31 December 1916. The circumstances were bizarre. His assassins poisoned, shot and threw Rasputin into the River Neva before they could be sure he was dead.

◀ *Christianity was not adopted as a state religion until AD 989.*

Serfdom in Russia

FEUDAL SERFDOM LASTED LONGER IN RUSSIA than almost anywhere else in Europe, though officially it began rather later, in 1649. Serfdom was not exactly slavery, since individual serfs could not be sold. However, they were tied to their lords' estates and could not leave them without his permission. If those lands were sold, the serfs were sold with them. They were, of course, at the mercy of their lords' will and justice, which could often be extremely harsh.

In Russia, as elsewhere, the serfs were obliged to labour on their lords' lands for two or three days a week, and put in extra days at harvest time and other, similarly busy, periods in the year. They were also liable to military service. Serfs were allowed to cultivate a portion of the estate to support their own families, but had to pay their lords a share of the food they produced.

The serfs were freed by the modernising tsar Alexander II on 3 March 1861 and afterwards became independent small farmers. However, after the communist ruler Josef Stalin (1879-1953) ordered the collectivisation of Russian agriculture after 1929, the peasant farmers, or *kulaks* were savagely persecuted, and many were deported to labour camps.

Cartoon depicting the Soviet leader Joseph Stalin. ▶

Prince Peter Kropotkin

PETER ALEXEIVICH, PRINCE PETER KROPOTKIN (1842–1921), was, despite his noble birth, an anarchist and revolutionary as well as a man of remarkably diverse talents. He was a leading geologist, geographer, biologist and anthropologist with a highly individual view of evolution. In his book *Mutual Aid* (1902), Kropotkin rejected Social Darwinian support for capitalism as a means to ensure the survival of the fittest. The book demonstrated that in very many cases, evolution resulted in mutually beneficial co-operation between animals and between peoples in primitive societies.

However, Prince Kropotkin also rejected Leninist Communism which he considered was the work of 'aliens, enemies of Russia and gangsters'. In particular, he objected to the imposition of state controls after the Bolsheviks assumed power in Russia in 1917. Kropotkin felt his research proved that co-operation could arise naturally without being imposed by the state. Another of Kropotkin's books, *Fields, Factories and Workshops* (1899), was a study of how small villages and decentralised communities could produce all their own food and material needs without relying upon landowners, big business, factory owners or governments. After several periods of imprisonment and exile, Kropotkin returned to Russia in 1917, but shortly afterwards retired from politics.

▲ *Prince Peter Kropotkin rejected the theories on evolution proposed by Darwin.*

South America

The First South Americans

FROM THE TIME IMMIGRANTS FROM ASIA began to enter America from Asia some 30,000 years ago, it took about 15,000 years for them to spread through South America and almost another 15,000 for their first major civilisation to appear.

South America, like North America, offered vast areas where the hunting and gathering was fruitful, such as the pampas of present-day Argentina or the rich regions of Brazil, for instance, where the mighty River Amazon extended across the continent and thick, impenetrable jungle grew. Here, Nature's gifts were bountiful and even today, some Amazonian tribes still lead the hunter-gatherer life of their far distant ancestors.

The long 'spine' of South America, the Andes Mountains, offered far less bounty. Those who settled there were confronted with living in a punishing environment, with mountains soaring over 4,000 m (13,123 ft) high into the thin air around the peaks, bringing freezing conditions, as well as the regular danger presented by active volcanoes. In time, the Andes-dwellers adapted physically to their surroundings, with large chests to contain lungs of adequate capacity and the splayed feet needed for gripping the sloping terrain.

▲ *The rainforests of South America provided everything man needed to survive: animals and vegetation for food, shelter and water.*

Towards the First Andean Civilisation

BY 4000 BC, AROUND THE TIME farming reached Europe, people in the Ayacucho region of Peru had domesticated llamas and alpacas and were cultivating maize, potatoes and cotton over a wide area. Fifteen hundred years later, also in Peru, the Waywaka people were fashioning objects from gold, and elsewhere in South America, farming had proved so successful that the population was growing and large permanent villages were being established. Trade routes came into being,

▲ *Ceramic plate depicting a dancing jaguar, crocodile or supernatural creature.*

and in around 1800 BC, the Chavin people near Lake Titicaca in the high Andes were exchanging goods with coastal dwellers.

Around this time, too, the Chavin were moving towards civilisation with the construction of a temple complex at Chavin de Huantar in northern Peru which was dedicated to a feline deity. Both animal and human sacrifice was practised there. The Chavin, whose influence reached as far as the Nazca valley in the south by 1000 BC, were skilled at stone work and gold work, pottery and the making of textiles.

However, after some 1,500 years, the Chavin culture was falling into decline by about 290 BC, and a new culture was replacing it some 70 years later around the Nazca river on the narrow coastal plain beside the Pacific Ocean.

The Nazca and Other Cultures

THE NAZCA WERE JAGUAR-WORSHIPPERS, with a well-organised society centred on their capital, Cahuachi which was dominated by a large, stepped pyramid some 20 m (66 ft) high. Irrigation was the key to successful Nazca maize cultivation. Nazca textiles were brilliantly multicoloured and often embroidered with jaguars.

The region around Lake Titicaca, the world's highest navigable lake some 3,650 m (1,975 ft) up in the Andes, and the desert country around it proved to be the crucible of all the early civilisations in South America and in about 10 BC, another people, the Mochica, were proving their skills in pottery which involved modelling in both high- and low-relief. Some of their ceramics celebrated coca-leaf rituals. Chewing coca, the powerful narcotic from which cocaine is derived, is still used in the Andes as a stimulant and a protection against the fierce mountain cold.

In the Moche valley, the Mochica constructed roads and irrigation channels, and temples to the sun and moon. The sun temple rose 45 m (148 ft) high and was made from some 50 million bricks. The interior featured multi-coloured frescoes.

In time, the Mochica culture spread southward, by conquest, from the Chicama and Moche valleys along the coast until its empire extended from the Andes to the Pacific.

Tihuanaco, Chimu and Inca

MEANWHILE, TWO OTHER CULTURES had developed in the area around Lake Titicaca, whose southern shore saw the rise of the city of Tihuanaco in about AD 400. Tihuanaco was the capital of a large empire now covered by parts of Bolivia, Chile and Peru. Decorated pottery and large, warlike statues have been found there, as well as a 'Gate of the Sun' cut from a single large stone.

Tihuanaco had faded away, in about 1000, while the Empire of Chimu, 1,300 km (808 miles) north-west of Lake Titicaca, was rising to power. The capital of Chimu, Chan Chan, was a splendid centre, with some 250,000 inhabitants, 10 large walled palaces and tombs containing gold and silver objects. However, within 500 years, by 1466, Chimu fell to another, mightier power – the Incas – whose subsequent Empire was to stretch some 6,500 km (4,036 miles) from present-day Ecuador in the north, through Peru and Bolivia to Chile in the south.

It took eight years of warfare before the Chimu succumbed. Inca expansion began from their capital at Cuzco in about 1438 when Pachacuti Inca Yupanqui (r. 1438–71) assumed power and set out to subdue the surrounding peoples, a policy continued by his son Tupac Inca Yupanqui (r. 1471–93).

◄ *The maize cobs on this effigy jar are gods associated with fertility and food.*

Conquered by the Incas

THE INCAS ORIGINATED IN ABOUT 1100, when Cuzco was founded by the legendary first 'emperor', Manco Capac. The Incas were made for conquest and empire, with their austere militaristic society and their unquestioning loyalty to their Sapa Inca (Supreme Lord) who was regarded as the Son of the Sun and therefore divine. Strong centralised government and extraordinary technological skills completed the equipment needed to suppress neighbouring peoples and as early as 1350 the Incas, led by the Sapa Inca Roca, constructed a bridge across the Apurimac river as a prelude to later conquests.

These conquests took savage form. In 1463, Sapa Inca Pachacuti waged a war of extermination against the Lupaca and Colla tribes around Lake Titicaca, and having accomplished that, went on to dismantle the power of Chimu. After him, in 1480, Tupac Inca began a programme of road-building which in the Andes meant long, steep staircases and travelling in the thin air which only the strongest and fittest could survive.

The purpose of these vertiginous mountain roads was to open the way for the conquest of Chile, which went ahead in 1492 when Tupac Inca overran the whole country all the way to the Maule River.

▲ *South Americans were a superstitious people, worshipping gods that protected them against everyday hazards. This is a statue to the goddess of childbirth.*

The Spaniards Arrive

BY ABOUT 1500, THE INCA EMPIRE, known as Tahuantinsuyu, Land of the Four Quarters, had become the greatest of all native South American empires, and covered the Andes from the Ecuador-Colombia border in the north through Peru and Bolivia and on to Chile in the south – a distance of some 5,230 km (3,248 miles).

Tahuantinsuyu, however, was destined to be very short-lived. After 1525, when Tupac Inca's son, Huayna Capac (r. 1492–1525), died, the empire was divided between his two sons Huascar and Atahualpa. The natural weakness caused by a divided legacy was exacerbated by the presence of the Spaniards whose intrusions into Central and South America and greed for gold had become known to Huayna Capac in 1521.

Huayna was also aware of the destruction the Spaniards had already wrought in Panama, Nicaragua, Honduras and the islands of the Caribbean. For the superstitious Incas, all this tied in alarmingly with bad omens – violent earthquakes, tidal waves which swept away Inca villages along the west coast and a moon surrounded by three rings, one of them the colour of blood. The three rings, the *aumatas* (seers) informed a horrified Huayna Capac, were portents of plague, war and the end of the Empire of Tahuantinsuyu.

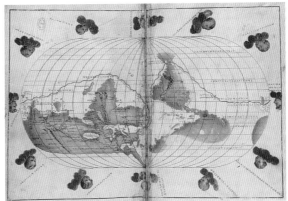

▲ *Map showing the route taken by Spaniard Ferdinand Magellan on his first voyage of circumnavigation.*

The Spanish Conquest

THE PREDICTION OF THE AUMATAS proved all too accurate. The Spaniards had brought with them several infections, which spread among the Incas, drastically reducing their numbers. Huayna Capac, who died of smallpox, was among the victims.

Next, civil war between Huascar and Atahualpa for possession of Tahuantinsuyu ended when Atahualpa had his half-brother murdered in 1532. Two months later, on 15 November, the conquistador Francisco Pizarro (1475–1541), with 177 soldiers and cavalry, arrived at Cajamarca after seven gruelling weeks traversing the Andes.

Conscious of the danger confronting his small force, who were isolated amid thousands of Incas led by a ruler whose word was divine

law, Pizarro imprisoned Atahualpa as insurance. However, even after Atahualpa had 'purchased' his freedom by giving Pizarro a roomful of gold 33.5 sq m (360 sq ft), with treasure piled 2.7 m (9 ft) high, and another full of silver, the alacrity with which his subjects had gathered this fabulous ransom underlined the danger he still presented.

The Spaniards therefore tried Atahualpa for the murder of Huascar and, on 29 August 1533, executed him. Afterwards, against little resistance, the Spaniards conquered all of Tahuantinsuyu by 1535, so bringing to an end the last and greatest of the native South American empires.

▲ *Francisco Pizarro, who conquered the Inca Empire.*

Technology in Ancient South America

IN PRE-HISPANIC SOUTH American terms, most technology was strictly related to everyday life. The tools which were developed – such as blow-pipes with poison darts as used by the hunter-gatherers tribes of the Amazon – were designed to make food-gathering, and therefore survival, easier rather than to promote the advance of science.

This applied even to the Inca astronomers, who were more advanced than their contemporaries in Europe. There were observatories in many Inca cities where, scholars and archaeologists believe, astronomers studied the movements of the sun, moon and planets such as Jupiter, Mars or Mercury, using an Intihuatana, or 'hitching post of the Sun', which had angles pointing to the four directions of the compass. The Inca astronomers could predict solstices and equinoxes, too, but all of this was for religious purposes – in order to calculate the proper timing of festivals, sacrifices and other important events in the year.

The Incas were master craftsmen; this two pronged silver diadem would originally have been part of an elaborate head-dress worn by chiefs and shaman. ▶

Farming

IN THE AYLLU, OR COMMUNITIES OF ordinary Incas, the great majority were farmers and used *taclla* or foot-ploughs to turn the earth. The *taclla* was a shaft of wood, 1.83 m (6 ft) long, hardened at the point by fire or tipped with bronze. *Lampa*, (hoes) were used to break up the clods of earth. Farming, however, was a challenge in the high Andes. Fields had to be terraced, each terrace representing a small field to be cultivated separately.

The cultivable areas of Tahuantinsuyu were divided in three. The food and plants grown on one part went to the gods and their priests. The produce of the second was for the government and from this, the nobles, government officials, craftsmen and the army were supplied with food. Everything grown on the third part of the land supplied the ordinary people.

The boundaries between the different types of land were carefully and clearly marked. Anyone who dared move the markers was very severely punished. So was anyone who failed to work the different fields in the proper order – the gods' first, then the government's, then the people's. Families received topos of land according to their numbers, one topo measuring about 4,000 sq m (43,057 sq ft).

Walls, Bridges and Boats

THE MOST REMARKABLE FEATURE OF INCA cities, and one which can still be seen in places like Cuzco or the fortress of Sacsuhaman today, was the ability of stonemasons to cut huge blocks of stone, limestone or volcanic rock so that they fitted together exactly, without the use of mortar. Rocks prepared centuries ago for splitting, with precise and careful measurements, can still be seen in Maccu Picchu, one of a ring of fortresses built to protect Cuzco. The Spaniards searched long and hard, but never found it and it was not until 1911 that an American, Hiram

The lost city of Machu Picchu, never found by the invading Spanish. ▶

Bingham (1875–1956), finally discovered its hiding place.

Inca builders also became very skilled at constructing heavily-knotted rope bridges across ravines and gorges, bridges which were so strong that, as the Spaniards discovered, it was possible to ride a horse across them at full gallop but in perfect safety.

In this, Inca technology was responding to the peculiar circumstances of Andean life, just as their roads had to be stepped, or the boats constructed around Lake Titicaca had to be made of reeds, in the absence of other usable material, or irrigation channels lined with stone, had to be used to nourish the land.

The Incas at War

LIKE THE AZTECS OF MEXICO, war as waged by the Incas was primitive in European terms. Their weapons, however, were none the less effective for that.

One Inca weapon consisted of three stones tied to the ends of cords. When thrown at an enemy's legs, the cords effectively tied them together, making him fall to the ground. Another simple, but still very deadly weapon, was a stone- or metal-headed club with six sharp spikes. Battle-axes were fashioned from stone, bronze and copper. Double-edged broadswords were made from Chinta wood and spears, 183 cm (6 ft) long were fashioned from long shafts of wood with fire- or metal-tipped points. There were also the usual bows and arrows.

Inca soldiers were protected when fighting in battle by a sort of armour made from thick, quilted-cotton tunics and helmets made of wood or strips of cane. They carried two shields. One, made of strips of palm and cotton was worn slung across their backs. The other was made of round or square wooden boards covered in metal or deer-hide. A further protection was to wrap long shawls round parts of the body or round an arm or leg to shield soldiers from enemy arrows or spears.

▼ *The Inca's weapons and style of combat were adapted to the perilous high mountain terrain they occupied. Familiarity with their inhospitable surroundings would have given them an advantage over their foes.*

Inca Society

THE EMPIRE OF TAHUANTINSUYU was a society under strict state control, but also one which was conscious of popular welfare. The cardinal principle of Inca rule was that everything and everyone under the sun belonged to the sun and, in therefore to the sun's representative on earth, the divine Sapa Inca. Whatever the Sapa Inca commanded was done and, if the common people were able to cultivate the land, pan rivers for gold or do anything else, it was only because he permitted it.

This was a strictly stratified society, in which everyone, from nobles to peasants, knew their place and where the tasks most vital to its continuance such as religious ritual or leadership in war, were reserved to the nobility. The government's duties were equally clear. They had to make sure everyone received a fair share of llamas, alpacas or *vicunas*, the pack-animals of the Andes. In times of bad harvest, earthquake or storms, the government distributed food and grain from its storehouses. They also supported the blind or crippled and could not do their full share of work on the land. Conversely, when the harvest was particularly good, extra food was shared out equally among the people.

Creation Myths of the Andes

AS IN MESOAMERICA, THE CREATION MYTHS of the Andean
cultures centred round the relationship between light and darkness and
the endeavours of the gods to perfect their handiwork.

The Incas believed that the god Viracocha created a world of
darkness, inhabited by giants made of stone. However, Viracocha sent a
great flood to destroy them when they ignored his wishes. The only
survivors were a man and a woman who were transported by magic to
Viracocha's abode, Tiwanaku.

Next, Viracocha made people
out of clay and painted on them
the clothes whose design and
colours distinguished one nation
from other. Each group was given
its own customs, language and
way of life. Viracocha breathed life
into them and sent them to
Earth, commanding them to
emerge from caves, lakes and
mountains where they were to
honour their maker by building
shrines for worshipping him.
Viracocha then created light from
darkness – or order out of chaos –
so that the people could see and
live in an orderly world. Then, he
caused the Sun, Moon and the
stars to rise up to the heavens from
the Islands of the Sun on Lake Titicaca, which
the Incas saw as their place of origin.

▲ *Viracocha, a creator deity, god of rain who is believed to have created the sun and the moon.*

The Amazon Creation Myth

THE DESANA OF THE COLOMBIAN AMAZON believe that creation occurred when an invisible Creator Sun exploded yellow light into the void. Pagë Abé, the Sun Father then set about creating the natural world, its animals, plants and forests, each with its own identity, habits and places. The Sun laid down the principles of existence, spreading brilliance and understanding throughout the universe, then delegated further creativity to a host of supernatural beings. These were the masters of individual realms such as the sky, river or the animal kingdom.

Dramatic acts of transformative creation were carried out by females, such as the Daughter of Aracú Fish. The task of these culture heroes was to invent many of the details of existence and cultural life, including the shapes and colours of animals, the techniques of hunting and food production and the symbolic domains of ritual and art.

The Sun now took two forms, by day residing in the sky, providing heat, light and fertility. On Earth he was the protective supernatural Jaguar, a feline being of the sort which frequently appeared as a motif in pre-Hispanic South American art. Another supernatural, Pamurí-mahsë, was transported the first human beings to Earth in a large canoe.

◄ Gold bead in the form of a snarling jaguar, signifies chiefs association with spirits.

The Beliefs of Amazonia

THE PEOPLES of the tropical lowland of the Amazon never reached the heights of civilisation attained in the Andes. yet their life of hunting, gathering, horticulture and farming included distinctive art in pottery-making, and sophisticated religious beliefs, rituals and spirituality. They, too, shared the view of a world animated by spirits and controlled by ancestors.

The most abiding belief among the peoples of the Amazon and lowland South America was trust in the transformative powers of shamans. The shaman was the keeper of the tribal mythic traditions and knew how to interpret myths meaningfully. For the shaman, myths were powerful tools which he used to speak to the ancestors and by which he could account for every aspect of life and death. The shaman was also a protection against capricious and powerful spirits. He confronted them in trance having taken on the shape of a spirit-bird or jaguar.

The main themes of Lowland mythology were those concerned with regulating human society and its relationship with the natural world. Their creation myths relate the ways in which light and order came into being, how animals and sometimes women were the original masters of the earth and how men usurped their position.

Magic and Medicine

MEDICINE IN THE INCA WORLD was intimately tied up with religious rituals, superstition and magic although Inca doctors were aware of the importance of disinfectants, were skilled at trepanning and at setting broken bones.

In the case of illness, the first thing to do was to make sacrifices to the gods with the help of a priest. If this did not provide a cure, then the *hampi-camayoc*, or remedy-keeper, was called in. The *hampi-camayoc* was both a sorcerer and a homeopathic doctor and he decided how the illness came about by making sacrifices and consulting the spirits.

Sickness was sometimes regarded as a punishment for wrong-doing, such as failure to observe religious duties. In this case, the *hampi-camayoc* placed a mixture of ground seashells and black and white maize in the patient's hand. The patient then recited certain magic words and blew the mixture towards the place where the offended gods lived. To complete the cure, the patient offered coca to the sun god, Inti, and scattered small pieces of gold and silver on the ground as an offering to Viracocha, the creator god. The cure was completed by medicine made from drug-plants such as quinine or cocaine.

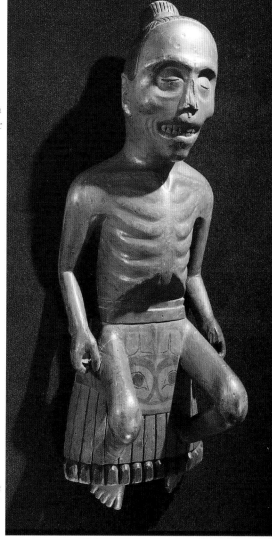

Carved figure of a medicine man. ▶

Spain

Origins

IN ABOUT 680,000 BC, HUMANS OF THE SPECIES Homo Erectus, or Hominids began to infiltrate Europe. They appear to have entered the continent by way of the Straits of Gibraltar and from there, into Spain. Some continued on north and settled in southern France, where their crudely made stone tools have been found at Vallonet Cave.

Others remained in Spain and in around 300,000 BC could be found hunting elephants around Torralba and Ambrona, about 97 km (60 miles) north-east of Madrid. Here, in prehistoric times, there were deep and extensive mudflats. The hunters drove the elephants into the mud, where they were inextricably trapped, and slaughtered them.

Immigrations into Spain continued with the main input, in around 3000 BC, in the south-east and consisting of Hamitic Berbers from the area round Oran, in present-day Algeria. This ancestry appeared to be borne out by Roman descriptions of the Iberians, as ancient writers called them. They had dark complexions, small frames, small features, prominent cheekbones and prominent lower lips. By the time the Romans took over the Carthaginian colonies in Spain after their victory in the Second Punic War in 201 BC, Iberian civilisation was well advanced, with walled towns, distinctive pottery and sculpture which clearly reflected a warrior society.

The Cave Paintings of Altamira

IN 1868, A HUNTER DISCOVERED THE OPENING to a cave some two km from Santillana-del-Mar, to the west of Santander in northern Spain. Seven years later, the cave was investigated, and animal bones and flint

Painting from the caves of Altamira. ▶

implements were found there. Then, in 1879, what looked like paintings of 'bulls' were seen on the roof of the cave and with that, one of the most remarkable finds from far-distant prehistory was made.

In 1901, when the paintings in the 270 m (886 ft) long Altamira Cave were professionally examined, it was realised that in around 10000 BC, cave-dwellers had painted reproductions of the animals which were their prey probably in order to increase their chances of success in the hunt. The paintings, remarkably lifelike and skilfully executed, had been made by lamp-light deep inside the cave, and depicted mammoth, horses, wild oxen, reindeer and bison, among other beasts. The materials used were yellow, red and black pigments made from minerals, some of which had had to be fetched from 48 km (30 miles) distant. Scaffold-ing had ob-viously been used to paint animals in some of the more inaccessible parts of the cave. Similar paintings, dating from around the same time, were discovered at Lascaux in southern France.

A Multi-Ethnic Society

THE EARLY IMMIGRANTS INTO SPAIN were only the start of a constant flow which ultimately made Spain into a multi-ethnic, multi-cultural society.

The Phoenicians saw the geographical convenience of Spain as a trading base and founded Gades, or Cadiz in 1100 BC as a replacement for the Iberian fortress of Tartessus which they destroyed. Then, in the sixth and fifth centuries BC, several waves of Celts arrived from France by way of the Pyrenees. Greeks from Phocea followed not long afterwards, establishing the port of Marseilles in southern France in about 600 BC and more settlements near Malaga in Andalusia, southern Spain and also in the far north, at Ampurias at the foot of the Pyrenees near the

present-day frontier with France.

The Romans followed and after their Empire fell in about AD 476, the Germanic Visigoths and Vandals took over, and after AD 494, some 200,000 of them arrived to establish kingdoms which persisted until the last of them fell to the forces of Moorish Muslims from Tangier on the Morrocan coast in AD 711.

With this began the longest occupation of Spain in historical times, a period of nearly eight centuries in which Moorish influence permeated Iberian society and made it unique in Europe.

▲ *The effect of different cultures meeting clearly shows in, amongst other things, works of art. Here we see a mixture of Greek, Roman, Spanish and Egyptian styles.*

The Beginnings of Moorish Spain

THE PHOENICIANS HAD BROUGHT TRADE to Spain, the Greeks trade, art, architecture and coinage, and the Romans organised rule, roads, forts, laws, municipalities and the Christian Church.

The Muslim Moors, however, brought a much wider and deeper spectrum of influence. Their conquest was in itself fairly straightforward. Visigoth power had been in decline for many years before the invaders landed and they met with little serious opposition. By about AD 714, the Moors had overrun most of Iberia, including present-day Portugal, as well as Spain. They continued to raid into France for many years, but were finally thwarted in AD 732, with their base at the old Roman settlement of Narbonne, eight km from the Gulf of Lyon, holding out against the French until AD 751.

In Moorish Spain, known as al-Andalus, the defeated Visigoths, even those who did not convert to Islam, suffered little serious interference and the Jews, who had been persecuted under the vanquished regime, gained an unaccustomed measure of freedom. Both formed substantial and wealthy communities within the new Moorish cities. The Jews, in fact, came to regard their sojourn in Moorish Spain as a 'golden age' of art, science and architecture in which they and the Moors lived in remarkable accord.

◄ *Moorish art infiltrated into Spain and introduced people to an entirely different culture, faith and way of life.*

Trouble in Al-Andalus

THE CHIEF PROBLEMS FOR MOORISH RULE in Spain came less from
the indigenous population than from quarrelsome and anarchic new
immigrants who came from north Africa and Syria. Internecine warfare
ensued on a damaging scale, with revolts and civil wars punctuating
several years until the enlightened Abd-ar-Rahman (AD 912–961)
managed to vanquish all rivals, reunite al-Andalus and declare himself
Caliph in AD 929.

This, however, was the classic situation,
duplicated many times in Europe, where peace
and order depended on a strong, just and
determined ruler. Abd-ar-Rahman's grandson,
Hisham II (r. 976–1013) proved too weak to
prevent the rise of a military dictatorship which
exacerbated all the old antagonisms. The
political crisis which resulted in 1009 almost
wrecked Moorish power in Spain as the royal
guard of Berbers and Slavonians, or slaves,
became kingmakers, proclaiming and breaking
rulers at will. As a result, al-Andalus broke up
into a mass of petty, perennially quarrelling
principalities.

Meanwhile, Christian Spain, though
subordinate to Muslim power, still existed in
the mountains of Asturias where the Visigoth
nobles had fled while Iberia fell to the invaders.
Here, the Christian reconquest of Spain was an
enduring idea although four centuries were to
pass before it began to take shape.

◀ *The Christian faith was practised almost in secret, and only
in remote areas of Spain as the Muslim faith introduced by the
Moors took over.*

Christian Spain

THE FIRST APPRECIABLE MOVE TO OUST Muslim power in Spain came after 1230, with the Christian King Ferdinand III (1201–52) unified the provinces of Castile and Lean. Subsequently, Ferdinand, a religious zealot, drove the Muslims from most of southern Spain, leaving them only Granada in present-day Andalusia, where a Moorish kingdom was set up in 1238. Granada survived until 1492 and an important reason for this survival was rivalry among the Christians.

Already, in the tenth and eleventh centuries, the kingdoms of Lean, the Basque realm of Navarre, and later, Castile and Aragon had arisen to complicate the separatist tendencies of Christian Spain. Civil war, usurpations and violent clashes between kings and their nobles amounted to more than two centuries of upheaval until, in 1469, the marriage of Isabella of Castile (1451–1504) and Ferdinand II of Aragon (1452–1516) united their two realms on their accession in 1479 and the final conquest of Granada became possible. Granada fell on 2 January 1492.

Ten months later, on 12 October, Christopher Columbus (1451–1506) sailing in the name of Spain , landed in America, so opening up in the same year the prospect of a unified state at home and a vast empire abroad.

▲ *Christopher Columbus sets sail from San Domingo.*

Trade in Early Spain

SPAIN BECAME A CENTRE FOR TRADE very early on in its history. After about 3000 BC, it is possible that copper and silver were being exported to the nearby Mediterranean islands – Sardinia, Minorca, Mallorca and perhaps as far as Malta. In addition, archaeologists have discovered similar types of pottery in Spain and these islands, suggesting their use as barter goods.

The Phoenicians used Spain and in particular their port at Cadiz, as a site for trading stations, but there was little evidence of settlement and apart from some trinkets and jewellery which were probably used for barter, they left behind few proofs of their presence.

Greek traders took Spain more seriously, establishing firm settlements and importing art objects which greatly influenced the styles of native art. The Greeks were also adventurous. The Roman history Herodotus (484–424 BC) recorded the voyage made in about 630 BC by a Greek sailing ship from Samos which was driven by a storm through the Pillars of Hercules – the Straits of Gibraltar – and 'at last reached Tartessus. This trading town was in those days a virgin port unfrequented by merchants and the Samians in consequence made a greater profit than any Greeks before their day.'

Spain as the Heart of an Empire

THE VAST SPANISH EMPIRE IN AMERICA which grew out of Columbus' voyages of discovery in 1492–1504, both made Spain and broke it. The phenomenal wealth in gold, silver, pearls and other precious stones that poured across the Atlantic brought unimaginable riches to a country only just emerging from centuries of warfare and dispute, but also laid on it enormous expenses for defence against rivals, the equipping of the fleets which brought the treasure home, the support of the missionaries who went out to convert the 'heathen' natives and the

Queen Christine of Spain is seen here with the philosopher, Descartes. ▶

cost of the large bureaucracy needed to run the new colonies. There was also the vast expense of conducting wars against Spain's rebellious colonies in the Netherlands and also against Britain.

The Empire did, however, give Spain an eminence it might not otherwise have acquired. Spain gained enormous prestige in Europe and became the prime champion of the Catholic Church.

In more practical matters, the Spanish silver dollar became the basic currency in Europe even in those parts of America ruled by Britain, France or the Netherlands. In fact, the first coins introduced into the British West Indies were fractions of the dollar, as were the famous 'Pieces of Eight'.

Spain as a Military and Naval Power

WITH ITS LONG EXPERIENCE OF WAR, Spain was a great military power in the sixteenth century. This eminence was based on both weaponry and tactics. Swords made in Toledo, which introduced an elaborate hand guard, were widely accounted the finest in the world. The *arquebus*, the first hand-held gun to be used in war, was developed in Spain and in 1503 showed its effectiveness in Italy, when the French were plastered with fire from a modest-looking line of arquebusiers.

The Spaniards became experts at using 'shot and ike' tactics which provided continuous fire from up to 25 ranks of arquebusiers drawn up on battlefield and firing in turn before withdrawing to the back to reload.

The Spaniards were, in fact, at the forefront of military technology, although they had to learn a hard lesson when the Armada sent to invade England in 1588 suffered a humiliating defeat. The cumbersome Spanish galleons, which carried troops for fighting on the enemy's decks, were no match for the smaller, nimbler English ships in which the space normally reserved for troops was occupied by guns. The Spaniards, however, were not slow to learn the lesson and within a short time themselves adopted the new galleons.

▼ *The defeat of the Spanish Armada by the English.*

Treasure Fleets and Trade

THE SPANISH TREASURE FLEETS were first organised in 1535 to provide safety for the wealth extracted from the American colonies on the long Atlantic voyage to Spain. An important element in this was the quinto, the fifth part of a cargo reserved for the monarch. As early as 1505, the quinto amounted to some £28,000, but had risen by 1518 to more than double that sum.

The chief import from America before 1530 was gold, but silver soon represented up to 99 per cent of the precious metals sent to Spain. Ultimately, the annual value of these imports averaged about £4 million.

The ground rules for the American trade were laid down by Queen

Isabella not long after Columbus made his first voyage in 1492. All goods were to come into Spain through a single port, at first Cadiz, but after 1503, Seville. Trade was controlled by the Contratacion or House of Trade which laid down all ordinances about the loading of ships and registration of cargoes and policed smuggling and unlicensed emigration to the colonies. The Contratacion also served as a school of navigation and in time became one of the prime mathematical and scientific research centres in Europe.

◀ *Queen Isabella I of Spain.*

Muslim Influence

THE MUSLIM OCCUPATION OF SPAIN lasted some 780 years, although during the last 254, Muslim rule was confined to the Kingdom of Granada in the south. Nevertheless, Moorish presence over such a long period had a profound effect on Spain and the Spaniards.

For instance, Muslim fatalism introduced a 'sad' trait into Spanish music and literature. The typically Andalusian temperament expresses itself in emotional and aesthetic music and verse of distinctly Muslim character.

Spanish architecture, especially in the south, followed Muslim custom which favoured the inward-looking house with whitewashed, windowless walls on the outside and a deep well in the centre affording

▲ *The whitewashed, flat roofed, small windowed houses seen in modern Spain reflect the influence the first Muslim settlers had on architectural styles.*

light in the interior, but reducing the heat of the fierce Spanish sun. Typical, too, is the central patio with fountains surrounded by citron trees flowering shrubs and fragrant myrtle. The elaborate irrigation systems built by the Muslims are still in use today, and retain their Arabic names, such as *aljibe*, a well, *acequia*, water channel, or *noria*, water wheel.

In practical matters, the Muslim Moors had an ongoing influence on the crops grown in Andalusia. For instance, they introduced sugar-cane, apricots and almonds. Andalusian cooking also shows Muslim influence in its copious use of olive oil.

The Alhambra

THE ALHAMBRA, THE PALACE AND FORTRESS of the Muslim Kings of Granada, is only one example of the delicate beauty and eloquent form which Muslim architects left behind in Spain. Built between 1238 and 1358, the palace was wrecked and defaced by the Christians after the Muslims were expelled in 1492, but was later partially restored.

Set in a park, the Alameda de la Alhambra, the palace was surrounded with roses, oranges and myrtle in typical Muslim style. Its serious purpose, however, was also obvious. The Alcazaba or citadel of the Alhambra was built on a virtually unscaleable promontory which overlooked the countryside below. The outside walls were massive, and the Alhambra was well equipped with ramparts and towers. Within these defences, the Muslims built a court of justice, approached through the horseshoe-shaped Gate of Judgment and surmounted by a large square tower.

Inside the palace of the Alhambra, there were several patios, including the impressive Patio de los Leones – Court of the Lions – which was surrounded by a gallery supported on 124 white marble columns. Blue and yellow tiles covered the walls to height of 1.5 m (4.9 ft), with an enamelled blue and gold border above.

Bullfighting

BULLFIGHTING, THE NATIONAL PUBLIC SPECTACLE OF SPAIN, is not a sport and for the Spaniards has a certain spiritual, even religious, slant. Corrida de Toros, the Spanish name for bullfighting, has its origin in 228 BC, when the Carthaginian general Hamilcar Barca (270–228 BC)

attacked the town of Ilici. The defenders attached horned animals to war chariots and tied lighted resin torches to their horns, then let them loose among the Carthaginians. The tactic annihilated the Carthaginians and Hamilcar Barca was killed.

Later, games were held in Bética, in Andalusia, in which men eluded the wild charges of horned beasts with a mixture of suppleness and courage and finally killed them with an axe or lance. The Romans, it seemed, were impressed and imported bullfighting for their own arenas.

When the Muslim Moors conquered Spain, they modified bullfighting from the displays of brute strength they had become under Visigoth rule to something more balletic, rhythmic and mystically oriental. Moorish and Christian knights rivalled each other in the bullring, which was either a restored Roman amphitheatre, the city square or an open field outside a town. After the Muslims were driven out of Spain in 1492, bull-lancing remained a favourite diversion for the aristocracy.

El Cid

RODRIGO D'AZ DE VIVAR (1043–99) was a medieval Spanish captain, better known as El Cid, from the Arabic *sid*, or lord. Vivar became a legendary national hero in Spain for his valiant deeds in the struggle against the Muslim Moors, where he acquired a reputation for invincibility.

Vivar, however, was more of a mercenary who at one time or another sold his services to both Christians and Muslims. Born at Vivar near Burgos, into the minor Castilian aristocracy, he was brought up at the court of King Ferdinand I (1016–65) He first demonstrated his military prowess during campaigns which enabled Ferdinand's son Sancho II (1038–72) to seize the throne from his younger brother Alfonso VI (1042–1109)

In 1079, however, Vivar was serving in the Muslim army which defeated an invasion from Granada. He came under some suspicion for his loyalties and was forced into exile. Vivar fought for several more years for the Muslim kingdom of Saragossa, but later appeared to switch sides once more and undertook the conquest of Muslim Valencia between 1089 and 1094. In 1094 and 1097, Vivar fought off Muslim attempts to retrieve Valencia and, by the time he died in 1099, he had attained his legendary status.

◄ *The Muslim knights preferred the more 'civilised,' sociable sports such as group hunts than the violence of the Spanish bull fights.*

The Morality of the Spanish Empire

IN ABOUT 1550, PERHAPS SURPRISINGLY for a people with a reputation abroad for cruelty and arrogance, the Spaniards worried greatly about their moral right to own and rule colonies and therefore to subject, and perhaps destroy, foreign cultures.

On the one hand, humanitarians fiercely condemned the brutalities practised on the native Americans by Spanish soldiers and colonists, who thought nothing of working them to death or killing them at will.

Opposed to this was the view that the Americans were barbarians, barely human, given to practising hideous rites and the adherents of a impious heathen religion. In this state, it was only right, they argued, that such uncivilised savages should be conquered and controlled by the pious

and most just King of Spain. 'Go out into the highways and hedges and compel them to come in', was a Biblical text which was much quoted by adherents to this view.

They were, however, strongly challenged in their turn by the Jesuits who went to America to convert the natives to Christianity. They also found themselves physically protecting them from the colonists, a policy which eventually led to their expulsion from America after protests to the king from those they hindered.

The Spanish Inquisition

THE INQUISITION WAS NOT PECULIAR TO SPAIN, but the Spanish form was the most famous, and most dreaded, due chiefly to the activities of Tomas de Torquemada (1420–98) the Spanish Dominican monk who revived the system in 1483. Originally, the Inquisition, which was also set up in France, Italy, the Holy Roman Empire and later in Spanish America, was established in 1233 to punish heresy within the Catholic Church. The Roman Inquisition was established in 1542 in response to the Protestant Reformation.

Originally, those found guilty were sentenced to excommunication, a fate which was pronounced after a religious ceremony, the *auto da fé* (act of faith) as it was termed in Portuguese. In Spain, however, the *auto da fé* was a preliminary to punishment by the secular authorities, and that usually involved burning. The ceremony included a procession, solemn mass and a sermon before sentence was pronounced. Apart from burning, penalties could include fines, flogging or imprisonment. Trials by the Inquisition were held in secret, and the accused was customarily tortured to confess.

The Spanish Inquisition was not abolished until 1834, by which time it had tried some 60,000 cases of heresy. Of these, Torquemada alone condemned some 2,000 to be burned.

◀ *The Church and Christianity has had much to do with the turbulent history of the Spanish.*

Glossary

ANGLO-SAXON
Germanic Angle and Saxon tribes settled England from the fifth century, taking advantage of Roman withdrawal to set up kingdoms.

ANTHROPOLOGY
Academic pursuit following Darwin's theories, to study human evolution, differences in lifestyles, cultures and societies across the world.

APARTHEID
Afrikaans word to describe the segregation of races in South Africa, based on a belief in white superiority.

ARABS
Title first used in the ninth century BC for Semitic people from Arabia, whose descendants settled throughout North Africa and the Middle East.

ARISTOCRACY
Ruling class or elite of western Europe, whose political power was based on landed wealth and patronage.

BABYLONIA
Ancient civilisation on the Euphrates River, now Iraq; site of the Hanging Gardens of Babylon.

BOERS
Seventeenth-century Dutch, Flemish and Huguenot settlers in South Africa; Boer descendants, who call themselves Afrikaners, introduced racial apartheid to the country.

BRONZE AGE
Period after 2000 BC when people began using metal-making technology based on copper and its alloys.

BUDDHISM
Religion based on the life of the sixth-century Buddha, whose teachings were that the destruction of mortal desires and anguish could be attained by following virtuous paths.

CELTS
Ancient European people, whose art and languages were marginalised to Wales, Scotland, Ireland and Brittany by the Romans and successive invaders.

CHRISTIANITY
World religion derived from the life of Jesus Christ, the son of God, who came to earth, suffered persecution for his teachings, was crucified and rose again.

BYZANTINE EMPIRE
Greek Mediterranean empire with a distinctive architecture and orthodox religious art; Byzantium lies at its centre.

CATHOLICISM
Division of Christianity marked by worship of the Virgin Mary, repentance and forgiveness, and the power accorded the Pope.

CLANS
Social grouping based on kinship, theoretically descended from a single ancestor who is sometimes represented as a spirit being.

COMMUNISM
Classless economic system of public ownership, where producing goods and food is a communal activity for the general good.

CONFUCIANISM

Chinese beliefs and practices based on the teachings of Confucius, relating to nature gods, imperial ancestors and the balancing of yin and yang.

COSMIC MYTHS

Common creation myths where primeval earth is separated from the sky, and stars and planets created by gods or humans.

CREATION MYTHS

Most cultures have a myth to explain the origin of the world; these frequently tell how the world and order was created out of chaos.

DARK AGES

Period in Europe from the fifth to eleventh centuries, noted for its lack of enlightenment in thought or government, law and order.

DIVINE TRICKSTER

African and North American mythological creation god who can also be profane, playing tricks to suggest that order is an illusion.

DRUIDISM

Pre-Christian pagan religion of the Celts, where priests were learned, artistic and important members of the social order.

FEUDALISM

Social and legal system whereby peasant farmers worked a lord's land and in return would receive protection from them.

FRENCH REVOLUTION

Eighteenth-century popular uprising that saw a decadent monarchy overthrown and its aristocracy stripped of land and power.

HITTITE EMPIRE

Ancient civilisation from the third to the first millenium BC, with advanced literacy and legal systems; particularly great between 1400–1200 BC, overthrowing the Babylonian Empire.

HUGUENOTS

Calvinist Protestant group who fought the French Wars of Religion against Catholics (1562 –98); there followed a period of co-exisitence before they were forced to flee from persecution in 1685.

HUMANISM

Belief from sixteenth century Renaissance Europe in the individual potential of human beings rather than religious values, expressed through art and philosophy.

GAUL

Area of Europe during Roman times covering what is now France and stretching to northern Italy and the Netherlands.

HINDUISM

Dominant religion of India, comprising a complex system of customs and beliefs, including numerous gods, reincarnation and a caste system.

ICE AGE

Period of widescale glaciation; up to 20 have occurred in the earth's history, the last immediately preceding historic times.

INDUSTRIAL REVOLUTION

Process by which Britain and other countries were transformed into industrial powers during the eighteenth and nineteenth centuries.

INQUISITION

Practice that operated across Spain, France, Italy and the Holy Roman Empire between the thirteenth and nineteenth centuries to suppress heresy for the Catholic Church.

IRON AGE

After 1000 BC barbarian tribes used iron rather than bronze; contemporaries of classical Mediterranean and African civilisations.

ISLAM

Founded in the seventh century by the Prophet Muhammad, messenger of Allah, Islam emphasises God's omnipotence and inscrutability.

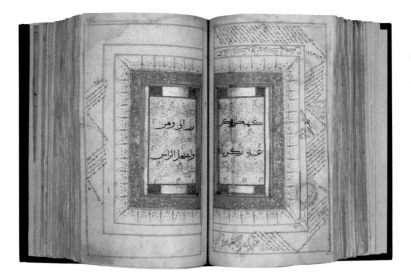

JAINISM
Ancient ascetic Indian religion emphasising non-violence and compassion for all forms of life, but not a belief in deities.

JESUITS
Roman Catholic order founded in the sixteenth century, aiming to protect the church against the Reformation through missionary work.

JUDAISM
Religion and cultural tradition of the Jewish people; Judaism follows one God and is based on the Pentateuch.

MEDIEVAL
Cultures and beliefs of the Middle Ages, after the Roman Empire's fifth-century decline to the fifteenth-century Renaissance.

MESOPOTAMIA
Site of powerful ancient civilisations of Sumer and Babylon, now Iraq, with a wealth of art particularly sculpture; dates around 3500 BC.

MOGUL EMPIRE
North Indian dynasty (1526–1858) of great artistic, architectural and commercial achievement; eventually overthrown by the British.

MONGOL EMPIRE
Nomadic tribes which conquered central Asia and attacked eastern Europe in the thirteenth century, building an empire under Genghis Khan.

NATURE GODS
Animist cultures believed that Spirits, sometimes ancestors, inhabited trees, rocks or rivers; this explained their changing appearance.

NEOLITHIC PERIOD
Final part of the Stone Age, marked by the development of agriculture and forest clearance, around 8000–3000 BC.

NORMANS
Viking 'Northmen' who settled France, then expanded and took control of what is now Normandy, then conquered England under the leadership of King William.

OTTOMON EMPIRE

Turkish Muslim empire (1300–1920), stretching to Hungary, South Russia and North Africa; crumbled after supporting Germany during the Second World War.

PAGANISM

From the fourteenth century worshippers following religions other than Christianity were regarded as pagans, a state associated with superstition and sorcery.

PALEOLITHIC

From two million years ago up to Mesolithic Stone Age period, Paleolithic times saw modern man develop from earlier types.

PATRIARCHY

Situation in which male heads of family or politicians act for and determine the lives of others, particularly women.

PHILANTHROPY

Act of giving to others from kindness or charity; may perpetuate poverty if means of production are not given to recipients.

PHOENICIANS

Mediterranean civilisation of explorers and traders which flourished from 1200 BC until conquered by Alexander the Great in 332 BC.

PRIMEVAL

Relating to the earliest period of the world; in mythical terms perhaps the period after creation and before foundation.

RELIGIOUS CULT

Many ancient cultures worshipped numerous gods but those following one of these, or an ancestor god, were called cults.

ROMAN EMPIRE

The Roman republic (510 BC– AD 476) occupied most of Europe, the Middle East and North Africa, introducing its architecture, engineering and art.

SEMITES

Peoples of ancient cultures in the Middle East, speakers of Semitic languages and founders of Islam, Judaism and Christianity.

SHAMANISM

Oldest known form of organised religion; belief in the power of Shamans who transact between the human and spiritual worlds.

SIKHISM

Religion founded in the eighteenth century by Nanak originally as a Hindu sect, teaching the belief in one god.

STONE AGE

The earliest period of human culture marked by the use of stone implements and covering Paleolithic, Mesolithic and Neolithic times.

TAOISM

Chinese philosophical system from sixth century BC, involving a belief in yin and yang, which balance the universe and the 'way', which stresses harmonious existence with the environment.

VIKINGS

Medieval Scandinavian warriors, traders and settlers; Vikings travelled vast distances by sea and river often plundering from gold and land.

Acknowledgements and Picture Credits

The following authors contributed to this book:

Loren Auerbach, Professor Anne M. Birrell, Rev Dr Martin Boord, David Boyle, Paul Brewer, Alan Brown, Miranda Bruce-Mitford, Malcolm Chandler, Gerard Cheshire, Peter Clayton, Ingrid Cranfield, Ray Driscoll, Dr Ray Dunning, Deborah Gill. Dr James Grayson, Dr Niel Gunson, David Harding, Stephen Hodge, Dr Gwendolyn Leick, Brenda Ralph Lewis, Dr James Mackay, Dr Helen Morales, Martin Noble, Mark Nuttall, Richard Prime, Professor James Riordan, Dr Nicholas Saunders, Anthony Shaw, Dr Harold Scheub, Karen Sullivan Jon Sutherland, Robert Vint, Bruce Wannell, Professor James F. Weiner and Rana K. Williamson.

AKG London: 37, 198, 209.

Christie's Images: 20, 24, 34, 35, 46, 67, 74, 91, 107, 127, 132, 133, 141, 158, 164, 166, 169, 176, 214, 228, 242, 268, 290, 292, 295, 302.

e.t.archive: 167, 175.

Foundry Arts: Nick Wells 11. David Banfield 16, 89, 93, 96, 100, 101, 102, 105, 106. Claire Dashwood 32, 72.

Image Select: 49, 64, 86, 92, 123, 125, 138, 161, 168, 173, 185, 213, 233, 238, 247, 248, 262, 277. **Image Select/FPG:** 10, 12, 28, 61, 63, 146, 155, 162, 174, 218, 245, 250, 259, 260. **Image Select/Giraudon:** 47, 56, 78, 99, 120, 140, 148, 154, 165, 182, 199, 203, 210, 211, 216, 229, 232, 246, 255, 267, 291, 300. **Image Select/Ann Ronan:** 14, 57, 70, 80, 134. **Image Select/CFCL:** 43, 137, 139, 159, 180, 236, 298.

Mary Evans Picture Library: 13, 15, 18, 19, 27, 30, 31, 41, 52, 55, 58, 59, 60, 62, 69, 77, 81, 88, 124, 126,

135, 136, 142, 144, 145, 151, 163, 170, 171, 172, 181, 184, 186, 202, 208, 219, 230, 234, 235, 243, 254, 256, 264, 265, 266, 270, 271, 278, 293, 296, 297.

Peter Clayton: 94, 95, 103, 108, 109, 110, 111.

Still Pictures: 17, 42, 82, 143, 221, 272.

Topham Picturepoint: 38, 48, 53, 54, 65, 76, 112, 147, 149, 157, 177, 192, 196, 197, 204, 205, 207, 217, 244, 251, 289.

Travel Photo International: 183, 215.

Visual Arts Library: 50, 51, 66, 79. **Visual Arts Library/Artephot:** A. Held 21, Varga 23, J. Lavaud 36, J. Lavaud 73, Ru Sui Chu 90, Varga 113, Nimatallah 114, Nimatallah 115, Varga 128, Nimatallah 129, Ogawa 178, Lavaud 179, René Roland 190, Periheron 191, Oronoz 195, Nimatallah 252, Nimatallah 257, Nimatallah 258, Faillet 276. **Visual Arts Library/Bridgeman Art Library:** 33, 39, 45, 75, 83, 97, 116, 117, 118, 119, 121, 122, 130, 131, 152, 153, 200, 201, 206, 240. **Visual Arts

Library/Werner Forman Archive:** 279. Private Collection 26. National Museum of Anthropology, Mexico 40, 193. Aboriginal 44. National Museum, Copenhagen 68. British Museum, London 71, 275. Museum fŸr Vπlkerkunde, Berlin 187, 284. Museum fŸr Vπlkerkunde, Basel 188. Dr Kurt Stavenhagen Collection, Mexico 194. Maxwell Museum of Anthropology, Alburquerque 220. H W Read Collection, Plains Indian Museum, Wyoming 222. James Hooper Collection, England 224. Museum of Anthropology, Vancouver Canada 225. Denver Art Museum, Colorado 227. Toni Ralph Collection, New York 273. Saunders, N. J 281, 283. David Bernstein Fine Art, New York 285. Schindler Collection, New York 286. **Visual Arts Library/ Kharbine-Tapabor:** 239. **Visual Arts Library/Edimedia:** 25, 29.

Every effort has been made to trace the copyright holders of pictures and we apologise in advance for any omissions. We would be pleased to insert the appropriate acknowledgement in any subsequent edition of this publication.

Index